TAN WEE

HOT SPOTS AND DODGY PLACES

TRAVELS THROUGH NORTH KOREA, SUDAN AND DISTANT LANDS

Marshall Cavendish
Editions

Cover art by Opal Works Co. Limited
Design by Rachel Chen

Copyright © 2009 Marshall Cavendish International (Asia) Private Limited

Published by Marshall Cavendish Editions
An imprint of Marshall Cavendish International
1 New Industrial road, Singapore 536196

Other Marshall Cavendish Offices

Marshall Cavendish Ltd. 5th Floor 32–38 Saffron Hill, London EC1N 8FH • Marshall Cavendish Corporation. 99 White Plains Road, Tarrytown NY 10591-9001, USA • Marshall Cavendish International (Thailand) Co Ltd. 253 Asoke, 12th Flr, Sukhumvit 21 Road, Klongtoey Nua, Wattana, Bangkok 10110, Thailand • Marshall Cavendish (Malaysia) Sdn Bhd, Times Subang, Lot 46, Subang Hi-Tech Industrial Park, Batu Tiga, 40000 Shah Alam, Selangor Darul Ehsan, Malaysia

Marshall Cavendish is a trademark of Times Publishing Limited

National Library Board Singapore Cataloguing in Publication Data
Tan, Wee Cheng.
Hot spots and dodgy places : travels through North Korea, Sudan and distant lands / by Tan Wee Cheng. – Singapore : Marshall Cavendish Editions, c2009.
p. cm.
ISBN-13 : 978-981-4276-15-3 (pbk.)
1. Tan, Wee Cheng — Travel. 2. Voyages and travels. I. Title.
G465
910.4 — dc22   OCN427798416

Printed in Singapore by Utopia Press Pte Ltd

Contents

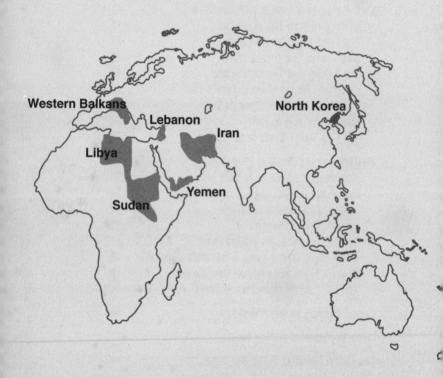

Acknowledgements

My thanks to my many friends scattered across the world who have assisted and advised me during my journeys; those who had accompanied me — Kelly Cheng, Gary Choa, Kenneth Loh, Tan Eng Teck and Kris Yap — in what otherwise could have been lonely ventures to remote parts of the world. Also thank you to those among my friends who have encouraged me not only in my travels, but also helped to turn this book into reality, in particular, Vernon Voon, who spent many tortuous days reviewing and proofreading the book. And to my parents and sister, who have been most worried for my safety and well-being during the past decade or so of my nomadic wanderings. Thank you, everyone!

While the stories in this book are records of my travels and encounters, certain names and circumstances have been modified to preserve the privacy of those concerned.

Introduction

All preconceived notions and beliefs concerning cosmology, history, politics and society were made ridiculous by the new discoveries. The world had been opened up by the fanatical self-confidence of visionaries, and had proved to be wilder than their wildest fancies. Now kingdoms were to be had for the taking.
— W. Raleigh, *The English Voyages of the Sixteenth Century*

North Korea, classified as a sponsor of terrorism by the US for most of the last few decades. Seen by the West as a brain-washed state ruled by what the West sees as a reclusive, isolationist dictator who occasionally threatens to nuke all his enemies.

Sudan, seen by many as a religious fundamentalist state ruled by brutal rulers accused of murdering hundreds of thousands of innocent civilians.

In short, North Korea and Sudan are at the pinnacle of global hot spots, the very opposite of nice, gentle Orchard Road in Singapore.

Why would anyone want to go to North Korea and Sudan?

》》》》》

My first foray to a political hot spot began one morning in late May 1995, in Ljubljana, when I got into a train for Zagreb, capital of Croatia. I was still a novice traveller, on my first journey to Eastern Europe. I had begun my journey in Vienna and gone south to Slovenia. My plan was to make my way to Hungary, Romania, Bulgaria and Turkey, skirting around the war-torn mess that was Croatia, Serbia and the other former Yugoslav states further south. In fact, dad, who was getting concerned about my never-ending nomadic inclinations, had warned, "Don't you step into Yugoslavia. Too dangerous!"

But Zagreb is only 130km away from the cafès of Ljubljana, the idyllic capital of Slovenia, the northernmost of the former Yugoslav states. Slovenia had gotten away free from the clutches of the Serbian generals after a ten-day war in 1991, whereas Croatia and Bosnia-Herzegovina were now bitter battlegrounds. I thought hard about whether to cross the border, but what the heck, a ceasefire had been in force for two weeks — if I didn't go then, when would I do it?

And so I got onto a quiet train, during which I learned proper Serbo-Croat[1] pronunciation from a Bosnian refugee. Marko, 37 years old, who once lived in Sarajevo but was now a refugee in Zagreb; a jovial fellow whose jokes I only half-understood due to his thick Slavic accent. Even then, it was that one-hour long pronunciation lesson that taught me the finer tones of the Slavic "vic's" and "j's". Marko also reminisced about the green pines and spires and minarets of multi-ethnic Sarajevo, which sparked off dreams of visiting this former Winter Olympic city.

I was in Zagreb for one day; merely two weeks after the Krajina Serbs[2] bombed the city when Croatian forces took over the small Serb region of Western Slavonia in a sudden offensive which was their first major military victory in the war.

The chessboard national flag of Croatia flew everywhere while a band played in the central park. Soldiers patrolled streets marked by massively-fortified garrisons at every corner. Sandbags and barbwire were commonplace. Yet this beautiful near-Parisian city had a surreal atmosphere, as teenagers roller-bladed in the park, and pensioners and lovers strolled along its wide boulevards sparkled with cafès, like people do everywhere else in the world. Little did I know that in less than five months, the Croatian-Bosnian forces would rout the Serbian army, and the war would be over in Croatia and Bosnia.

There weren't many tourists — I only saw one, an African-American who jokingly wondered when the next bomb would fall. The cheapest hotel in town with available rooms was charging US$100 per night —

---

[1] This language has since become officially known as Serbian, Croatian, Bosnian and Montenegrin in the respective countries that broke away from Yugoslavia.

[2] The Krajina Serbs live in a number of regions along the border of Croatia and Bosnia-Herzegovina. In 1991, when Croatia declared independence from Yugoslavia, the Krajina Serbs declared themselves independent of Croatia, and quickly overran huge stretches of Croatia with the help of the Yugoslav Federal Army.

refugees occupied the rest, and only diplomats and peacekeepers on expense accounts were in town. I contemplated going south to Dubrovnik but it was too dangerous then. If the ceasefire had broken down, I would have been trapped in a region surrounded by enemy artillery. And so I hopped onto an overnight train to Budapest, Hungary.

Hot spot. A google search revealed a website that defines it as "a place of political unrest and potential violence," although it is a term that has increasingly been taken to refer to places where one could surf the internet through wireless means.

Why go to hot spots and politically unstable places when there are many safer places to choose from? I have no simple answer to that. Perhaps it was nomadic instincts, or even a distorted sense of romanticism. Or blame it on my DNA — a great-great-granduncle-multiple-times-removed was known to have departed Hainan Island in Southern China in the mid-19th century for the wild pirate isles of Nanyang, never to be heard of again.

But world affairs, politics, history and economics have always been my passion, and I often dream about the places I read about. Perhaps, I was influenced by George Mallory, the famous mountaineer who perished climbing Mount Everest in 1924, who, when asked during an interview with the *New York Times* in 1923, why he wanted to climb Mount Everest, said simply "Because it is there," or by St Augustine, the 4th century philosopher and theologian, who said: "The World is a book, and those who do not travel read only a page."

One would miss out a lot if one completely ignored places in the news, which in any case could be what the great powers wanted you to believe. Iran, despite constantly being accused by the US as a sponsor of terrorism and a hotbed of Islamic fundamentalism, is to most world travellers, one of the safest and most hospitable countries in the world. Those who are interested in world affairs should discover for themselves the world beyond the thousands of pages of propaganda churned out by the sometimes-biased international news networks.

And it all became so easy after the first hot spot. After that short foray into Croatia in 1995, a whole series of global hot spots past and present followed: Central Asia in 1998, Caucasus in 2000, Colombia in 2002, North Korea in 2004, Yemen in 2007, and the Horn of Africa, Libya, the Sudan, Iran and Lebanon in 2008.

Hot spots do not necessarily imply physical danger. Libya, which used to be regarded by the US as one of the "Axis of Evil" states, has always been a safe place to visit. North Korea, despite a recent shooting incident that resulted in the death of a South Korean tourist, is generally safe so long as one participates in Disneylandesque rituals such as bowing to the giant statue of Kim Il Sung when instructed by one's North Korean tour guide.

There are certainly very dangerous places, such as Iraq and southern Afghanistan where I would not go now, where a casual foreigner walking on the street is practically courting suicide. But in most other places, such as Yemen and the Sudan today, and the Balkans and Caucasus during parts of the 1990s [3], it is a matter of taking a calculated risk.

Even for countries in the news, there are places in those countries that are safer than other parts. For instance, Iraqi Kurdistan is, to many intrepid travellers, a safe haven compared to the rest of Iraq. Khartoum is an oasis of comfort and security compared to the wild, messy Darfur. It is up to one to decide the threshold of danger and plan one's journey accordingly. We live in a world with a proliferation of hourly-updated news, blogs and other websites that provide more information than we could ever read.

Singaporeans are already in hot spots across the world. I have met an adventurous Singaporean lady in a dilapidated hostel in northern Colombia as well as a handful of brave entrepreneurs in Dili, Timor Leste. As I write, a brave young Singaporean has just completed an internship in Afghanistan. It was an open secret that during the era of sanctions against Vietnamese involvement in Cambodia in the 1980s, some Singaporean businessmen were trading with these regimes, providing them with valuable hard currency for commodities and supplying them with critical supplies.

---

[3] The Balkans is almost completely safe today, apart from occasional sparks of border tension, rioting and demonstrations.

It is in hot spots like these that interesting business and social entrepreneurial opportunities abound, and where the most creative and entrepreneurial businessmen prosper in extraordinary environments and times. Such people are always on the lookout. Ethical and moral concerns aside, wars and conflicts have always provided the creative with a rich environment for business experimentation. The moment a conflict ends, businessmen rush in to provide incoming peacekeepers and diplomats with creature comforts.

More importantly, it is also during one's travels, even in hot spots, that one realises that we live in a world of exuberant ethnic and religious diversity. Whilst every group celebrates their uniqueness in customs and traditions, people often have common hopes for a better life, peace and harmony, and the desire to do good. This is no different irrespective of their race, culture, religion and sexual orientation.

One who travels to hot spots and conflict zones never ceases to ponder how nations — in particular those which had once prospered — fall into chaos and destruction. I have long concluded that it is often religious and ethnic jingoism that destroys peace, harmony and social fabric of nations. History has shown how extremists exploit religious sentiments of perfectly reasonable men-on-the-street to gain power.

Often, such extremists exploit age-old prejudices and irrational fear of a bogeyman to stir the ordinary citizens towards their goals. The Nazis railed against the "immoral Jews", "homosexual perverts", "criminal foreign immigrants" and "expansionist neighbouring states"; and held rallies to uphold "good old German family values". Milosevic blamed the Albanians for everything that went wrong in order to win Serbian support. The Iranian revolutionaries saw (and still see) a "Zionist-American plot" at every corner. Rival Lebanese groups smell a "genocidal conspiracy" every other day. Even in the US and Singapore today, there are organised groups who, illogically, blame homosexuals and abortion laws for growing divorces among heterosexuals, SARS and all social ills.

Those of us who live in prosperity and harmony must be vigilant against those groups that exploit freedom of speech to belittle, demonize and discriminate against ethnic, religious and sexual minorities. These groups use misinformation, fear-mongering and self-righteous moralizing to seek to impose their intolerant views on secular states inhabited by many diverse ethnic and religious groups as well as sexual minorities. If we were not careful, hard-earned peace and social harmony would be eroded and irreparably damaged.

Travel opens one's mind, and alerts one to the many fascinating as well as worrying issues the world faces. Why hesitate? Go forth and explore our diverse and amazing world.

North Korea: Dear Leader's Flower Show (May 2004)

Come, Celebrate Day of the Sun

"Bodies Formed To Celebrate Day Of The Sun," screamed the headlines of *Pyongyang Times*, distributed free on the Air Koryo flight. Something about nudism and the body-beautiful cult making headway in sunny North Korea?

"Preparatory committees have been set up in many countries worldwide including Russia, Belarus, Mongolia, Austria, Egypt and Guinea and many other countries to celebrate the Day of The Sun, 92nd birthday of Great Leader President Kim Il Sung," the article continued. "Various countries have broadcast special programs praising the feats he performed for the Korean revolution and humankind's cause of independence... Famous art troupes and artistes from scores of countries are putting on stage beautiful songs and dances reflecting the unanimous reverence of the world progressive people for the President."

Welcome to the Democratic People's Republic of Korea (DPRK), more commonly known elsewhere as North Korea. Founded in the Soviet-occupied zone in the northern half of Korea in 1948, the DPRK was led by President Kim Il Sung (known as "Great Leader") until his death in 1994, and since then, by his son, Kim Jong Il ("Dear Leader").

In the DPRK, the Kims are worshipped as virtual Gods. Everything that is good is attributable to the two leaders, and anything bad to the "imperialist Americans and their South Korean puppets in Seoul".

Even today, Kim Il Sung remains the "Eternal President" and "Sun" of the DPRK, which makes the country the only one in the world with a dead president. His son, whom the official media proclaimed as "Sun of the 21st Century", is merely the Secretary of the ruling Korean Workers Party and Chairman of the Central Defense Commission.

On that fine spring day of Juche 93 (the DPRK uses the "Juche" calendar that starts counting from the year Kim Il Sung was born), or 2004 elsewhere in the world, we arrived in Pyongyang on a rather bumpy Air Koryo flight that had caused more than a few passengers to shed tears of fear. Our tourist cards were duly stamped and we then met our guides, Mr. Roh and Ms. Park. In this age and time, the DPRK remains one of the few countries that only allow visitors on guided package tours.

Tourists are not allowed to wander about by themselves; they have to be accompanied by an official tour guide. Indeed, we had been told that one should request the guide's permission before taking photos, something hardly heard of anywhere else. As it turned out, we could pretty much take any pictures we wanted, although most of us did exercise a certain degree of discretion and restraint, particularly at the beginning of the journey.

We were driven to Pyongyang city, through the fresh green, fertile countryside of Taedong River valley. The highway was good and almost entirely empty. This is a nation renowned for clean and empty streets. Few people own cars, but the public transportation network has also collapsed due to the shortage of fuel and foreign exchange to purchase oil and spare parts. Indeed we saw people walking alongside highways in the middle of nowhere. Those who live in the suburbs of Pyongyang probably spend two to three hours walking to work everyday, each way!

I wonder if that was in the spirit of Chollima (*"qian-li-ma"* in Chinese), the legendary horse which was supposed to be able to run 1000 *li* (about 500 km) a day. The Chollima was a political campaign waged by Kim Il Sung in the 1960's to hasten post-war reconstruction and economic development — "Transform Korea at the speed of the Chollima," he urged the nation.

Communism has the power of mobilizing manpower and resources for grandiose projects, due to the low cost of labour and negligible economic rent. Such power, however, often leads to even worse wastage and more inefficient use of resources that Karl Marx thought communism would

resolve. In North Korea, this culminated in the great famine of 1996/7, in which as many as 2 million people, or about 10% of the population, died.

PYONGYANG, CAPITAL OF THE DPRK. At first glance, this looks like a modern city of skyscrapers and massive monuments, towering above the agricultural plains whose flatness gave the city its name (Pyongyang literally means "flat"). Once you are in the city, you notice the rough, unpainted walls of most of these ten-to-twenty-storied buildings. Many flats have broken window panes; some are boarded up, others taped over to keep the glass in place.

Yes, the same kind of degradation, neglect and decay one sees everywhere else in cities in the Socialist and ex-Socialist world. Because the buildings belong to the state and not the people who live in them, no one takes care of them. The monolithic state, which has too many things to look after with a limited budget, has not set aside any funds for assets that have no tangible productive value, thus the decaying architecture in places such as Havana, Khabarovsk, Murmansk, Odessa and Tirana.

The streets were clean, but had a cold, almost Spartan look. Commentators often say that Pyongyang looks like a ghost town, with nobody on the streets. This is an unfair statement. If you are out during the morning or evening rush hours when people commute to or leave work, you will see crowds on the streets or waiting for buses in disciplined, military-like lines.

The difference from the rest of the world is, people in Pyongyang go to work from home, and then head back straight from work to home. They do not get distracted by the bright lights of new shops and fancy advertising billboards, simply because in a total socialist system, there are no shops, department stores or public advertising apart from functional state outlets that distribute necessities which come without brands or frills. And quite possibly, a society with no advertising executives unless you count state propaganda functionaries and artists.

The super-efficient state budget apparatus decides what everyone in the country needs in one year, be it shirts, underwear, tea, pork, toothpaste or pencils, allocates funds for their production, and then distributes them via ration coupons to the glorious working people. As they say in the Communist World, miners and farmers get the most coupons, but as we all know, it is those guys in the party HQ that get real dollars and spend them on the most unrevolutionary goods from imperialistic foreign countries.

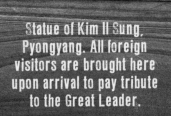

Statue of Kim Il Sung, Pyongyang. All foreign visitors are brought here upon arrival to pay tribute to the Great Leader.

As we speak, the system is fast evolving. It has been more than a decade since the Soviet Union fell, and Eastern Europe is joining the European Union. China is socialist only in name and perhaps more capitalistic than many countries worldwide. North Korea, long subsidised by the USSR and China, is now bankrupt. Struck by famine and gross mismanagement, then by the failures of its experimental special economic zones, the DPRK has now silently begun its economic reforms.

Indeed, kiosks and carts selling simple merchandise such as sweets and cigarettes have appeared on the streets of Pyongyang. Billboard advertisements have appeared in Pyongyang for cars called Huiparam, or the "Whistle", to be assembled in North Korea with Fiat-manufactured parts — the very first in this country. Maybe these are meant for a new elite that have benefited from this tentative economic reform.

Reports also say that new private markets have been set up though foreigners are forbidden from visiting any, and a mobile network is being set-up by a joint venture with a Thai company. And deep in the countryside, local governments are allowed to set up import-export companies and retain 70% of the earnings from such ventures. These are interesting developments. I wonder, when we will see the first McDonald's in the DPRK?

Yanggakdo, Goat's Head Island, lies in the middle of the Taedong River that divides Pyongyang into two. This was where we were to stay . One of three "deluxe" hotels in the country, the Yanggakdo Hotel's height and location provide a wonderful panoramic view of the city and its many huge monuments. More importantly for the authorities, its location on an island means that the tourist cannot easily wander off on his or her own.

Two bridges link the isle to both sides of Pyongyang but tour programmes are deliberately tight so that nobody has time to wander off during the daytime. During the night, however, the lack of street lights (or rather, the lack of electricity) means that one does not want to risk getting knocked down by a car. Besides, none of us wanted our guides to get into trouble by breaking the rules.

And so, the authorities keep the tourist occupied by having a Macau-run casino with Mainland Chinese staff in the basement of the hotel. Drop by and you will find plump, middle-aged, cigar-smoking Chinese gamblers and working ladies by their side — typical officials and businessmen from Dongbei (i.e. Northeast China) in Pyongyang to launder cash.

Nearby, there is a large "international cinema hall" that hardly ever opens. Look out for the Pyongyang International Film Festival every September, they say. Perhaps, one could then look forward to Soviet oldies and blockbusters from revolutionary studios in Cuba, Mozambique and Vietnam!

≫ ≫ ≫ ≫ ≫

I bought a book[4] on what it calls "famous" North Korean films. Here are excerpts on some of the country's most exciting movies:

The First Party Commissioner — *The film delineates the struggle for founding the Party right after liberation. Chol Jin, a former anti-Japanese revolutionary fighter, is sent to a county with the assignment of forming a Party organisation. The state of affairs is very complex. The anti-party factional elements and class enemies do various harms and even conspire to kill Chol Jin. Chol Jin crushes the subversive moves of the reactionaries and succeeds in organising the first Party cell in the smelting works.*

The Problem of Our Family — *The feature film and its nine sequels criticise all the outdated customs and modes of life and incorrect ideas on the glorious road of revolutionising and working-classising the whole of society and show that only when the families which constitute the cells of society are revolutionised will the revolutionisation and working-classisation of the whole society be successfully realised.*

The Choe Hak Sins — *This film deals with the tragedy of the family of a clergyman who worships America like God. During the temporary strategic retreat in the Fatherland Liberation War American imperialist troops of aggression come to a town in North Korea. Choe Hak Sin who has lived in the town as a minister for over 30 years has an illusion that the Americans are as good as their*

---

[4] *Korean Film Art* published by Korean Film & Import Corporation, 1985

noisy words about "philanthropy" and "liberty" and expects them to act from a "humanitarian" standpoint. But the American imperialist aggressors arrest, jail and murder people without discrimination. Choe Hak Sin loses his beloved wife, elder daughter and son at the hands of the murderers. Only now he opens his eyes and curses himself for having implanted the spirit of flunkeyism towards and worship of America in the minds of his children and believers. He earnestly calls for wiping away all the American imperialist aggressors.

The Story of a Nurse — During the Fatherland Liberation War Nurse Kang Yon Ok assigned to the medical post of a field unit is picked out for a casualty evacuation team. She is deeply impressed by the fight of the Party members on the height of the outer perimeter... she finds herself in a difficult position... nevertheless she pushes on looking up at the respected Supreme Commander... One day the hospital is brutally bombed by enemy planes. She saves a wounded soldier by shielding him with her own body. She is seriously injured. Breathing her last, she asks that her Party card and her Party fees be forwarded to the Party Central Committee, and dies a heroic death.

The Fate of Gum Hui and Un Hui — Gum Hui and Un Hui are twins born when the country is liberated. On their birth their mother dies. Their father, too, dies soon later while heading for the north with the twins in his arms... Gum Hui was picked up by painter Ok Hyon San who took her to the North, while Un Hui by fisherman Han Byong Ho who took her to the South. Gum Hui grows up to be a dancer under the blessed socialist system and gives full play to her artistic talent. But Un Hui taken to the south grows up suffering from poverty and hunger. She becomes a singer in the bar. Scenes of Un Hui's hard life in South Korea make a strong appeal that Korea must be reunified as early as possible.

»»»»»

FIRST STOP: THE GRAND MONUMENT OF KIM IL SUNG. This is an obligatory stop for every visitor to the DPRK. Here, a 20-metre high statue of "the Man" stands on a hill overlooking Pyongyang, with his arm stretched forward, pointing the way to Kim-ian paradise. This was built in 1972 to celebrate his 60th birthday. Here, following instructions, we bought a bouquet of flowers at the unsocialist price of five euros, walked to the front of the monument solemnly, formed a line, bowed to the Great Leader and placed the flowers at his feet.

Of course, if you did not want to do that, nobody would point a pistol at you. But that would be most rude. It would just upset the guides, and set a negative tone for the rest of the trip. Fortunately, everyone on the tour took the whole thing in the spirit of fun and teamwork. When in Rome, do as the Romans do. Or don't bother to come at all!

Loud military music blaring out loud, small crowds of people — men in formal suits and ties and women in the bright traditional Korean gown - walked up the hill in neat files and paid their respects to the dead man who remains the president of the country. The birthday of Kim Il Sung was approaching and it was going to be 10 years since his death. "It's a big occasion," Ms. Park said, "and so everyone comes here on his or her own accord to mourn the Great Leader".

The sun set over Pyongyang as its citizens laid their flowers at the gigantic feet of the humongous statue of the "Sun of DPRK and All Humankind", so huge that one immediately sympathised with the minuscule men and women who live in this socialist paradise. A paradise in which the leaders are everything and everyone else mere sidekicks in the many political murals that adorn the otherwise bare walls of this city.

» » » » »

Juche, meaning self-reliance, is the official ideology of North Korea. Developed by Kim Il Sung, its main tenet says that man is the master of his own destiny.

When I asked Ms. Park whether people in North Korea were religious, she said, "No, we don't believe in anything superstitious. We believe in the Juche idea, that man directs his own destiny and decides what he wants to do. We do not rely on others and it is through our efforts that we change nature as well as the environment, and ultimately shape our own destiny."

According to DPRK official sources, people in more than 160 countries have set up study groups and associations to promote the Juche idea, proclaimed in the official press as "the most significant development in the history of philosophy and ideology in human history."

» » » » »

Dinner time! Our first dinner was at what was supposed to be a "famous restaurant" in town, though one that had merely "Restaurant" on its signboard, once again illustrating the functionality of everything in this

Political mural depicting the return of Kim Il Sung to Pyongyang after the defeat of Japan.

Mural of Kim Il Sung, this time as popular commander of the Army.

country. There we had lots of wonderful traditional Korean dishes. And so much that we could hardly finish them all. This was to be the trend for most of our meals in North Korea. What famine? I guess that was the message the regime wanted the world to get, and they would make sure the tourists had more food than they ever wanted.

Karaoke time! North Koreans love karaoke, and all of them seemed to sing well. Mr. Roh and Mrs. Park both had a go, and the restaurant waitresses entertained us with the North Korean top of the charts, which included all-time favourites such as "Song of General Kim Il Sung" and "Song of Dear Comrade Kim Jong Il". I guess, in a society where the TV — provided there is electricity — contains hardly anything beyond "Dear Leader Visits The Cherry Farm Number Three" or "Concert of The Patriotic Soldiers of Fifth Artillery Division In Honour of the Great Leader", people indulge in simpler pleasures of life like singing, dancing and sports.

The Light of the Great Leader

DAY 2, 6AM: We were woken by revolutionary music calling the people to get up to work for the glory of the Nation. Communist countries have an efficient way of dealing with alarms — they simply set a common alarm for everyone. No more wastage of resources so common everywhere else in the world!

We began the day on a "pilgrimage" to Mangyongdae, the birthplace of Kim Il Sung, 12km from Pyongyang city centre. Welcome to the Mecca of Kimilsungism!

As our bus rolled along the highway, we passed thousands of adults and school children on their way to Mangyongdae as well. They waved red flags and branches of pink and red flowers, the Kimilsungia and Kimjonglia respectively, walking to the "sacred" ground like pilgrims, sometimes singing patriotic songs along the way. Some saluted as we passed them. It was an amazing sight.

MANGYONGDAE — This group of thatched huts is one of the most sacred spots for the worshippers of the Kims. According to official accounts, Kim Il Sung was born here in 1912, in a family so poor that his mother bought a huge damaged jar to hold water. This pathetically punctured jar was proof of the family's poverty and yet, one might question how a poor family managed to have so many family photos taken in that era.

The huts displayed many photos of Kim Il Sung and his extended family, most of whom, according to official accounts, were martyrs of the struggle against the Japanese occupation of Korea. At the age of 13, he left home to fight the Japanese, and founded the forerunner organisation of the ruling Workers' Party of Korea at the age of 14. He was a great guerrilla leader in the deep mountains by 24 and liberated the country from the Japanese in 1945, when he was 33. What a child prodigy, master strategist and brilliant general!

South Korean, American and Russian sources are less flattering. They say he was a refugee in neighbouring Northeast China, who later fled to Russia as the Japanese nearly wiped out the guerrillas. It was in a Russian camp that his son, Kim Jong Il, was born, although DPRK official accounts claim that Kim Jong Il was born on sacred Mt Paektu, the Korean mountain of the Gods, on the day a bright star and double rainbow appeared over the skies.

»»»»»

Back in Pyongyang, we visited the other gigantic monuments to the country's leaders and ideology, such as the Juche Tower and Monument to the Party Foundation. Pyongyang is a city of monuments. Many of these tall monuments were built in symmetrical patterns to fit in with other grand public buildings that offered incredible straight-line views across the city. It was as though the two Kims were also *feng shui* experts and urban planners in addition to the other skills for which they are renowned. How I would love to have them rule the whole world!

Political banners are everywhere, with slogans such as: "Long Live The Great Leader!", "Long Live the Ideas of General Kim Il Sung!", "President Kim Il Sung Lives Eternally In Our Hearts!", "Long Live The Sun Of The 21st Century, General Kim Jong Il!", "Drive Out American Imperialists & Reunify The Country!", "Crush The Nuclear Provocations of the US Imperialists!"

We also visited the Pyongyang Metro. As one descended on the amazingly long escalators, loud military music and exclamations over the radio system called on the commuter to "work for our strong country under the guidance of the party and the ideals of Great Leader Kim Il Sung".

Inside, beautiful mosaics showed the Great Leader in various poses, in his long gray coat with the usual trinity of worker, peasant and soldier, not to mention other standard DPRK icons such as Mangyongdae, the Chollima horse and Mt Paektu. It was like time-travelling to Moscow during Stalinist days or Beijing under Mao Zedong.

One grand structure that we saw was the pyramid-shaped 105-storied Ryugong Hotel, which was never completed. It was intended to be the world's tallest hotel with five revolving restaurants on top (for unknown reasons, this country loves revolving restaurants!) — surely the DPRK, the world's tourism paradise, needed lots of new hotel rooms. However, the Russians messed up the job and construction stopped in 1992. It was said that the lift shaft structure was listing dangerously and could collapse at any moment.

More than a decade since construction was interrupted, the empty shell of the 330-metre structure has remained the most obvious landmark of the city, visible from anywhere in the city and suburbs, and most certainly, a symbol of the monumental "success" of the regime.

》》》》》

Have you heard of the term "on-the-spot guidance"? The Great Leader and Dear Leader, as supreme leaders of the country and geniuses of humankind, give advice and guidance on everything under the sun. Such advice is duly documented and plaques or monuments put up on the spot to commemorate such guidance, which could range from anything from choice of water taps for public housing projects to fish farming and furniture design.

A CNN report provided some interesting examples of the leaders' on-the-spot guidance activities, as disclosed in the sixth part of "The Legend of Blossoming Love for On The Spot Guidance"[5]. In this episode, the Dear Leader was seen advising the mountain folk on nutrition and food safety, and giving a female soldier a karaoke machine and tips on how to use it. He gave further "on the spot guidance" on fashion. "All these uniforms," the narrator announced, "were made with the love of the Great Leader," who wanted to be sure the colours matched and the jackets were warm enough. And because Kim wanted his soldiers healthy, he even gave some guidance about how to brush their teeth.

According to North Korean publications, the Great Leader and Dear Leader are renowned geniuses hardly matched anywhere in world history. The North Korean people as well as world civilisation have benefited from their great works in politics, history, philosophy, military-strategy, economics, nuclear science, aeronautics, electronics, culture, and film-making, among countless other topics. North Korean undergraduates use

[5] http://edition.cnn.com/2004/WORLD/asiapcf/02/24/nkorea.tv/index.html

textbooks written by the two leaders on mathematics, physics, chemistry, computer science, biology, geography and history.

According to a report from the Korean Central News Agency (KCNA), "the respected Dear Leader is a genius well-versed in the latest science and technology. He gave on-site guidance to the Academy of Sciences and other scientific research institutes and gave clear-cut instructions on scientific and technological problems which even specialists could hardly understand."

The report continued, "When an institution developed a new world-level programming system, he personally operated a computer to learn its level, stated its shortcomings and clearly indicated the ways for overcoming them."

The two leaders are also authors of all-time best-selling literature works and winners of major literary awards. In fact, Kim Jong Il was known to have written 1,500 books during his university days, that is, more than one book per day.

The Dear Leader is also said to be an accomplished rocker, singer and composer, although the only public recording of his voice any foreigner could find was made during a 1992 military parade, when he said, "Long Live the heroic Korean People's Army!"

According to the local press, "famous" actors, actresses, acrobatic troupes and artists from 40 countries worldwide have arrived in Pyongyang for the "Spring Friendship Arts Festival to celebrate Day of the Sun", Kim Il Sung's birthday. We met some of these people in our hotel; they included Mainland Chinese, Russians, Indonesians, Vietnamese, Finns, Indians, Japanese, Uzbeks, Syrians, Egyptians, Zimbabweans and even Korean-Americans. "The whole world is celebrating the glories of Kim Il Sung and Ideas of Juche," the North Korean press noted.

»»»»»

We drove south across flat agricultural plains and rolling hills to Kaesong, capital of the Koryo dynasty (918–1392 AD), and a provincial capital with more than 300,000 people. From here, Panmunjom in the Demilitarised Zone (DMZ) is only 8km away.

Kaesong is the site of a special economic zone that is being developed with Hyundai Corporation of South Korea. Here, Hyundai and other South Korean companies will set up factories employing cheap labour from North Korea. This is a major step towards cooperation between the two Korean states, and one that would help the South Koreans to compete more effectively with the economic prowess of China.

Tourists come to Kaesong for two things — the ancient relics of the Koryo dynasty and Panmunjom. Upon arrival, we headed for the royal tombs of King Wan Kon, the first king of Koryo, who reigned when England was ruled by the Saxon kings of the House of Wessex, the Scandinavian Vikings struck fear across the seaside communities of Western Europe and about the same time the first images of the use of gunpowder were drawn by an unknown artist in the Buddhist grottoes of Dunhuang in the deserts of Western China. Koryo, according to the DPRK, was the first unified Korean dynasty. King Wang Kon had united the remnants of the Koguryo (spelled "Goguryeo" in the South) Kingdom with the much-weakened Silla Kingdom of the south.

South Korean and international historians, however, say that Silla (57 BC–935 AD) was the first unified dynasty of Korea. Based in the South Korean city of Gyeongju, Silla was founded in the same year the legions of Julius Caesar defeated King Galba of the Belgian tribes; and it united Korea after the defeat of Koguryo and Paekche in the 7th century, whilst China indulged itself at the height of the Tang dynasty's golden age. Modern political considerations often affect the interpretation of history. The North Koreans often emphasize the importance of Koguryo and Koryo because their capitals were in the north, whereas the South Koreans emphasize the Silla and Ri dynasties because their capitals were in the south.

As with the royal tombs of Silla at Gyeongju, the tomb of Wang Kon was a huge round mound surrounded by carvings of the 12 Chinese zodiac animals as well as sculptures of officials and generals. Looking at how "new" the sculptures were, it seemed as if the North Koreans had completely reconstructed the tomb complex after its destruction during the Korean War.

We drove back to town where we put up at the Kaesong Folk Hotel. This comprises traditional Korean houses and courtyards converted into a hotel complex in the middle of Kaesong's wonderfully preserved old town of narrow alleys, square compounds and quaint old houses.

To protect honoured tourists from the harassment and dangers of excessive interaction with residents of the old town, our beloved Dear Leader has turned an entire area of the old town into the Folk Hotel, where tourists can stay in the traditional houses and wander along a few short alleys within the walled confines of the hotel beside a picturesque stream, without ever stepping on to the open streets of Kaesong.

Dear Leader further pampered us with a wonderful traditional Korean dinner specially prepared in the traditional fashion, and we were asked to join in the fun, crushing soya beans and milling flour. It was a wonderful evening, where we indulged in lots of fun and laughter with the hospitable staff of the Folk Hotel.

We walked back to our room after dinner. It was pitch dark as the country faced serious power shortages. The only source of brightness was the brightly lit golden statue of Kim Il Sung overlooking the city. Yes, give me the light of the Great Leader!

Arch of Triumph of Pyongyang, exactly one meter taller than the Parisian version. Built in 1982 to celebrate Kim Il Sung's 70th birthday and to commemorate his "victorious liberation of Korea from Japanese occupation".

Who Started The Korean War?

On a misty morning, we drove southeast towards the 4km-wide DMZ. Near its entrance, we got off to take pictures of the highway sign pointing south: "Seoul 70km". On this godforsaken ground of rice fields and occasional concrete anti-tank barriers, it was hard to believe that Seoul and its bright lights, glass towers, hedonistic discos, massive shopping malls and bustling streets were only an hour and a half away. Isn't it a twist of fate that these poor farmers could well have been ploughing the fields with modern semi-automatic tractors rather than the poor overworked oxen they were using?

We stopped briefly for our guides to complete the paperwork and also to wait for the DMZ military guides to arrive. "This is a high-alert zone," Ms. Park said, "everyone has to be vigilant in case the enemies do anything. There'll be a few soldiers coming with us to ensure our safety."

One must not forget that the DPRK, with more than a million men under arms and reserve forces of 6 million, has the third largest armed force in the world. According to Michael Breen's *Kim Jong Il*, the DPRK "spends only US$5.1 billion per year on defense, less than half South Korea's defense budget, but this amount represents a staggering 31.3% of the country's GDP. This small country of only 22 million is the most militarised nation in the world."

Even then, Michael Breen commented that "the economy is so shattered that there is scarcely any fuel… the North has suffered so much food shortage… that, if South Korea reinforced the DMZ with a line of food courts offering free Big Macs for North Korean customers with rifles, it would all be over in minutes."

Ironically, security on the North Korean side appeared considerably less tight than in the South which I visited late last year. Over on the South Korean side of the DMZ, one came across numerous American and South Korean troops and military installations, ranging from huge concrete anti-tank barriers to electric fences and endless military checkpoints. I was also required to sign forms acknowledging the dangers of the excursion and agreeing to various rules of conduct and waiving the right to sue the authorities if accidents occured.

The most ridiculous thing in the South was that no one was allowed to wear jeans in the DMZ, for they say that would justify (in what ways I still do not know) North Korean claims that the South is an American colony. On the other hand, no one cared what you wore in the North. Some in our group wore jeans and we didn't have to sign any forms nor were we warned about any precautions.

Our DMZ guide was a good-looking and rather confident officer in his thirties. He gave an interesting introduction over a large relief and model map of the area and then we were driven into the DMZ, where we had a distant view of the ridiculously large North Korean flag (largest flag in the world) and the equally huge flag of the South on the other side of the demarcation line.

We headed for the Joint Security Area (JSA), a compound that used to be jointly maintained by forces from both sides. However, as a result of the infamous Axe Incident in 1976 during which an American army captain was axed to death by North Korean soldiers for chopping down a tree that affected the view of a US/UN checkpoint, the JSA was divided into two and no one was allowed to cross the demarcation line to the other side. The US/South Korean side had proclaimed the dead captain a martyr of freedom whereas the North described the incident as further proof of US aggression. Who's right and who's wrong?

From a huge building overlooking the compound, we watched the tall American and South Korean (which the North calls the "south Korean puppet regime") soldiers. We visited one of the meeting buildings that straddled the demarcation line — what a thrill, entering the same building we did last year from the other side!

It was also interesting that US and South Korean soldiers wore dark glasses that made them look dubious and forbidding, which was not helped by the rather stiff "ready-to-fight" *taekwando* posture they adopted in the DMZ grounds. In contrast, the North Koreans wore no dodgy dark glasses, and walked around in an easygoing manner. In fact, this was exactly what we had observed during our visit from the South last year, so it wasn't just a show put on by the North.

The Armistice Talks Hall one kilometre from the JSA was next, where our officer guide (who was quite guarded about revealing his rank or name) gave us a brief introduction to the DPRK version of the Korean War. "The American imperialists started the Korean War," he said, "and the DPRK, under the leadership of the Great Leader, defeated them upon a few kilometres of their incursion."

Once again, one gets an alternative version of history so different from the ones we are familiar with. Of course, he did not explain how the North managed not only to defeat American incursions but also to capture Seoul within three days and 90% of South Korea within one month.

He did, however, raise a few valid points. Nuclear weaponry is the cheapest and most practicable way for the DPRK to protect itself. The DPRK's actual nuclear capability forces the US to negotiate with North Korea instead of invading the country as it did Iraq, which was only trying to develop nuclear capability. And he said, "Why is it that the US can have the largest nuclear arsenal in the world and yet does not allow anyone else to develop nuclear capabilities?"

Anti-US billboard in Pyongyang.

It was with great pride that in 1998, the North Koreans launched a Taepodong missile over Japan, into the Pacific Ocean. Not only did that show the world North Korean missile capability (and the fact that it could soon reach the North American coast) but also demonstrated the helplessness of Japan, a much larger and richer country. Despite the animosity between the North and the South, the South Koreans viewed the incident with barely-concealed delight, for they tended to dislike the Japanese more and hoped to inherit those missiles once reunification had taken place.

Here in this mini-museum where armistice negotiations took place, we found the axe (murder weapon to the South Koreans and Americans) used in the Axe Incident as well as a whole lot of "evidence" proving that the Americans had started the Korean War — in fact, we bought a little booklet *The American Imperialists Started the Korean War*, and another, *America — The Empire of Terrorism*.

» » » » »

Forget about Reuters, AFP or AP. North Korea's KCNA[6] is one of my favourites. Here's one of their eternal pieces:

Marshal Kim Jong Il, how does the world name him.

The political, military, business, academic and publishing and press circles in more than 160 countries over the world attached the most honorific appellation to Marshal Kim Jong Il.

The titles summed up so far numbered more than 1,200. Some of them are as follows: The great star of Korea, born by the great sun/ the sun of the revolution/ the sun of Juche/ the sun of mankind/ the sun of the 21st century/ the sun of hope/ the sun of life/ the eternal sun/ the unparalleled hero/ the greatest saint/ the paragon of loyalty/ the skillful and veteran statesman/ fascinating statesman/ the master of diplomacy/ the supreme incarnation of faith / the ever-victorious commander/ the symbol of invincibility and ever-victory/

---

[6] http://www.kcna.co.jp/index-e.htm

the greatest general/ the perfect military strategist/ the marvelous strategist and tactician/ the heaven-sent hero/ the high intelligent and almighty leader/ the unrivaled great man/ the greatest personifier of human wisdom/ the master of philosophy/ the incarnation of might displaying infinite creative ability / the master of literature and art and architecture/ the genius of human music/ the world-level literary giant/ the great veteran of humanity/ the heaven of all the people/ the destiny of the world/ the helmsman of the world/ the top brain of the world revolution/ the heart of the world/ the great leader who will lead the 21st century / the guardian of our planet…

The world progressives boundlessly revere and follow Kim Jong Il as the great sun, legendary great man and outstanding leader of the 21st century. Human history has recorded many great persons. However, it has not witnessed such a great man as Marshal Kim Jong Il who is worshipped by all people of the world with different nationalities, social systems and political views.

Under the leadership of the Marshal, humankind is vigorously advancing toward a bright future of the 21st century. With the national pride of being led by the great Marshal who enjoys absolute respect and reverence of the world progressives, the Korean people will wage a more vigorous struggle for the independent reunification of the country.

》》》》》

After leaving the DMZ, we headed back to town and then picked up another military officer for a visit to the Concrete Wall. Located on another part of the DMZ, accessible from Kaesong only via a bumpy, winding road, the Concrete Wall is, according to the North Koreans, the equivalent of the Berlin Wall on the Korean Peninsula, and it prevented all contact and links between the people of the North and South. Sure, as though there were no other barriers between the two states.

We strained our eyes looking for the wall through telescopes but none of us were sure of what we were actually seeing, especially since it was rather misty and everything in the background — whether trees, bushes, ground or installations — looked blurry from such a distance. The South Korean military post 4km away saw us and spoke (in Korean) using their loudspeakers — "We notice you tourists over that side!"

Back to Kaesong at the exuberant Unification Restaurant on the slopes of the hill on which the golden statue of Kim Il Sung stood, we had a wonderful lunch of royal Koryo dishes served on gold- and silver-coloured tableware. Crowds holding bouquets of flowers were walking solemnly uphill to pay their respects to the Great Leader. Royal food in a royal place at the foot of a royal hill!

We also stopped by the Sonjuk Bridge where an official and his servant were assassinated in 1392 for being loyal to the overthrown Koryo dynasty. The blood of the murdered, the Koreans claimed, could still be seen on the bridge. Yes, there was a pinkish patch on the bridge indeed. Next to the bridge is a shrine dedicated to the murdered. This has become a pilgrimage spot devoted to loyalty, one of the supreme virtues of Confucianism. Here, an older ideology and value system was at work, and it was worth noting that the Kims are keeping this alive. Maybe Confucianism would be a more lasting and viable ideology than any other currently in force in the land.

»»»»»

Driving back to Pyongyang, we passed the gigantic Reunification Monument which comprised statues of two ladies in *hanbok*[7] stretched out over the highway. This highlighted the Korean desire for reunification and Kim Il Sung's proposal for a Koryo Democratic Confederal Republic to be formed between the North and South. As we sped through town, many parts of Pyongyang were celebrating the birthday of Kim Il Sung, with public concerts and marches. The whole city was in a carnival mood, with colourful banners and billboards.

We dropped by the Foreign Languages Bookshop but the employees had shut down early to do the "Kim Il Sung pilgrimage". We went to the

---

[7] *Hanbok* also known as *Choson-ot*, is the traditional Korean dress worn for formal and semi-formal occasions today.

Stamp Shop instead and there all of us went crazy buying North Korean stamps, most of which depicted themes relating to the country's leaders. We also bought quite a few stamps showing anti-US motifs. At the bookshop at Koryo Hotel next door, we bought a book written by Kim Jong Il on filmmaking. Yet another masterpiece by this glorious leader.

Buying things in this country can be a big hassle. Anything on sale for foreigners is quoted in euros but change is often lacking. Instead, cashiers would give you assorted notes and coins in various currencies, principally Chinese RMB and US$. On one occasion, I got change back in Euro coins, RMB, yen coins and a chewing gum!

Kim Il Sung Won The Korean War

We dropped by the War Victory Memorial, a huge monument to commemorate North Korea's "victory" in the Korean War. Yes, I also remember Saddam Hussein's "victory" in the Mother of All Battles in the First Gulf War.

There were many huge sculptures depicting major episodes of the war, all built in the usual typically dramatic socialist style. One of my favourites was named "Citizens of Seoul welcoming the Korean People's Army". (The KPA is the official name for the North Korean Army.) Quite amusingly, the South Korean War Memorial in Seoul also comprised equally monumental sculptures in the same style.

Nearby is the War Victory Museum, a huge complex devoted to the same. In this complex, we were shown a huge treasure trove of not only military hardware and war pictures, but also "evidence" of the American launching of the Korean War and American atrocities in Korea.

The Korean War was a brutal military conflict during which between 2 and 4 million civilians died. Both sides committed many atrocities. Many cities changed hands several times as pitched battles were fought throughout most of the Korean peninsula. In recent years, several major massacres committed by US forces in the North have been revealed in the American and South Korean press.

Patriotic sculptures at Kim Il Sung Monument.

Unfortunately, instead of using more reliable and objective sources, the museum squandered goodwill by putting up some dubious displays and statistics. Examples were an irrelevant portrayal of an American priest shown as a sadistic torturer of Koreans and crudely modified photos of US soldiers surrendering. Another display claimed that the Americans murdered 140,000 South Koreans before the Korean War broke out while a publication we found at the museum put the figure at 1 million.

While the display devoted huge sections to "evidence" of the US launching the war and the DPRK's rapid advance through the South, there was little devoted to the radical routing of DPRK forces after UN forces landed in Incheon and their march into Pyongyang and eventually to the Chinese border on the Yalu river. There was instead some mention of the "strategic withdrawal" northwards and the atrocities committed by US forces in Pyongyang.

The most notable omission was the Chinese involvement — the last two years of the war were in reality a war between the US and China. The latter had gotten involved, as they were afraid this was a prelude to an American invasion of China, in support of their Kuomintang allies in Taiwan.

International sources indicated that half a million Chinese soldiers died fighting for North Korea, including Mao Zedong's son. We asked about that and were told that only "a few Chinese volunteers" participated in the war. The museum guide added that it was Kim Il Sung's excellent leadership that turned the tide of the war and led North Korea to "victory". I think Mainland Chinese visitors would be very upset if they heard this version of the events.

»»»»»

The *USS Pueblo* was an American spy ship captured by the North Koreans in January 1968 off the coast of the port city of Wonsan. One US officer was killed during the event and 82 men ended up in North Korean captivity. The North Koreans secured a propaganda coup when the US Government was forced to apologise in exchange for the return of the 82 captured men and the remains of the dead officer.

The ship remained in DPRK possession as a war trophy, in an episode similar to the US spy plane incident off the coast of Hainan Island, China, in 2001. I think the Americans would have done the same to North Korean or Chinese spy planes or ships captured off the coast of California.

We visited the *USS Pueblo* which has become a tourist attraction in Pyongyang. We watched an interesting documentary of the incident, and were shown the bullet holes at the spot where the US officer was killed, as well as the espionage and radio equipment, US Army manuals and maps.

Nearby was where the *General Sherman*, yet another US armed ship, was destroyed in 1866, the year Jesse James and his infamous gang committed their first bank robbery on the dusty main street of sleepy Liberty, Missouri. By the 19th century, Western powers had been intruding into Korean territory demanding that it opened its gates to trade as well as missionaries. French, British, Russian and American gunboats attacked Korean ports from time to time to extract concessions. The Korean imperial court became hostile to foreigners and banned conversions to Christianity.

In 1866, the *General Sherman*, a US metal-clad, merchant marine schooner owned by a British trader, sailed up the Taedong river for trade and some say, to evangelize. Clashes broke out. The ship was captured and burned after a four-day battle, and all its crew was killed.

The Ri court then had stelae put up across the country to commemorate the event, and they proclaimed: "Posterity should remember the unwillingness to fight Western intrusion means reconciliation, and that insisting on peace negotiations means selling the country."

Whilst there were no clear historic records on who might have been responsible for the capture of the *General Sherman* and the killing of the invaders, DPRK authorities had declared the obvious heroes — they claim that Kim Il Sung's great grandfather was the one responsible, once again proving the heroic lineage of the Kim family!

»»»»»

Here are the lyrics to a North Korean top of the chart song:

General Kim Jong-Il
1. *From Paek-du mountains, 1,000km long beautiful realm*
   All look up to the General and cheer him.
   He is the people's leader to inherit the great work of the Sun.
   Long live, long live, General Kim Jong-Il !
2. *Millions of flowers on the earth tell us his love.*
   Blue waves of the ocean sing of his work.
   He is the creator of happiness to grow the garden of Ju-che.
   Long live, long live, General Kim Jong-Il !
3. *He protects socialism with his courage like steel.*
   He makes our country famous in the world.
   He is the defender of justice with a flag of autonomy.
   Long live, long live, General Kim Jong-Il !

» » » » »

According to our guides, 20,000 tourists visited North Korea in 2003, most of whom were from China, especially from the Dongbei region just next door to North Korea; which also explained why most of the tour guides spoke Chinese. The great majority of Chinese tourists visit the casinos of the Rajin-Tumen region in the tri-national northeastern corner of the country on the border with China and Russia.

North Korea's "peak" tourism seasons are spring and summer. The rest of the year is just too cold. Even then, there are times when the tour guides do not have much to do, even during the high seasons.

What do they do then? "We study," according to Ms. Park, and Mr. Roh added, "We study in the Grand People's Study House." He was referring to the huge national library on Kim Il Sung Square, built to celebrate Kim Il Sung's 70th birthday in 1982. "And during harvest time, the whole city, including the tour guides, go to the countryside to help the farmers. University students would preach the ideas of Juche to the farmers."

Huge government buildings in central Pyongyang.

The Dear Leader and the Great Leader in an official painting at the crater lake at the summit of Mt Paektu, site of the mythological birth of the Korean people.

Classic sculpture of the socialist worker.

We visited a school in the afternoon. This was probably a regular feature on all tour programmes in the DPRK. We were shown a biology class, a computer class (with very old Singaporean Datamini computers — I haven't even seen them for ages at home!) and an ideology class.

The students were no strangers to foreign visitors and were very friendly. However, at the ideology class, it was quite startling that the students didn't even dare turn their heads to look at us, concentrating instead on a presentation on the life of heroic teenager Kim Jong Il. The walls of the school were full of murals devoted to, guess what, the deeds and lives of the two leaders of the country.

After a walk-around, we were treated to a pleasant song and dance performance by the students during which we were invited to join in the dance. I wonder how much time they devote to such displays of "normality" for foreigners. The guide said, "This is an ordinary school where students are children of intellectuals and workers." What do you think?

Military Circus was next. We watched an amazing display of North Korea's world-class circus — not surprising since circus arts have always been a core competence of communist countries. In a society where propaganda movies and speeches by the leaders can only distract the people to a limited extent, circus and gymnastic performances are areas that provide some variety in the lives of the people.

Apart from the usual circus and gymnastic stunts, there was a comedy play about how a nasty American soldier was punished for mistreating the "oppressed South Korean people". The audience, comprising largely young military cadres in smart uniforms, had a really good laugh. I wished I understood Korean too!

When the performance ended with all performers appearing on stage to wave farewell, (Surprise, surprise!) a huge projected image of the Dear Leader appeared on the screen. All in the audience stood and clapped. I'm not sure who they were saluting, but, yes, I should thank the Dear Leader for this wonderful performance! Then off we went to Mt. Myohyang (meaning "Mountain of Mysterious Fragrance") on an expressway specially built for tourists. The night was to be spent at the pyramid-shaped Hyangsan Hotel.

Electricity for the Great Leader's Toys

The International Friendship Exhibition is the star attraction of Mt. Myohyang and its beautiful pine valleys. In addition, it has to be one of the world's most bizarre museums, the ultimate temple to Narcissism with a capital N! This is a complex of two huge palatial buildings with intricately carved traditional rooftops, built deep into the mountains and permanently exhibiting more than 200,000 presents to Kim Il Sung and Kim Jong Il from leaders and "admirers" from over 170 countries worldwide.

The visit began with the now familiar Greet-the-Great-Leader ritual. To the tunes of military music, the huge elaborately carved doors to the first hall were opened, and as instructed, we walked in to find ourselves face-to-face with a life-sized wax figure of Kim Il Sung — so lifelike that I would have thought that it was the Old Man Himself. We formed a line in front of the Man, and at a signal from our guides, bowed to this god of the DPRK.

And then we began a tour of this gigantic complex full of endless high-ceilinged corridors, and huge bunker-like exhibition halls, complete with chandeliers, air-conditioning and taps that had running water — all these were incredible considering the state of the economy, the appalling energy shortage and the complete breakdown of the water supply system which meant that running water was a rare occurrence outside the hotels. I suppose the power used in this complex could have lit up half of Pyongyang!

As the guides explained, Kim Il Sung and Kim Jong Il are world-beloved leaders, and people from all over the world have showered them with gifts to show their admiration of these great men.

Among the notable presents were armoured train carriages and limousines from Joseph Stalin and Mao Zedong, a bizarre standing stuffed crocodile presenting a tray of cups courtesy of the Sandinistas of Nicaragua, silver coconuts from Saddam Hussein, and a basketball autographed by Michael Jordan presented by Madam Albright. The guides were at pains to explain why this basketball was a worthwhile present — the fact that basketball players could be as popular as political leaders is a concept difficult to understand in a country where the only well-known people are the Great Leader and Dear Leader.

China, Hong Kong and Taiwan were the most generous donors of presents — perhaps 70% of the presents were from companies and organisations in these countries, mostly extravagant gold, silver and jade carvings of themes such as Kim Il Sung, Kim Jong Il, Mt Paektu and traditional Chinese auspicious symbols (e.g., longevity, traditional gods, fortune, etc) — a reflection of the economic and political ties between Greater China and the DPRK.

There were also many presents from illustrious characters from the "World Dictators Hall of Fame", such as Yasser Arafat (intricate models of the Dome of the Rock in Jerusalem, a monument not under his control), Nicolae Ceausescu (hell of a bear's head), Erich Honnecker (sword and revolver, and some rather plain, utilitarian steel tables and chairs of the sterile sort one finds in hospitals) and Joseph Mugabe (I loved his silver lions and elephants!).

Singapore has a more modest corner with dozens of gifts, mostly from a relatively unknown company called Welcome Trading Co Pte Ltd, including two huge stone carvings of the Merlion, a symbol of Singapore. There were also two small gold trinkets from the Parliamentary and the Foreign Affairs Ministry delegations to North Korea.

In the USA section, the exhibition guide pointed at a framed-up full-page advertisement in the *New York Times* entitled "Korea prospers under Juche idea", and said, "Look — Even the Americans acknowledge the superior ideas of our leaders." One of our Swedish travellers and I had a closer look and saw the words "Advertisement" in the top margin. We had seen similar paid advertisements in Swedish as well as Singapore papers before. What a useful way to spread the great ideas of Juche!

It took two hours to walk briskly through just the highlights of the International Friendship Exhibition complex. At the end of the tour, the exhibition guide asked, "So are you convinced that the world loves our leaders? Do you still see the DPRK as an isolated country?"

»»»»»

We passed many towns and villages on the way back to Pyongyang. None of these had lights when we passed them the night before, to the extent that I had thought there was nothing but wilderness from Pyongyang to Mt. Myohyang. Lenin once said, "Socialism plus electricity equals communism." I wonder what Juche has got to say about electricity and the Great Leader's toy exhibition at Mt. Myohyang. Maybe something along the lines of "Juche plus the Great Leader equals electricity for the Great Leader's toys, statues and palaces!"

Just outside Pyongyang, we stopped by the Revolutionary Martyrs' Cemetery. In this magnificent memorial set on the slopes of Jujak Peak overlooking the city, there were busts of 120 guerrilla leaders and "revolutionary martyrs" who had lost their lives during the anti-Japanese struggle.

Sombre piped music added to the dignified, moving atmosphere of the site. The busts were built to face Pyongyang so that the martyrs could "see the new Korea", the guide said. Ironically, the most prominent building they could see from here was none other than the empty skeleton of Ryugong Hotel, whose 105 storeys rose high above any other construction in Pyongyang, the very tribute to Kim Il Sung's "new Korea". Ten years had passed since construction ceased and funds dried up. Would this stir the spirit of the revolutionary dead?

Nearby is the Kumsusan Memorial Palace, once Kim Il Sung's lavish residence and office, now converted into his mausoleum after his death. It is also here that his US$100 million-embalmed body rests. This is again another astonishingly colossal complex which takes a few minutes to drive past, even when there is no traffic. Soldiers guarded it ceremoniously as though the Great Leader were still alive. Surely a great leader needs a great palace! It was a pity it wasn't included in our itinerary. In any case, it only opened twice a week and one would need to give advance notice and visit in formal shirt and tie.

We visited one of the few operating Buddhist temples in Pyongyang, the one-thousand-six-hundred-year-old Kwangbok Temple, which was rebuilt in 1990 from the ruins of the Korean War. Here the abbot told us, "The Great Leader had done a lot to promote Buddhism in this country. Thanks to him, this temple was rebuilt." Words of a state functionary? Yes, only 10,000 Buddhists in a 22-million strong country once renowned for its Buddhist piety and scholarship.

Back to the city centre, we dropped by the Fountain Park where families were strolling and relaxing. The next day would be Day of the Sun and there was a festival atmosphere in the air. Department Store Number One was nearby and we asked if we could visit it. The place appeared rather dark although we could see shoppers walking around. (Obviously, the national electricity saving scheme was on! Have you ever gone shopping in the dark?) Our guides said that advance notice had to be given for any visit and it was too late to do so.

Instead we were taken to another store near Ryugong Hotel. We walked around and soon realised that everything was priced in Euros as well as the North Korean won. This couldn't be a store for ordinary Koreans. I asked Ms. Park and she admitted that most of the customers here were foreign diplomats and aid workers, and things here were too expensive for her.

In fact, this is owned by some Argentineans, which explained the large amount of Argentinean merchandise. We were not really disappointed. The bottled water was cheaper than in the hotel. We even found Tiger Beer here, at prices half that in Singapore! There were also quite a few varieties of hair products — I wondered if they would do Dear Leader's hair any good.

We dropped by the Foreign Language Bookstore, and topped up our growing collection of North Korean souvenirs. The many profound works and gems of wisdom by Kim Il Sung and Kim Jong Il have always been bestsellers with foreign tourists! All of us would have lots of coffee table propaganda books, parts of the series of selected works by the country's leaders (which run into volumes of 20 and 40), political posters, stamps of the Kims, kitschy miniatures of the Chollima Horse, and all sorts of DPRK treasures to carry home from this journey.

Considering the ridiculous sums they charge for these, we must have contributed a lot to Kim Jong Il's Cognac and Mercedes fund. Kim Jong Il was Hennessey's best customer for two years running in the early 1990's, and he bought two hundred S Class Mercedes at US$100,000 each in 1998.

We had dinner and then returned to the hotel. We popped by the revolving restaurant at the top of our hotel. It wasn't revolving and the city was largely dark apart from the few monuments. Roberto, one of our fellow travellers, decided to give on-the-spot guidance to the attending staff, "Why isn't it revolving? This isn't revolutionary enough. You should start the Revolution!" With that, he got the staff to press the button, and so the Revolution continued.

At the Day of the Sun celebrations.

The Weirdest Flower Show on Earth

DAY OF THE SUN. Loud band music started early on this important day of the DPRK calendar. It's the birthday of Kim Il Sung and a public holiday. The riverside was full of families on outings, rowing boats and simple merrymaking. We visited the Taedong Gate, an ancient portal that once guarded the city of Pyongyang. Nearby, a school was celebrating the birthday of Kim Il Sung by presenting top students with prizes.

We dropped by Kim Il Sung Square — this is the heart of Pyongyang where all the grand military parades take place — 75,000 sq. m. of concrete slabs surrounded by immense buildings such as the Grand People's Study House, the Korean Central History Museum with its Socialist-classical columns, Korean Art Gallery and various ministries. All these form part of a *feng shui*-like symmetry with the Juche Tower, Monument of Kim Il Sung and other monstrous memorials and concrete mammoths of Pyongyang's megalomaniacal city planners.

The visit to the Korean Central History Museum had to be my favourite alternative history lesson ever. It was interesting comparing the North Korean version of history with that of the rest of the world:

a.   Korea is the cradle of mankind. They claimed that ancient skulls, millions of years old, had been found in Korea which proved that Korea was where Man began and that the peninsula had been ethnically Korean since the beginning of time.

b.   Tangun was a real person who founded the first Korean state. They hadn't tried to explain how he was descended from the gods as well as a bear-woman. North Korea also claimed that they found the skeletal remains of Tangun near Pyongyang and had them carbon-tested to prove that those remains were 5,000 years old (which would mean that his contemporaries were the earliest Egyptian pharaohs and the first Mesopotamian kings). International historians and scientists, however, had cast doubts on the North Korean findings, especially on the methodology used.

c. Korea under the Koryo dynasty was the only country in
    Asia that defeated the Mongols. According to South Korean,
    Japanese and Chinese sources, however, Korea was repeatedly
    occupied and devastated by the Mongols, who used it as a
    launching ground to attack Japan, which was one of the few
    countries never conquered by the Mongols.
d. Kim Il Sung defeated the Japanese during WWII and liberated
    Korea. Nothing mentioned about the atomic bomb and the
    role of the Americans and Russians fighting the Japanese and
    Germans.
e. The US invaded North Korea and the North Koreans, under
    Kim Il Sung, defeated the Americans. Little is mentioned
    about Chinese involvement or Soviet aid.

The museum guide made references to the great deeds of Kim Il Sung
and Kim Jong Il from time to time — they were responsible for all the good
deeds, liberating the country, reconstructing the country and even for the
preservation of historical relics.

She pointed to some gold Buddhas found near Mt. Kumgang, "Under
the guidance of the Dear Leader, these golden relics were preserved and
now are presented to the world in this museum."

I was touched. I wondered what they would have done to the golden
Buddhas if the Dear Leader had not given special instructions — perhaps
some zealous functionaries would have melted them down to make golden
statues of our two great friends?

I shouldn't complain. In this wonderful depository of Korean historical
artifacts, I realised how foolish I was, believing the lies imperialists and evil
capitalists wanted me to believe all my life. Maybe I should repent by setting
up a Juche study group in Singapore, and spending my vacations teaching
Juche ideas to Thai farmers and Indonesian sea gypsies.

»» »» »» »»

Lunch was on Pyongyang Boat Number 1, which cruised along the Taedong River while we had wonderful *bulgugi* (Korean BBQ). The river was full of pleasure crafts and the riverbank crowded with families out on picnics and strolls. A crew from Pyongyang TV waved wildly on the riverbank, shouting greetings and filming us waving back. I could imagine this TV news commentary, "Visitors from afar celebrating the Day of the Sun on a cruise along the Taedong River".

Then off to the Arch of Triumph of Pyongyang, 60 meters tall — the North Koreans would point out to you that it is exactly one metre taller than the Parisian version. It was built in 1982 to celebrate Kim Il Sung's 70th birthday and to commemorate his "victorious liberation of Korea from Japanese occupation". Inscribed on different sides of the arch were the years "1925" and "1945", representing the year Kim Il Sung left home to fight the Japanese and the year he returned to Pyongyang as a victor.

About a hundred metres away is the enormous Kim Il Sung Stadium, with capacity for 100,000 people. Nearby is a huge wall mural depicting the arrival of Kim Il Sung in Pyongyang on 14 October 1945.

According to DPRK official accounts, the citizens of Pyongyang welcomed Kim Il Sung at this spot where he gave a speech about the Revolution and plans to reunify Korea. The murals also depict banners written in Hanja (which is basically Korean written in Chinese script, with the same meaning) "Long Live General Kim Il Sung!" and "Long Live Liberation of the Motherland!"

Everyone was elated to see this bright young man who had spent 20 years of his youth fighting for the liberation of his country. Kim Il Sung's grandparents hugged him and cried, asking, "Why did you return alone? Where are your parents, uncles and cousins? All dead? Why didn't you return with them?" Sob, sob…just try imagining a North Korean tearjerker. Once again, DPRK official history highlights the sacrifices of the Kim clan when liberating the country.

South Korean accounts, however, claim that when Kim Il Sung appeared at the venue, the gathering crowds were shocked that the great guerrilla hero the Soviets (who took over the northern half of Korea from the Japanese) had told them about, was only a highly confused young man who was not fluent in Korean. There was a lot of skepticism that Kim was anything but a Soviet puppet.

>> >> >> >> >>

Another gem of wisdom from KCNA. In this one, the Old Man (already dead for a decade) even received awards from Ecuador and Peru. Can anyone from either of these two countries confirm the accuracy of this report?

April Holidays Widely Commemorated Abroad[8]

> *Pyongyang, May 13 (KCNA) — Functions took place in over 100 countries to commemorate the Day of the Sun and celebrate the 11th anniversary of Kim Jong Il's election as chairman of the National Defense Commission of the DPRK and the 72nd anniversary of the heroic Korean People's Army this year. Kim Jong Il received gifts from the president of Pakistan, the Chiclayo Branch of the Peruvian-Korean Institute of Culture and Friendship, the honorary director of the Voluntad Publishing House of Ecuador, Juche idea study organizations and public figures of different countries. He was also presented with floral baskets by the Guinean president, the Political Bureau of the Party for Unity and Progress of Guinea, the Palestinian president, the prime minister of Thailand, the first vice-president of the Council of Ministers who is the minister of Revolutionary Armed Forces of Cuba and other state and party leaders, government ministers and figures from all walks of life of many countries.*
>
> *President Kim Il Sung was awarded certificates of honorary citizenship by the government of Canar Province of Ecuador and Magdalena del Mar District of Lima City, Peru[9].*
>
> *Kim Jong Il was also presented with certificates of honorary*

---

[8] http://www.kcna.co.jp/item/2004/200405/news05/14.htm
[9] A Peruvian reader of my original website report wrote to say that Peruvian municipal authorities are not allowed to confer honorary citizenship.

citizenship by Rafael Lara Grajales City of Puebla Province, Mexico, and Magdalena del Mar District of Lima City, Peru.

Commemoration and celebration functions marking the April holidays were held at least on 1,000 occasions under the sponsorship of over 2,000 political parties, organizations and institutions in more than 100 countries.

The functions were held in more than 20 forms such as meetings, national seminars, "cultural evenings to commemorate the Day of the Sun", the opening ceremonies of the week of Korean culture, art performances, sports contests, book and photo exhibitions, film shows and lectures.

Over 600 media of 130 or more countries featured the commemoration and celebration events more than 2,500 times.

Upwards of 380 newspapers of over 90 countries dedicated articles to the events with portraits of Kim Il Sung and Kim Jong Il and over

More political monuments, Pyongyang.

The uncompleted Ryugong Hotel, which was supposed to be the tallest hotel in the world, when completed.

100 TVs of 50 odd countries made special telecasts of films recording the revolutionary activities of the peerlessly great men.

At least 100 radios of over 70 countries aired brief histories of revolutionary activities of Kim Il Sung and Kim Jong Il and articles on the indomitable might of the KPA and the revolutionary paeans "Song of General Kim Il Sung" and "Song of General Kim Jong Il" and other Korean songs.

Every April, Pyongyang plays host to the International Kimilsungia Festival, which must be one of the largest flower shows in the world by visitor number. Held at the modern, very grandiose Kimilsungia-Kimjonglia Exhibition Hall, this must be the only flower show in the world devoted to only two flowers — none other than the Kimilsungia and Kimjonglia, flowers named after the Great Leader and Dear Leader.

We arrived at the venue to find the whole area crowded with disciplined Korean families and groups of workers — men in formal suits and ladies in flowing traditional gowns — walking in file to the exhibition hall. As tourists, we were given priority entry and were greeted by an enormous full-wall painting of Kim Il Sung and Kim Jong Il with the crater lake of Mt. Paektu in the background. Hundreds of pots of blooming Kimilsungia and Kimjongilia were placed in front of the painting, turning the whole area into a symphony of pink and red.

Hundreds of people — families, co-workers and friends — queued patiently for their chance to have their photos taken in front of the painting, and more people streamed into the building — once the ushers had cleared the earlier group. It was an incredible sight, with loud piped military marching and patriotic music. Definitely a pseudo-religious ritual of pompous proportions. Although we were now used to unreserved displays of piety for the Kims by this sixth day of our tour, what appeared in front of us was nonetheless spectacular.

I asked the exhibition guide how many visitors there were. "800,000 people attended the last exhibition held here two months ago, during the birthday of the Dear Leader Comrade Kim Jong Il — the 8th Kimjonglia

Festival. We expect the number to exceed a million this time, during this 8th Kimilsungia Festival."

Wow! This must be the weirdest and most assiduously attended flower show in the world!

We were quickly taken into a few rooms where there was a display on the history and background of the two flowers. The pink Kimilsungia is a species of orchid, first bred by an Indonesian botanist, and presented by Sukarno to Kim Il Sung in 1965 when the latter visited Indonesia. It was named after Kim Il Sung, a gesture which North Korea's KCNA called "a symbol of the great love and genuine admiration the people of Indonesia have for the Great Leader".

Before long, this tropical orchid became the symbol of the regime and over 250 greenhouses have since been built to grow this tropical hybrid all over this country of harsh winter. Despite the shortage of electricity, the greenhouses of Kimilsungia are always looked after very well. During the famine and energy crisis of the late 1990's, KCNA carried reports about how patriotic citizens asked the state energy bureaus to shut down their home heating systems during winter so that there would be enough electric power for the glories of Kimilsungia.

How can there be a flower for the father without one for the son? The Dear Leader's cause was answered by a Japanese botanist in 1988. The Kimjonglia is a variety of the South American begonia. Huge and red, some critics say the Dear Leader needs flowers larger than his father's to make up for his father's greater stature in history. Whatever it was, the Kimjonglia took off in a big way too, with huge Kimjonglia festivals every year as well.

Into the exhibition proper. Numerous provincial and municipal authorities, military units, factories and even foreign embassies seemed to have sponsored displays of the two flowers. A typical display comprised a wall-sized panel with one or both of the Kims, either in formal suits, in military uniforms, on a running horse, with children, with workers/ farmers/soldiers, with people of all colours from around the world, or Mt Paektu/Kim Il Sung's birthplace, or the Chollima horse in the background. And in front of every panel, countless pots of Kimilsungia and Kimjonglia.

They even have prizes for the best exhibits!

The whole exhibition centre, probably the size of a few football fields, was jammed with massive crowds. What a nice family or office outing opportunity! Great music such as the Song of General Kim Il Sung and the Song of General Kim Jong Il, lots (or rather many of two kinds) of beautiful flowers, not to mention an excellent venue for people watching. All the hunks and babes of Pyongyang are here for the flowers… oops… I mean for the admiration of the exquisite Kimilsungia and Kimjonglia.

» » » » »

NIGHTTIME — THE GRAND FINALE OF KIM IL SUNG'S BIRTHDAY CELEBRATIONS. We went to the big square named after the God himself, to watch the celebrations from a grand stand full of foreign diplomats, tourists, the top brass of the Korean People's Army in their full uniform splendour and the well-dressed, well-fed elite of DPRK society (the "New North Koreans"?) in expensive, almost bourgeois outfits.

What a breathtaking sight! On the enormous square was a huge colourful platform with a symphony orchestra and numerous singers surrounded by a hundred thousand Korean dancers, in a kaleidoscope of amazingly colourful traditional costumes. Balloons were released into the skies, huge banners everywhere on the dazzling square overlooked by the oddly solemn portraits of Kim Il Sung, Karl Marx and Vladimir Lenin. An exuberant sight which only became eerie when one realised they were celebrating the birthday of a man dead for a decade and yet still the "eternal president" of the country.

Before long, beautiful Korean girls rushed up the viewing platform to get the foreign guests onto the square. And so we went, dancing with the people of Pyongyang. A dozen Sikh dancers from India, complete with turbans and flowing Punjabi robes, ran around the splendid square in a line, wildly waving the flag of the DPRK. Yes, these were the people who appeared in the local papers today, praising the Book of Juche, in total admiration.

That night, Pyongyang suffered no power shortage. All the buildings were brightly lit, and I presume, the lifts and taps worked as well.

Whither the Axis of Evil?

We drove west to Nampo City, a port of over 750,000 inhabitants at the mouth of the Taedong River. Although Nampo is an important city, the bare austerity of communism has turned this into what looks like a bare, ugly city of unpainted run-down buildings and smoky chimneys.

We headed for the West Sea Barrage in the city's suburbs, passing fish farms and salt fields. Completed in 1986, this is an 8km wide dam built over five years across the estuary of the Taedong River. It not only controls the tide of the Western Sea and hence enhances flood-control, but also regulates the passage of huge vessels through three locks, and enabled the reclamation of many hectares of land for agriculture.

Once again, this engineering wonder, which they claimed to be the world's greatest dam project (though I could not find it on any world ranking) was credited to the "heroic army-constructors under the revolutionary leadership of Great Leader General Kim Il Sung and Dear Leader General Kim Jong Il, who visited many times and gave numerous on-the-spot guidance."

One of us asked whether the Great Leader had engineering know-how and how many workers died in the construction. The local guide looked a little puzzled and said, "We had ensured the highest engineering and safety standards. The Great Leader himself, who is a genius, conceived the idea and designed the whole project. How could anyone have died in the construction?"

»»»»»

Summarised extracts from a DPRK book, *Kim Jong Il — The Great Man*[10]:
    Phone Call at Dawn

   An official received a phone call from Kim Jong Il's secretary at dawn one day. "Dear Comrade Kim Jong Il wants you on the phone. I will put you through."

---

[10] Li Il Bok & Yun Sang Hyon, *Kim Jong Il — The Great Man*, 1989, p. 13.

Sprang to his feet, the official said when the phone is connected, "Dear Comrade Leader! I am on the phone."

There was a strange silence. The official's heart throbbed with fear. Had he done something wrong? 15 minutes past before Kim Jong Il's tender voice was heard, "I'm sorry. I called you up but dozed off." Fatigue was felt in his voice.

The official said in a trembling voice, "Dear Comrade Leader! What time is it now? I'm worried that you do not go to bed every night like this."

"Well, the same story over again. Excuse me." Said the Dear Leader Kim Jong Il.

The official listened to him silently, his eyes glistening with tears.

» » » » »

Back in Pyongyang, we visited the National Art Gallery and its exquisite display of the ancient murals of the Koguryo Kingdom (57–668 AD), which straddled the Chinese-North Korean border. The kingdom, founded seven years before the Great Fire of Rome in Nero's reign, is famous for its tomb murals, found in both North Korea and China, which depict life in this martial kingdom with strong cultural influences from China.

Both China and North/South Korea are now submitting these ancient tombs for listing as World Heritage Sites, even though a dispute has broken out over the Chinese claim that Koguryo was a Chinese regional state rather than Korean kingdom. It is astonishing to see how politicians make a mountain out of an anthill.

We strolled around the serene greens of Moran Hill, where families had a relaxing day dancing and picnicking. Here, we saw the Koreans as a people no different from you and me. They too, like us, laugh, cry, joke, dance, run, walk and sleep. That evening, on the bus back to the hotel from dinner, Ms. Park sang a song of farewell dedicated to us. As night descended over the city, I felt a sudden sense of sympathy for these people.

Over the past week, we had gained great respect for the North Korean people. They are friendly, helpful and polite. They often bow when saying 'thank you' and they take interest in people as individuals. They have hopes and aspirations for their lives, and they have suffered terribly in recent times. Whatever misgivings I may have had for the way the country is being run, I cannot condemn the ordinary people as terrorists or evildoers. If George W. Bush and his neo-con imperialists had decided to launch a military adventure in North Korea, my support — not that it means anything substantial — would have gone immediately to these people.

Political painting depicting Kim Il Sung as world leader, admired by people everywhere.

The Yalu Bridge Leads to the Future

DAY OF FAREWELL. At the Pyongyang Train Station, Mr. Roh and Ms. Park sent us off. After confirming for the last time that we could not get hold of their Great Leader badges (they were specially issued to individuals by the state and had to be properly accounted for), Mr. Roh became our model of the day. All of us zoomed in on his tiny badge with our cameras.

Onto the Chinese carriages, hitched onto a North Korean locomotive and meant-for-locals carriages that were barred to us, plus a few Russian carriages from Vladivostok. The train limped through the wretched-looking countryside, taking five hours to cover 120km. We passed farmers ploughing their fields with oxen, red flags flapping in the wind, towns of rusty factories and unpainted concrete, and railway stations whose only hint of colour was the portraits of the two leaders.

We must have passed through the small town of Ryongchon, where a train accident a few days later led to a major disaster that killed hundreds. I have no idea exactly which stop it was but it could well have been the one where I was stopped from snapping a picture for the first time on this journey.

A cargo train full of coal and timber was travelling parallel to our stationary train. People were holding on tight to the rooftops of the carriages, not unlike a typical railway scene in India and Bangladesh. I clicked away with my camera, but a soldier on the station platform shouted, strangely, in Russian, "*Nyet, foto!*" A Chinese passenger standing near shouted in Chinese, "*Ta suo bu ke pai zao!*" ("He says, no photo!")

I put away my camera. Fortunately, nothing more happened. The soldier didn't jump onto the train for an arrest, which could well have been the case five years ago. The country is changing, though hardly fast enough.

A large city soon came into sight. This was Sinuiju, the capital of North Phyongan Province which lies on Yalu river, facing the Chinese city of Dandong. This was also the site of the Sinuiju Special Economic Zone, which failed to take off after the Chinese arrested the dodgy Dutch-Chinese tycoon, Yang Bin.

Yang Bin was appointed by Kim Jong Il to be the Chief Executive of what was supposed to become the North Korean equivalent of Shenzhen (the booming Chinese city on the border with Hong Kong). The Chinese had accused Yang Bin of dodging taxes, although some observers said the move was taken to punish Kim Jong Il for disobedience to his Chinese overlords, while some suspected that it was a favour granted to the Americans who were anxious to see Kim Jong Il's experiment fail.

Sinuiju has long been exposed to the rapid economic reforms of China. Chinese businessmen and day tourists come here often, leaving capitalist influences dreaded and rejected in the rest of North Korea. As the train rolled across the city's tracks, casual glances revealed many small shops, kiosks and hawkers that might indicate the emergence of private enterprise in this country.

Even then, this was a pathetically run-down city, whose only saving grace was the gigantic statue of Kim Il Sung, with arms pointing south towards Pyongyang. We endured an incredible three hours of passport examination and customs at the railway station. Here, we dealt with a few rather rude, stiff-looking customs officials, who were the only fat people we had seen on the trip, not counting the portraits of our two best friends that we saw everywhere in this country. Obviously, we had learned who made the most money in North Korea.

The train moved again, and there it was, the splendid Yalu River that divides China and North Korea. On the North Korean side are the decaying, rundown facades and high-rise slums of the Stalinist state. On the Chinese side, nothing but the skylines of Dandong's dazzling glass towers and massive shopping malls and hotels, all recent monuments and evidence of China's new commercialism and economic superpower status in Asia.

Dandong may be among the poorest of China's medium-sized cities but compared to any of North Korea's cities including Pyongyang, it is the brave new world, a first-worldish place next to a miserable wreck of propaganda and lies. Even the Chinese customs service we would encounter later, though communist in name, was polite and efficient, and had the entry cards filled in for us.

The kilometre-wide Sino-Korean Friendship Bridge was a link between two economic systems. We saw the stumps of the old Yalu Bridge on the North Korean side of the river, mere remnants of the bridge destroyed by American bombers in 1950, as well as the still intact "half-bridge" over the Chinese half of the river.

Given the entrenched rule of the Kim family in the DPRK, it is inconceivable that the country will be ruled by anyone other than Kim Jong Il, at least in the next decade or so. Even South Korea probably dreads seeing the collapse of his regime, for the spectre of penniless refugees and a massive hungry army frightens economic planners in Seoul. As a result, Kim has been able to manipulate the South Koreans, so that the latter would continue giving millions of dollars in aid to the North.

Kim Jong Il, for all his misadventures, is not a frog in a well. In fact, former US Secretary of State Madeleine Albright, who has met Mr. Kim, said that he was rational, very well informed and "was not delusional".

The winds of capitalism and market economics have triumphed everywhere. Kim Jong Il had seen what happened in China and elsewhere, and there are signs that reforms are being gradually undertaken to save the regime. Whilst this is unlikely to lead to a new democratic North Korea in the short term, my bet is that Kim Jong Il would adopt the Chinese model of gradual economic reforms coupled with the existing iron-fisted rule.

Kim Jong Il's private kingdom, funded by a mixture of nuclear extortions and perhaps South Korean and Chinese investments in the coming years, could harness the nation's low-cost but highly educated workforce to turn itself into one of the largest chaebol in both North and South Korea.

Ultimately, Kim Jong Il might consider tweaking the outstretched arm of his father's statue, either northwards to Dandong, or slightly to the southeast, towards that state they currently denounce as the "American puppet government in Seoul". Perhaps then North Korea will be on track to become a worker's paradise.

Western Balkans: Field of Black Birds (June 2002)

"Violence was indeed all I knew of the Balkans,' writes Rebecca West, 'all I knew of the South Slavs."

Quoted from *The Atlantic*, January 19, 1941

"The Balkans, then, evoked not so much a specific area as the idea of localized chaos, of balkanization, of primitive quarrels and primeval ways of resolving them."

Bozidar Jezernik, Wild Europe
— *The Balkans in the Gaze of Western Travellers*, 2004

15 June 1389, St Vitus Day, Kosovo Polije. This was the year England and France signed a temporary truce during the Hundred Years' War; Queen Margaret I of Denmark united Scandinavia under the Kalmar Union; Hayam Waruk, the greatest ruler of the Majapahit Empire who ruled the sea lanes, ports and islands of Southeast Asia, died, signaling the beginning of the last great Hindu kingdom of the region; and the Sultan of Delhi and the boy-king of Korea were murdered. In the Balkans, a major battle was in the offing. Led by Prince Lazar of the Serbs, the princes of the Balkans — the Serbs, Bosnians, Albanians and Bulgarians — gathered on this flat plain for the day of reckoning. Against them, the Turks under Sultan Murad, had mustered the greatest invasion force ever on the Plains of the Black Birds — Kosovo Polije in the Serbian language.

The trumpets roared and 60,000 heavily armoured men clashed. At the end of the day, vultures encircled the plains of corpses and the river turned into lakes of blood. Both Prince Lazar and Sultan Murad were dead. So were thousands of their men.

The flower of the Serbian nobility had been wiped out in the battle and the landscape of the Balkans was changed forever. The Turks regrouped under a new sultan and soon overran the entire Balkans. The Serbian nation was gone, except in ballads and folklore, to be passed down through generations, who would learn about the glories of its great kings and princes, as well as the tragic battle of Kosovo.

15 June 1989, St Vitus Day, Kosovo Polije. The revitalised Serbian nation was more than 100 years old, and now part of a larger Yugoslav Federation. A crisis had broken out, and the new Serbian President, Milosevic, had called for a million citizens to gather on the plains of Kosovo on the 600th anniversary of the Battle of Kosovo.

The coffin of Prince Lazar, holy saint of the Serbian Orthodox Church, was opened for the masses. The crowd roared in this fanatical display of religious piety in a state that was only a few years before officially atheistic. "Never again Kosovo!" Milosevic vowed. "Serbia will never fall again!" With that, the parliament of Serbia abolished the autonomy of Kosovo and set off the wars of Yugoslav disintegration.

The Balkans is the geographical expression for the countries in southeastern Europe, in particular those parts of Europe once occupied by Ottoman Turkey. This term arose in the 19th century with the need to define those regions of European Turkey where rising nationalistic passions were stirring with the corresponding decline of the Turkish Empire. 'Balkans' has since become a byword not only for the ethnic diversity and perceived backwardness of the region, but also for complicated ethnic issues and dysfunctional politics which have led to many tragic wars and untold suffering since then. This term has become unfashionable. Slovenia and Croatia now prefer to call themselves Central Europe whilst some in Romania and Bulgaria, among the European Union's newest members, now call themselves Southeastern Europe.

From June to July 2002, I travelled around Southeastern Europe, in Albania and what used to be the former Yugoslav republics. This was a region of bloody warfare and chaos in the 1990's, beginning with the dramatic assertion of Serbian rights at the historic Field of Black Birds in Kosovo, leading to the declaration of independence of Slovenia and Croatia and a series of wars across the region, which only ended in 2001 when President Milosevic of Serbia was overthrown not long after Serbia was forced to evacuate Kosovo. This was a journey into the region's bloody decade where I met many colourful characters on my travels in old battlefields.

This was not my first trip to the Balkans. I was in the region in 1995, when I travelled overland from Vienna to Istanbul, passing through Slovenia, Croatia, Hungary, Romania and Bulgaria. Full-scale war was on at that time in Bosnia and I could not travel south of Zagreb as the Croatian capital was cut off from the southern half of the country by the Serbians who controlled the territory in between.

Map showing countries in the Western Balkans

Macedonia: Your Name or Mine

Macédoine — a French salad of mixed fruits and vegetables. Some say the diverse ethnographic mix of the Balkans region of Macedonia inspired the expression.

THESSALONIKI, OLD SALONIKA. PEARL OF THE AEGEAN, SECOND CITY OF THE BYZANTINE EMPIRE. I arrived in Greece's second largest city and the capital of Greek Macedonia on Thursday morning. Ouzo billboards, strong Greek coffee, gyros stalls and loud Greek music suggest nothing more Greek than Thessaloniki. But good old Salonika, as the city is also called, hasn't always been as Greek as the Thessaloniki of today.

Two hundred years ago, the city was ethnically more diverse — with Greeks, Jews and Turks living together. Kemal Mustafa Ataturk, father of modern Turkey, was born in a town house in the centre of Salonika in 1881, the same year Pablo Picasso was born and Thomas Edison and Alexander Graham Bell formed the Oriental Telephone Company. Venture to the countryside and an 18th century visitor would have found Turkish landlords

and Slavic Macedonian farmers, Vlad shepherds — these are descendants of Roman soldiers who still speak a tongue similar to Latin and Romanian — and Roma gypsy nomads. By the start of WWI, the ancient region of Macedonia had been subdivided by the Greeks, Serbians and Bulgarians.

The Treaty of Lausanne, which settled the post-WWI Greco-Turkish War, implemented the Great Exchange of Populations between Greece and Turkey — the Turks of Macedonia departed for Turkey, to be replaced by the Greeks of Pontus and Anatolia. Hitler moved the Jews to the death camps of Mitteleuropa, and intense Hellenisation led to the departure of Slavic Macedonians to Bulgaria and Yugoslav-controlled Macedonia, as well as Australia. Greeks left other parts of the Balkans for Greece as the Iron Curtain fell across half the continent. Old Salonika became a mono-ethnic city. This was a scenario being played repeatedly across the Balkans, especially in the past decade of the wars of Yugoslav succession.

It was no accident that I chose Thessaloniki as my beachhead into the Balkans. Salonika, founded by one of Alexander the Great's generals and his successor in Greece in 315 BC and named after Alexander's sister, is the largest city of both Greek and Slavic Macedonia. The crossroads of history, it was the homeland of Alexander the Great, the conqueror whose forces defeated the Persians, and created an empire of their own, stretching from Egypt to Ferghana Valley in Uzbekistan, which I visited in 1998. The Macedonian kingdom that propelled into the Classical Age was, to the Greek city-states, a semi-barbarian, newly Hellenised upstart formed by Alexander's father, Philip II, whose armies marched into the Greek peninsula to enforce the right of imperial power. It was feared and despised by the city-states in equal measure.

Philip's tomb was discovered in the 1970's in Vergina, a village to the west of Thessaloniki. Also discovered there was the emblem of the Macedonian dynasty, the Golden Star with outstretched rays. The newly independent Macedonian Republic adopted this famous logo in 1991 upon the collapse of the Yugoslav Federation — a move that infuriated the Greeks, who demanded for a change of name for the country and promptly declared a blockade of poor little Macedonia.

Eventually tiny Macedonia, with 2 million people, was forced to change its national flag, and was only admitted into the UN and international organisations as the Former Yugoslav Republic of Macedonia, a bizarre, cumbersome mouthful which only UN bureaucrats could think of. Utterly ridiculous, considering that even Serbia and Montenegro would soon no longer call themselves Yugoslavia[11]; and yet Macedonia is forced to hold on to that outdated title.

After the collapse of Alexander's empire, Macedonia became a mere geographical expression for two millennia. The Slavic tribes came and intermarried with the local semi-Hellenised Macedonians. Even then, ethnic Greeks continued to live in the city and the Turks arrived here too, when the Ottoman Empire captured the region in the 14th century and ruled the region till the start of the 20th century. So what do you call the people here? Aren't they all Macedonians, whether Slavic, Greek, Turkish, Teletubbie or whatever? Should anyone have a monopoly on the name 'Macedonia'? Welcome to the Balkans, land of confused politics and identities!

After a relaxing day in Thessaloniki visiting the numerous ancient Byzantine churches (as well as Ataturk's house museum which was heavily guarded against anti-Turk activists) and thoroughly bored with the numerous slogans like "Macedonian is Greek", I took a train across the border to the Republic of Macedonia.

When I bought the ticket, I had to say "Skopje, the Yugoslav Republic". The Greek press calls it the "rump Skopje Republic". If you took the train the other way, you would see the large Greek billboard "Welcome to Macedonia" — later I was to meet people who were confused by these signboards on their way to Thessaloniki and thought they were still in the Republic of Macedonia".

I met Alexis, a Greek engineer, on his way to Skopje to meet his Macedonian girlfriend. They met each other in an Internet chatroom a year ago and since then, he has been making almost fortnightly trips to Skopje. He took out her photo from his wallet — a girl with most engaging features that reminded me of a Slavic Monroe. Was politics a problem? No, Alexis

---

[11] This was written in 2002, before the dissolution of Serbia and Montenegro into two separate states.

said, love is love, and love transcends boundaries. And he whispered into my ears, and sex is sex, and sex transcends boundaries too. Only politicians argue about those meaningless issues of how Macedonia should be named, he said. And of course, he won't even utter a word about politics when he's with his prospective parents-in-law.

After an hour of rolling hills and lush green valleys, I entered the territory of the Macedonian Republic.

» » » » »

Skopje, the capital of Macedonia, was a dilapidated city of 500,000 people. It was destroyed in the great earthquake of 1963 and huge ugly complexes were built after that. After the following decades of socialist decay and the economic collapse due to the break-up of the Yugoslav Federation, everything started to fall apart again.

Even the famous Stone Bridge, which is a symbol of the city, was out of bounds for repairs, for god-knew-how-long. Rubbish and rubble were piling up in open spaces in the city centre, and plastic mineral water bottles and the ever-present black trash bags — symbol of modern consumerism and non-biodegradable wastage — were floating through the Vardar River on its lazy meander to the Aegean Sea. It was unbelievable that this dirty, dilapidated city was linked to two great figures in Byzantine history.

It was here in Skopje that the Byzantine Emperor Justinian (482–565 AD) was born. He succeeded his uncle Justin I as emperor in 527AD

Alexander the Great:
Does he belong to
Greece or the Slavic–
Macedonia of today?

around the time the Saxon kingdom of Essex was founded in England and the great Buddhist complex of Bulguska was built in Korea. Not satisfied with being merely the emperor of the Eastern Roman Empire, he set off to conquer Rome and the West, together with much of the Middle East and North Africa, bringing the Byzantine Empire to its greatest territorial extent with the help of his capable generals, Belisarius and Mundus. He also wrote Roman Law, which remains the basis of civil law across much of the world even today. His architects left a wonderful legacy of spectacular masterpieces, in particular, the Hagia Sophia, which remains the most visited monument in Istanbul today.

More controversially, he married Theodora, a courtesan, though she had proven to be a good advisor who was credited with many of Justinian's wise policies. On Theodora's advice, Justinian crushed, with great resolution and brutality, the Nika Riots, which had almost toppled his government. 30,000 rebels were killed in the heart of Constantinople during the suppression. Justinian was also a champion of Christianity, and issued decrees and actively sought the suppression of all other religions. He shut down famous temples and religious shrines of the ancient Greek and Egyptian religions, and persecuted the Jews across the Empire. Some historians believe that it was Justinian's suppression of religion and popular dislike of Byzantine rule that led to the rapid conquest of the Middle East by the armies of Islam, decades after the reign of Justinian.

Skopje was also once the capital of the Serbian Tsar Dusan Stefan (1308–1355), the greatest of the Serbian monarchs, who ruled lands from the Danube to the Aegean Sea about the same time Western Europe lost between 30–60% of its population as a result of the Black Plague. He conquered all Byzantine lands west of Constantinople, codified Serbian laws and founded the Serbian Orthodox Church as a separate church. It was his military victories that forced the Byzantines into inviting the Turks into the Balkans, thus leading to the eventual conquest of the Byzantine Empire by the Turks and their subsequent expansion all the way to the gates of Vienna.

Despite the downright decrepitude, Skopje had its charms. Six hundred years of Turkish rule have left the city full of tall, magical Turkish minarets along the skyline, like a mini Istanbul of mesmerizing towers and unspoken secrets. As I stepped into the Old City, which was still largely inhabited by local Turks and Albanians, I felt as though I was in Turkey or Albania, with loud energetic Turkish and Albanian pop music bursting out from the many cafes in its winding streets and the bazaar, described by *Lonely Planet* as the last Oriental bazaar of its kind in Europe. Across the river in New Skopje, young fashionably-dressed Slavic Macedonians strolled around in its wide avenues and leafy squares. Nearby was the statue of saintly Mother Theresa, born here to an ethnic Albanian family.

In the cafès in this city, spies, revolutionaries and conspirators once met a hundred years ago to plot the expulsion of the Ottomans and its replacement with Greek, Serbian or Bulgarian rule — Macedonia as a separate nation state from its neighbours is a new concept, not fully evolved even here. Today, spies, revolutionaries and conspirators probably continue to meet in this city, discussing the latest intrigues involving the young Macedonian state and its Greek, Kosovar Albanian and Serbian neighbours — some players have changed but the stake remains this sleepy land of green meadows and slow, winding rivers.

With the Kosovo conflict of 1999 and the subsequent Albanian rebellion in Macedonia of summer 2001, Skopje has, most unexpectedly, experienced an unusual boom of sorts. The large number of NATO troops, UN personnel, aid agencies, EU bureaucrats, assorted diplomats, intelligence services and journalists have led to the appearance of numerous restaurants, bars, night

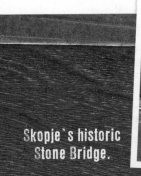

Skopje's historic
Stone Bridge.

clubs and even an Irish pub. I was told that the local Chinese and Indian restaurants were run by extremely entrepreneurial people who rushed to Priština to open branches very soon after NATO forces moved in.

Macedonia had few tourists and everyone thought that any foreigner here must belong to some international organisation. Indeed, KFOR (the NATO-led Kosovo Force) and UNPREDEP (the UN Preventive Deployment Force that patrols Macedonia's borders with Albania and Serbia) soldiers and vehicles belonging to UN, FAO, UNICEF and other international agencies were everywhere. I was asked many times to which organisation I belonged. One local even thought I was an Anglo-Chinese in the British Army given the slight hint of English accent in my speech after five years in London. They remained suspicious when I said I was a mere tourist. They probably thought I was a spy from somewhere. Maybe Beijing, or even Taiwan.

Macedonia is the site of some strange intrigues between the two Chinas. In 1999, China accused the Macedonians of treachery when the latter switched to recognition of Taiwan after the Taiwanese offered millions in aid. China then vetoed resolutions in the UN on extending the mandate of UNPREDEP in Macedonia. Since then, the Macedonians have switched recognition back to China, with millions in Beijing aid replacing that of Taiwan.

»»»»»

Macedonia is an easy country to travel around. Most Macedonians speak English very well — like the Scandinavians — and they are open about their political views. It was interesting to hear them but also depressing to notice that many believe that war would break out at some time. Between 20–40% of the population is ethnic Albanian (exact number depending on whom you believed) and since the liberation of Kosovo from Serbian oppression, many Albanians, especially those in Kosovo, believe in the establishment of a Greater Albania, including all the territories where ethnic Albanians live, i.e., southern Montenegro, Preshevo Valley in Serbia and western Macedonia.

Rebellion broke out in Tetovo, one of the largest cities in Macedonia, in summer 2001, the pretext being discrimination by majority ethnic Macedonians against the local Albanians. The small Macedonian Army was ill prepared for this insurgency and, many say, would have completely lost control of the situation if NATO had not intervened. Since then, a ceasefire has been in effect although political tension remains high. According to the "Internationals" I spoke to, the large western cities of Tetovo and Goristar have become 75% Albanian, as ethnic Macedonians have fled eastwards to more Slavic areas of the country.

David, a Macedonian I met, felt that Macedonia was a mere pawn in the big game. If the big powers wanted Macedonia to be partitioned, David reckoned, Macedonia would have no chance at all. Albanians and Slavic Macedonians — according to a number of people I met — are physically not overly different. People generally get along with each other. It's the politicians who create all the trouble. It is they who stir up the ethnic tensions and latent fear of being overwhelmed by the "enemy". Isn't that the same everywhere around the world?

»»»»

I took a bus to the UNESCO World Heritage City of Ohrid, passing the city of Tetovo with its beautiful Alpine scenery, although I also remembered the scenes on TV showing the Albanian rebels firing on Tetovo from those same mountains above. Ohrid is one of the oldest cities in the Balkans. Located on the shores of the lake bearing its name, Ohrid was the old capital of the Bulgarian Empire of Tsar Samuel, one of the greatest Bulgarian monarchs. Samuel, who was once called "invincible in power and unsurpassable in strength", fought the Byzantines and every other nation in the Balkans, and at one time established a huge empire in the region. Like other warlords in this tumultuous region, his empire, a military machine less successful at institutional building beyond the predominant ethnic group of the state, did not last beyond his death. In 1014, Samuel died of a heart attack after witnessing the return of 15,000 Bulgarian soldiers, who had been captured and then blinded in both eyes by the Byzantines after the Battle of Kleidion. One soldier out of every 100 had been spared an eye so that they could lead the rest back to their homeland. His empire collapsed four years later, conquered by the Byzantine emperor, Basil II, the Bulgar-slayer.

The Macedonian national identity has always been in a flux. Even its cities were once key centres of neighbouring states other than its own — Skopje, capital of Macedonia was once capital of the Serbian emperor, and Ohrid, Macedonia's jewel, was formerly capital of the Bulgarians. No wonder everyone has a claim on this land.

But beautiful Ohrid is more than the capital of a long dead Bulgarian empire builder. This city, also nicknamed the Jerusalem of the Balkans, was where the Slavic saints, Cyril and Methodius, invented the Cyrillic alphabet, used in languages such as Russian, Bulgarian, Serbian, Macedonian, Ukrainian and Belarusian. Ohrid is also famous for the amazing frescoes in its churches — 40 altogether. There used to be 365, one for each day of the year. Brightly coloured frescoes, some dating back to the 10th century, adorned its many churches.

For US$10, I rented a room from retired professor Kirste, his wife Olga and their jobless son, Mitko. The collapse of the former Yugoslav states had a dramatic impact on the lives of its citizens. My Macedonian friends lament the good old days under Josip Tito, the strongman who tolerated no racism and ethnic chauvinism. Those were the days when Yugoslav citizens needed no visas to visit the world, apart from Australia and the USA. Now

Sveti Naum Monastery by Lake Ohrid.

they cannot even step into neighbouring states. The loss of traditional markets and political instability has destroyed any prospects of economic growth. After 10 years of war, many wondered if only the political class has benefited from all the bloodshed, especially when so many in this group have become rich from smuggling, private deals and phoney privatisation.

It was also in an Ohrid cybercafé that I met a pretty local model, Jane, after a flirtatious exchange of eye signals and cryptic messages. We had a candlelight dinner at a pasta restaurant that was as romantic as a restaurant of this kind could get in a sleepy post-Communist town. We walked along the banks of beautiful Lake Ohrid, with the lit-up citadel of Tsar Samuel in the background. "Take me to Skopje or Belgrade, and out of this hopeless land to wherever you are going" Jane said in semi-jest. The miserably high unemployment rates meant few assignments; and Jane had to sign up with the local military police force instead.

The meeting of foreigners, mostly associated with international organizations and far-richer lands, bring some obscure hopes of a better future. Even Belgrade, capital of war-torn Serbia, was perceived as a more attractive place by some Macedonians. After all, Belgrade was the old metropolis of Yugoslavia, a worldlier city compared to sleepy provincial Macedonia. I wonder how lives can be different for people in different lands. A twist of fate at birth means a lifetime of different fortunes.

»»»»»

I returned to an alarmed Professor Kirste in the morning — he was relieved that I hadn't been murdered by bandits and rebels — and got on a local ferry to Sveti Naum, a 10th century Orthodox monastery near the border with Albania, which was famous for its fabulous frescoes. Here, I was blessed with a wonderful view of the lake. Its blue waters, and the green, sun-struck mountains with still, black shadows — this was purest Balkans in typical 19th century "acrylics". The crystal clear air and the fragrance of the morning grass masked the tension that prevailed in this land.

Serbia: Dreams Broken & Rebuilt

BELGRADE, THE WHITE CITY. Capital of Serbia and the soon-to-be-abolished Yugoslav Federation, at least to be in a form substantially different from the present one. Across the Danube, the city rises steeply onto a plateau. Here, fashionable Belgraders parade on its wide boulevards littered with numerous cafès and flashy emporiums of luxury goods. There was little sign of war, apart from the uncountable potholes and burnt-out frames of the Ministry of Defense and a few other buildings in hidden corners.

The Serbs are a beautiful people characterized by tall builds and sharp cheekbones. Stern, expressionless and reserved at first encounter, they melt into warm smiles and humble greetings when the stranger probes further. They are hardly like Milosevic or Karadzic with whom the world has grown familiar in the turbulent times of the 1990's.

The Serbs are a romantic people with a strong sense of history and sometimes, a skewed view of their national destiny. Throughout their troubled history, they have often seen themselves as a victimized nation, the defenders of European civilization and the ones destined to suffer for their love of their land and freedom. The mediaeval Serbian kingdom flourished under Tsar Stefan Dusan the Great, when its borders stretched from the Danube to the Aegean Sea. The enormous riches of the empire were manifested in the exuberant monasteries built in its heartland — in what is today the lost province of Kosovo — and the sacred monastic republic on Mt. Athos, northern Greece.

The empire scattered after Dusan died. Caught between the Christian West and Islamic East, the Serbs saw themselves as the defenders of Western Civilisation after the Ottoman conquest. The Serbian nation rose again in the 19th century and by the end of WWI, had transformed itself into Yugoslavia, a combination of the nations of the Southern Slavic peoples, namely the Serbs, Croats, Slovenes, Montenegrins, Macedonians and the Bosnian Muslims.

The Second World War rocked the foundation of the new state but Josip Tito, the charismatic strongman of Croat-Slovene origins, welded the country together with bullets and relatively fair distribution of jobs and wealth. The federation began to unravel after Tito's death in 1980. Nationalistic Serbs under Milosevic, President of Serbia, pursued a policy against minorities and increasing centralization; while other republics pursued greater decentralization and independence.

War broke out when the Slovenians and Croatians declared independence in 1991, followed by the Bosnians, actions which prompted the uprising of Serbs residing in these lands, who hoped to remain in the same state as Serbia. By 1995, the guns were silent in those lands but the thousand-year old communities of Serbs in Croatia had been all but expelled from their ancestral lands.

Milosevic's relentless policies of centralization and oppression drove the Albanians to rebellion, which only ended with the 1999 NATO intervention. Serbia was bombed, its infrastructure reduced to tatters — bridges, communication centers, oil refineries and more were left in ruins. Kosovo was evacuated and by the end of 2000, Milosevic was overthrown and arraigned in The Hague on war crimes charges.

History has come full circle. Not only has Serbia lost its battle for a more centralized Yugoslavia, the federation has fallen apart, Kosovo — a core autonomous province within Serbia — lost, and even the core republic of Montenegro and the autonomous province of Vovojdina are campaigning for independence.

In 2002, under EU pressure, Montenegro and Serbia agreed to abolish Yugoslavia, and set up a loose confederation known as Serbia and Montenegro. Critics doubt even this new creation would survive for long. As a Serbian businessman I met said, every town with half a million people would soon set up its own state.

Whatever the case, Serbia had lost big time. It is now but a much-reduced state with 8 million people, less than the population of Belgium. Its economy is in shambles. Serbia once had a medium-sized industrial economy. It exported cars, pharmaceutical products and other light manufacturing products. Now, many of the heavy industrial plants and its infrastructure have been damaged by war.

In the last few decades when Asia has been pursuing foreign investments and developing their key competencies, Serbian politicians talked politics and stocked arms. The country has a well-educated population and a skilled workforce, although some may argue that much of that workforce has to be retrained due to years of stagnation. Serbia's post-Milosevic government has announced investment incentives and privatization mandates, but would you want to invest in a country where every coalition government continues to be held hostage by radical right wing parties obsessed with lost territories?

I arrived in Belgrade after an overnight bus journey from Skopje, capital of Macedonia. The bus passed in creepy darkness, the wild borderlands of

Preshevo, where a new Albanian guerilla group is now campaigning for the incorporation of this smallish valley into Kosovo.

Whereas the ideas of Greater Serbia used to rock the Balkans, it was now the devilish dreams of Greater Albania that prevented those in Albanian-inhabited parts of western Macedonia, southern Montenegro and southern Serbia from sleeping well.

The bus also passed through Serbia's second largest city, Nis, where the infamous Skull Tower — a hellish structure built of Serbian skulls originally erected by the Ottoman Turks — reminds generations of Serbian children what could happen again if they lost another battle of Kosovo.

> *Belgrade is blessed as few cities are with natural beauty, lying high on the confluence of two great rivers, Danube and Sava; but it is like a pretty peasant girl with the carriage of a queen and the raiment of a dirty beggar.*
>
> — John Gunther, *Inside Europe*, 1938

Belgrade is a beautiful city at the junction of what was once the border between the Austro-Hungarian and the Ottoman Empires, as well as the frontier of Roman Catholicism and Eastern Orthodox Christianity. A statue of a naked man stood on the sharp apex of the fortress, looking northwards, as though to mock the Great Powers with his large, magical

Ministry of Defence building, Belgrade, bombed out by NATO forces.

tool. An ancient monastery graced its northern slopes, where the national saint, St Sava, was honoured.

A few miles further south were the centers of government. Violent events had taken place in these gigantic temples of power. The Old Palace, now the City Hall, was where King Alexander Obrenovic and deeply unpopular Queen Draga[12] were murdered in an army coup in 1903, their bodies mutilated, cut into pieces and then thrown over the balconies onto the front garden, where you can now sit for a picnic lunch. Across the street was the Federal Parliament, where in 1928, Radic, the Croatian nationalist leader was assassinated, an event that the Croats remember today. In 2000, this was the scene of a revolution in which the masses ransacked its halls and proclaimed the end of the Milosevic regime.

Across the park was the wreckage of Radio TV Serbia, bombed by NATO forces in 1999 — 16 people died. A monument stood nearby, with the word "Why?" on it. Was it worth it all? Milosevic knew that the building was a target but ordered the staff of RTVS to stay up late. The Federation needed its martyrs and NATO planes duly delivered the 16 deaths. Not far from here, a few streets further south, the twisted metal and hanging rocks of the Defense ministries greeted war tourists in a symphony of self-defiance. On the sidewalks of the main boulevard, kiosks sold postcards of the burnt-out buildings and of those denouncing NATO as barbarians. A rather humourous postcard depicts a Europe occupied by modern day Romans — the United States — and the Serbs as Asterix and the gallant tribes of Gaul.

The Serbs were a friendly lot. During my short stay, through contacts and the Internet, I was fortunate to be able to meet a number of interesting locals, ranging from news editors and émigré businessmen to human rights lawyers and artists. I also encountered much friendliness partly as the result of my ethnicity — the Serbian people see the Chinese as their allies due to the bombing of the Chinese Embassy in Belgrade by the US.

---

[12] Alexander became very unpopular when he married his mistress, Draga Mašin, a commoner ten years older who had been his mother's lady-in-waiting. Draga further got her brothers appointed prime minister and war minister, which infuriated the army and culminated in the coup of 1903.

A taxi driver in Novi Sad even gave me a huge discount! It was amazing to see that these were hardly the monsters that the Western media has portrayed all these years.

The Serbs have been a misunderstood people. Ethnic cleansing and the destruction of cultural monuments, such as the bombing of the ancient city of Dubrovnik, cannot be excused. But it is hard not to sympathise with the desire of the Serbian people to stay within the same country. Unfortunately, their efforts to maintain a dead federation led to much suffering for their enemies as well as for themselves. Most ironically, the whole region, including all the former Yugoslav states, might well be included in a united, borderless Europe within the next few decades.

I also took a bus to Novi Sad, capital of the Vovojdina Autonomous Province, home to 27 ethnic groups, including Hungarians, Croatians, Slovaks, Czechs, Ukrainians and Germans. This province has emerged from the decade of conflict relatively free of trouble. This is a tolerant region, where the locals understood the potential destructiveness of agitation and strove to avoid the type of rhetoric and bickering that led to disastrous consequences elsewhere in the Balkans. But even here, with a weakened Belgrade, local politicians were calling for a province with enhanced powers.

Public sculpture, Belgrade.

This flat land is the breadbasket of Serbia. Wheat, sunflowers, vegetables and rice flourish in the summer heat. I strolled along the leafy streets of Novi Sad; the gigantic ramparts of the Petrovaradin — Gibraltar of the Danube — rose to the skies above the NATO-blasted Danube bridges. The Petrovaradin once guarded the Austro-Hungarians against the onslaught of the Ottoman Turks, but today, it has become the site of the annual EXIT summer music festival, the Woodstock and Glastonbury of the Balkans.

Begun only in 2000, EXIT has caught the imagination of young Eastern Europeans and an increasing number of Western Europeans. I saw many enthusiastic young people setting up tents and festival installations. If only Serbian politicians could devote more effort to endeavours such as this than to struggle over causes to keep territories where the local population no longer saw themselves as Serbian.

I also had coffee with Mishko in a café overlooking the Danube. He is a social worker originally from central Serbia but now works with disabled children and orphans. Mishko has dense, curly black hair and a thick moustache; he chain-smoked throughout our entire conversation in the café. Mishko is gay and used to have a Bosnian-Muslim boyfriend from Sarajevo. The international press had written about the trails of heterosexual mixed race couples and the sufferings they had gone through when the ethnic conflicts of the former Yugoslav states tore families and friends apart. What was seldom covered were the experiences of mixed-race gay and lesbian couples such as the case of Mishko and his partner, Ali.

During the siege of Sarajevo, Mishko braved death and bribed corrupt soldiers so as to sneak into Sarajevo twice in four years to meet Ali and to bring him valuable supplies.

"Maybe I was younger then and love was everything." He stubbed out his cigarette on the long-abused plastic table, once bright yellow but now spattered with cigarette marks all over. "And I paid those bastard soldiers and militia with Deutschmarks I earned from black market trading."

Such was the power of love, which motivated people to do what they might not have done under ordinary circumstances. But life in peace was more mundane and the time apart which changed characters and habits caused greater damage to the relationship than war. Their love fell apart a few months after the war ended.

»»»»»

Back in Belgrade, however, I saw a people no longer interested in the politics of power and nationalism. The Serbia of today is tired after more than 10 years of political instability and warfare. In the Republic Square, the loud music of a local heavy metal rock band threatened to burst my eardrums. In flashy new hotels, foreign businessmen explored the prospects of upgrading local infrastructure long rotted by a wasted decade.

I see the shadow of a new phoenix rising from the ashes. Serbia, I wish her well.

Srpska: At Odds with the World

I left Serbia behind as the bus crossed the bridge over the River Sava. A billboard greeted the bus, "Bosnia and Herzegovina", the country commonly abbreviated as BiH[13]. Three meters behind, a much larger sign said, "Welcome to the Republic of Srpska".

Srpska, commonly known as Republika Srpska or the Serb Republic, is one of the two "entities" making up the BiH, as a result of the Dayton Agreement that ended the war in BiH (1992–1995). Srpska has 49% of the territory of BiH and is primarily Serb. The other entity is the Federation of Bosnia and Herzegovina ("FBiH") which accounts for 51% of the territory and is basically a federation of Bosnian Muslims (now known as Bosniak) and Croats. Let's take a step back and have a look at how all this began.

Bosnia, the crossroads of the Western and Eastern Roman Empires, was settled by Slavic tribes after the collapse of the Roman Empire. Its history has always been subject to debate by its three constituent peoples, the Bosniaks, Serbs and Croats, who account for 43%, 31% and 17% of its population respectively.

To the Bosniaks, they have always been the main inhabitants of this ancient land. Caught in the conflicting demands of the Roman Catholic Church and the Eastern Orthodox Church of the Byzantine Empire, the Bosnian people set up their own Bosnian Church, which some say are intertwined with the Bogomils, a dualist aesthetic sect considered heretical by others but related to the Cathars in southern France.

Under the Bosnian king, Tvrtko Kotromanic (1338–1391), who called himself "King of Serbs, Bosnia and the Seacoast", the Bosnian state extended into huge territories in what is today Croatia and Serbia, but again, like most Balkan monarchs who expanded through war, his empire didn't last long. The existence of a rival sect infuriated the Pope who raised a crusade against the Bosnians. Rivalries among the feudal lords tore the country apart.

---

[13] "i" is "and" in Serbian/Croatian/Bosnian/Montenegrin, whatever you call that language spoken by the former Yugoslav nations. These languages are virtually the same and are written in Latin as well as the Cyrillic script. They used to be regarded as a single language known as either the Serbo-Croat or Croato-Serb but with the breakup of Yugoslavia, individual countries declare that the national language is now known after the names of their respective countries.

The Ottoman Turks came soon after and took over this land torn by strife. The locals welcomed the Turks as liberators and converted to Islam en masse. This included the elite who were anxious to avoid paying excessive taxes from land ownership. For a long time, the Muslims of BiH had a confused identity, some calling themselves Muslim Serbs and others Muslim Croats. Tito, leader of communist Yugoslavia, however, recognized them as a separate nation in the 1960's, and since the end of the Bosnian War, they have renamed themselves Bosniaks, i.e., people of Bosnia.

Listen to a Serb and you will get this story: BiH has always been a Serbian land. Tvrtko Kotromanic was actually king of the Western Serbs. The Roman Catholic Church converted some of the Serbs who then called themselves Croats, and the Turks forcibly converted others who then

called themselves Bosniaks. But all these were once Serbian lands and should always have been. It was Tito who messed things up by giving them recognition as a separate people.

To a Croat, naturally, this was Croat land too, and Tvrtko Kotromanic was actually a Croatian duke who broke away from the Croatian state. So, which version do you believe? All sides have scholars and tons of scholarly work to prove their theories.

The Yugoslav Federation began to fall apart when Slovenia and Croatia declared independence in June 1991. By late 1991, the Bosnian Croats had convinced the Bosniaks that independence was the way to go. This terrified the Serbs, who suffered massacres by Croatian and Muslim Fascists known as Utashas during WWII, particularly, in the notorious Jasenovac concentration camp.

Firm on remaining in the same state as fellow Serbs, the Bosnian Serbs declared their own republic, Srpska, in April 1992. War broke out immediately and the Serbs laid siege to Sarajevo. The whole country burned as atrocities and massive destruction occurred everywhere. Ethnic cleansing, i.e., massive expulsion and elimination of a specific ethnic group, became the most famous by-product of this war.

The Serbs were the best armed and were initially successful, capturing over 70% of BiH. Many atrocities were committed, most of them by the Serbs, but war crimes committed by the Bosnian and Croat armies occurred, too. Rivalries between the Bosnian and Croats led to hostilities between the two supposed allies. 250,000 died in this war, most of whom were civilians. By 1995, infuriated by atrocities committed by Srpska, NATO launched air strikes against them. Coupled with victories by the Croats on the field, all parties were eventually forced to sign the Dayton Agreement, dividing BiH into FBiH and Srpska, a strange state of affairs that has lasted till today.

»»»»»

The first town I passed through was Bijeljina, where in April 1992, the Serbian warlord and gangster, Arkan[14], launching the first of the ethnic cleansing raids, killed a few local Bosniaks and frightened the rest into flight. Next was Brcko, in the so-called Posavina Corridor — a strip of Srpska-controlled territory 3km wide linking a wide swath of Srpska land around its largest city, Banja Luka, with Serbia itself. During the war, this was the lifeline of Srpska, through which supplies and reinforcements braved Bosniak and Croat bombardment to reach Banja Luka. The control of Brcko was so contentious that it has been made a special territory of the BiH not subject to either Srpska or FbiH control.

As the bus approached Banja Luka, the landscape became a chaotic mixture of lush green farmlands and rolling hills. Many houses looked newly refurbished since the end of the war, but one also passed by many ruined villages and burnt buildings, their previous occupants perhaps victims of ethnic cleansing. I wonder if they were now sitting in refugee camps abroad, or resting in unsettled peace under the rubble of their own houses.

It was 6:30am when I arrived at the bus station of Banja Luka. The city centre was 3km away. I didn't have any convertible marks (KM), the official currency of the BiH, but could find neither an exchange office, nor anyone willing to change money with me — not even taxi drivers were willing to do that. Classic chicken and egg story. I had no KM and so couldn't take a bus or taxi. And because no one was willing to take me to town, I would not have any KM. I could hardly believe how un-entrepreneurial these people were! In the end, I had to walk the 3km into town with my heavy backpack.

Due to frequent earthquakes, Banja Luka has few historic buildings. The local Serbs worsened the tourism scene by expelling all the Bosniaks in town, and blowing up all 16 of their mosques, including Ferhadiya, the famous architectural gem in the north of Bosnia, built in 1580 by a Bosnian-born grand vizier (senior minister) of the Ottoman Empire. His clan had persuaded the Turks to revive the Serbian Church following the conquest

---

[14] "Besides being a major criminal, political and military player during the Balkan Wars, Arkan was also owner of FK Obilić, which won the 1997/98 Yugoslav football league championship. He fathered nine children by five women, among them a Swede, a Belgian, a Spanish language professor, an actress, and a popular folk singer 21 years his junior. Arkan was assassinated in 2000 in the lobby of Belgrade's InterContinental Hotel, after which an indictment by the International Criminal Tribunal for the former Yugoslavia (ICTY) in The Hague was made public.

of Bosnia and so helped revive Serbian culture during the period of Turkish rule. So much for the repayment of good deeds. I took some pictures of the empty site, now fenced up with aluminum sheets and stone stools with the famous Serbian logo — 4 "S's" — "Only Unity Will Save the Serbs".

I checked into one of the three hotels in Banja Luka. There were hardly any tourists in town. The locals, aware of their international pariah status, are fairly open in expressing their views. My hotel receptionist, Slaven, a burly man in his late forties, soon spoke proudly of their struggle for freedom when we started the conversation about road maps. Slaven spoke nostalgically about his people taking to arms against the Mujahideen (that's how they refer to the nominally Muslim Bosnian Government forces) and the Utashas (the Croats, adopting the name used by the hated Croatian fascists during WWII).

Banja Luka: the famous Serbian logo — 4 "S's" — "Only Unity Will Save the Serbs".

Memorial to young dead Serbian fighters, Banja Luka.

"Yes, we heard the Muslim fundamentalists shouting Allahu Akbar all the time in the forest. They cut off the heads of any Serbs caught. After Sept 11, why is the US still supporting these Mujahideen?" he asked.

I have long heard about the Serbs' love for describing the Bosniaks as fundamentalists. If you go to Sarajevo, you will see how Islamic they are — girls walking around half naked in the summer heat. Well, Slaven warned me not to fall for Sarajevo's pretense that it was secular and multiracial. Even then, Slaven reckoned, the war years were hard, and he loved peace. But he and his countrymen, i.e., the people of Srpska, would readily take up arms again if their rights were infringed, although issues like war crimes and ethnic cleansing were considered by most Serbs to be enemy propaganda, and hence not worth speaking about.

Like many Serbs I have met, Slaven was also an enthusiast in all sorts of grandiose geopolitical conspiracy theories about why great powers did this or that. OK, it was not all talk about war and death. Slaven also spoke about his younger days, when he backpacked across Europe without the need for visas. His face glowed when he spoke about the amorous Swedish girls he met in summer while basking in Dubrovnik, now part of Croatia.

» » » » »

I also met Jasmin and his friend Paul, both talented locals about my age, with a lot of knowledge and war stories to share. Jasmin is a good-looking guy with apple-cheeks and penetrating eyes; he is currently doing his PhD. Paul, who runs a travel agency, has soft, blonde hair and flashes a broad smile whenever someone approaches. We had a great time chatting in a riverside cafe along the beautiful Unas River, and then at a great Serbian dinner in Banja Luka Castle, with live music by BiH's candidate at Eurovision — she's Serbian (of course, said Jasmin).

I tried the Karadjordje Steak, which is a huge lump of meat. It resembled a large, erect penis and was served with generous portions of tomato sauce and mayonnaise. The dish is named after the Karadjordje Dynasty that once ruled Serbia during parts of 19th and 20th centuries.

It was said that one of the Karadjordje monarchs had an unusually large organ which inspired this dish.

Jasmin is a mixed-blood Serb — a phenomenon common in all of former Yugoslavia where a middle-class lifestyle and educated population meant that people did not bother about ethnicity when choosing their life partners. In many parts of Yugoslavia, mixed marriages accounted for 20% of all weddings, and in an ethnically diverse region like Bosnia, the figure was as high as 30% in some communities. However, this fact did not prevent the war from happening. People, despite their ethnically mixed extended families, often chose sides when the war broke out. Many families split apart while some moved abroad to escape the stigma associated with such marriages.

In Jasmin's case, as in many others, they rationalized their circumstances and chose sides. Jasmin's father is a Bosniak who currently lives in FBiH and his mother is Serb. He moved to Banja Luka with his mother after his parents divorced. Jasmin was convinced that the Serbs were right in the war. "There is no such thing as the Bosniak nation. It is an artificial creation by people who want to destroy Serbia. The people here were all Serbs. It was the dirty Turks who converted some Serbs by force to Islam — look how dirty the Bosniaks are. Dirt and rubbish everywhere. Who would want to be Muslim by choice?" Jasmin said to a visibly shocked me. All my fine impressions of this smart, friendly young man instantly evaporated.

Jasmin unfolded a satellite map with red circles marked on it. "Look — these are locations of killing fields where Serbs were massacred by Muslims and Croats. Thousands of burial sites." He pointed to the circles, "Here, here and here as well." But Jasmin wasn't referring to massacres of the 1990's war; he was talking about WWII. Jasmin specialized in a macabre topic — mass murder of Serbs by Croats and Muslims of the Ustasi puppet regime during WWII, a prime justification for the recent war by the Serbs. Never again can the Serbs allow themselves to be ruled by anyone else, for they would be massacred like in WWII.

I wondered if it was his mixed ethnic heritage that turned Jasmin even more radical than other Serbs. I have read papers about the Basque separatists of Spain. Many of the top Basque terrorists are only part-Basque. Some theorise that it is the mixed ethnic heritage of these people that made them more determined to show their affinity or even loyalty to one side than others. And to show their ultimate loyalty, they became the most radical supporters of the cause of that ethnic group[15].

Paul's father was a Chetnik who moved to the UK after WWII. There he met Paul's mother, a Serbian girl who went to the UK to study. The Chetniks were members of a Serb right-wing paramilitary force during WWII, which was accused of many massacres of non-Serbs across Yugoslavia. They initially fought against the German and Italian invaders but later collaborated with them against the Communists. Many Chetniks were executed by the Communists after the war while the rest ended up in Western Europe as refugees. During the 1990's Balkan wars, many Serbian paramilitary forces called themselves Chetniks as well, thus bringing further disrepute to the term.

Paul came to Serbia more than 10 years ago after his parents' divorce, but he still owns a British passport and speaks good English. Paul saw himself as a Serbian patriot, and had seen action in the frontlines during the Balkan wars. He felt emotionally and intensely for the Serbian nation and the predicament it is in. It was absolutely bizarre having tea with this handsome, charming English native speaker and indeed UK citizen — talking casually about his support for militias notorious for ethnic cleansing and other war crimes.

The war had forced these well-educated young men to take up arms and the conflict had turned them into fierce supporters of their cause. I did not agree with all their beliefs and theories, but I admired their courage and strong personal sense of purpose in life. The Serbian people are passionate about their history and heroes, as well as the land where their ancestors had lived. I can appreciate why the Serbs would like to see all their people live in a common land. Unfortunately, the Serbs often failed to appreciate the irrevocable changes of the demographic landscape and that the views of the current inhabitants of these lands do matter. It is also highly regrettable that the struggle had led to such an atrocious loss of lives, something that most

---

[15] In recent years, we are also witnessing the increasing role of recent Muslim converts in the Al Qaeda terrorist acts. They could be anxious to prove their loyalty despite their non-Muslim birth.

Serbs do not want to know about even today. Even then, too often does the international press portray the Serbs solely as the villains and others as victims. The reality is a lot grayer than that.

» » » » »

Banja Luka was a town where few tourists ventured and any stranger aroused immediate interest. I received an invitation to meet Mr. Davidovic, owner of my hotel and one of Srpska's largest conglomerates, with interests in banks and all sorts of enterprises. I was surprised as to why an important man like him wanted to meet a Singaporean backpacker. I popped by his office at the top of his group complex overlooking the City, and there he was with his team of advisors and interpreters.

Not many tourists passed through town, he explained, and most either worked for UN, EU or NATO. He was curious what a casual Singaporean was doing in town. Since Singapore was an international financial centre, his guess was that I might be a banker of sorts, and he wanted to know my impression of Srpska and investment opportunities there.

And so we went into a two-hour-long conversation. I hated to burst any notion that Banja Luka might be a future Singapore or Hong Kong of the Balkans; any short-term hot money, fly-by-night type is probably fine if you are using private capital and have the appetite for risks. For longer term ventures, apart from the usual emerging market hazards, I don't think

Ruined buildings like this are found across the Bosnian countryside.

anyone wanted to sink long term money into a smallish state of 1.4 million people, whose unstable relationship with its neighbours was tainted by a recent and rather bloody war.

Srpska is forever bickering with FbiH and the EU High Representative. In addition, do you put money into companies that might own land taken over in an ethnic cleansing exercise, whose real ownership was uncertain, and who knows, might even have been involved in slave labour and concentration camps of the sort shown on CNN during those war years? Just look at how German and Swiss companies get sued for class actions relating to the Holocaust after all these years.

Srpska is a statelet built on the ruins of Yugoslavia. It is the symbol of Serbian desire for the unity of their lands. Unfortunately its more noble objectives have been tainted by an unsavory process. The problem with the Dayton Agreement was that the Serbs pretended that it was full international recognition of their state and a step closer towards unity with Serbia while the Bosniaks took it as a first step to full reintegration of all parts of BiH into a centralized country; the Croats believe that they might just agitate for their own constituent state. The result was that the struggle of the Serbian people — one which was neither wholly successful nor a complete failure — had resulted in the creation of a strange BiH whose state structure is inherently unstable and almost guaranteed to generate more threats to peace and economic development.

With a lot of mixed feelings, I hopped onto a train for Sarajevo.

Bosnia: Divided Paradise

Imagine a mini-Istanbul with all its Ottoman minarets, throw in some Catholic spires and Orthodox domes, and then dump the whole mixture into a snowcapped Swiss Alpine valley — the result is Sarajevo, capital of Bosnia-Herzegovina ("BiH"). Host of the 1984 Winter Olympics. The place where Austrian Archduke Franz Ferdinand was assassinated, thus sparking off WWI. And a heroic city under a horrifying over three-year-long siege in the last decade of the 20th Century.

I arrived in Sarajevo after a train journey from Banja Luka, capital of Republika Srpska, the Serbian section of BiH. Although officially part of the same country, the people of Srpska and its Bosniak-Croat counterpart of the south (FBiH) seldom cross that invisible border. People who board the train tend to get off before it reaches the border which used to be the ceasefire line of the Serbs and Bosniak-Croat regions. Only foreigners like me do the whole journey. The memories of the past were too painful. Too many have died and many do not want to be reminded of the past.

The train was driven by a Srpska Railway engine head and served by a Srpska conductor, complete with the double-headed eagle logo of the North. At Doboj junction near the FBiH border, the engine car was replaced with a BiH Railways of FBiH coach and a conductor from the BiH Railways. A few years ago, there were soldiers on the border between the two entities. They have since been removed.

Now, more observant visitors would notice the sudden appearance of mosques once the border is crossed. There aren't any mosques in Srpska because they have all been blown up, together with cemeteries and all sorts of monuments, so as to ensure that no one would remember that the north once had other ethnic groups.

The Bosniak-Croat Federation itself, which comprises 10 cantons each of which has its own prime minister and a full cabinet of ministers, is not an admirable Disneyland of peace. My Serbian friends spoke of the financial and moral corruption in FBiH with much contempt and disgust. Apparently, not too long ago, a cantonal minister in FBiH was driving while his secretary was performing oral sex on him. He made a sudden stop and his secretary inadvertently bit the ministerial organ and he had to be rushed to hospital. All Bosnia was talking about it when I was there.

»» »» »» »» »»

First built as a market town by the Turks, Sarajevo quickly became the center of this land. Beautiful Aladdin-like mosques rose above its skies, together with churches of the Catholic and Orthodox faiths. People of diverse groups mingled in its many cafes and restaurants. Loud Turkish pop was everywhere together with the aroma of strong Turkish coffee.

As you stroll westwards along the river, you enter the part of town built during the 30 years of Austro-Hungarian rule — the elegance of Central Europe, nice little squares, the first public tram service in Europe, and some of the most beautiful people living anywhere on Earth.

The city lies in a valley surrounded by mountains almost Alpine in appearance. On sunny days, light and cloud shadows constantly modeled and remodeled the ridges and dips of the pine-covered mountains. Nearby were the skiing resorts that played host to the Winter Olympics. Old Sarajevo also used to be the cultural hub and Hollywood of former Yugoslavia. This was the center of literature, performance arts and 20th Century culture par excellence.

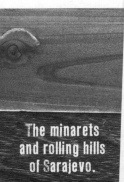

The minarets and rolling hills of Sarajevo.

All this was wiped away on 5 April 1992, when Serbian snipers attacked peace marchers from Holiday Inn. Immediately the city found itself surrounded by Serbian artillery and bombarded by Europe's fourth largest army, from the very mountaintops that gave the city its beauty and wonderful ski spots — these tools of death rained destruction on this amazing city, strangling its inhabitants and promising nothing but servitude to its multi-ethnic population.

From then till 1995, the city became a by-word for extraordinary courage and endurance, and for strength and resilience. This was the Balkan Leningrad, the city under prolonged siege, the suffering one.

> "Each person in Sarajevo is very close to an ideal microbiotician, a real role model for the health conscious, diet-troubled West… People are healthy, in spite of everything, for no one eats animal fat anymore, or meat, or cheese — meals are made without eggs, without milk, onions, meat, vegetables. We eat a precious mix of wild imagination."
> Sarajevo Survival Guide, FAMA, 1993, p. 19

I walked along that beautiful boulevard stretching from the airport to the heart of the Old Town. Just a decade ago, this was known worldwide as Sniper's Alley, where Serbian snipers took aim at the grandmothers out looking for bread now that their pensions were non-existent, the four-year old rushing out from his flat for a football that had gone out of the window, or a daddy just looking for some wood to make winter more endurable for his children. Thousands died this way, doing the simplest tasks of everyday life. But calling that avenue Sniper's Alley is a misnomer. The whole of Sarajevo was a huge sniper's alley, for the entire city lies in a slender valley along the river, and any gunner on top of the mountains could reach anyone anywhere.

> "Running — that is the favourite sport, practiced by everyone in Sarajevo. All crossroads are run through, as are all the dangerous neighbourhoods. One runs with stolen wood, to the line where others

*are standing. Something is on sale, and you will know it only when you
join the line."*

Sarajevo Survival Guide, FAMA, 1993, p. 51

The city's two main cemeteries lie in Serbian-controlled territory, and so
the dead were buried in the city's beautiful urban parks instead. As I strolled
in Sarajevo's beautiful Ottoman and Austrian parks that once played host to
generations of lovers, poets and writers, the numerous graves dating from
1992 to 1995 reminded me of the city's enormous suffering.

Eventually even the city parks were not enough for the dead. They
decided to use the Olympic stadium, too. I popped by the Kosevo Stadium,
where the 1984 Winter Olympics had its opening and closing ceremonies.
The striking number of graves in its football field almost melted me to tears.

The skyscrapers in the foreground — even these were without windows
for they had been blown out by the Serbian forces — the city's mosques and
churches, symbols of its multiethnic nature, plus the amazingly irrelevant
residential buildings, all combine to make this scene surreal. Imagine NYC's
Central Park full of graves, or London's Hyde Park with crosses and crescents.

I took a bus to the western suburbs, passing the offices of the newspaper
Oslobodjenje, whose entire complex had been destroyed by god knows how
many missiles, with twisted iron and huge boulders of debris around its
collapsed floors. Yet, the paper continued to be published almost everyday,
from its basement. It shrank from a broadsheet like the *Times* and *Washington
Post*, to an-A4 sheet, with eight, and then four pages. Sarajevo wanted to
speak to the world, even during the war. Sarajevo refused to be silenced. Its
silence would imply defeat by the criminal intent of its enemies.

In the far suburbs near the airport, I visited the famous Tunnel of
Sarajevo, where the Bosnians built a tunnel linking itself with the rest
of the world, under the runway which the UN had occupied but agreed
with the Serbs never to allow be used by the Bosnians. From this narrow
1.5m wide pipeline of life, Sarajevans received news of the life and death
of family, sent out the injured, got their supplies, and brought in arms to
fight their enemies.

Sarajevo graffiti.

Endless rows
of graves at the
Sarajevo Olympic
Stadium.

Sarajevo Tunnel:
Lifeline during
the siege.

Despite it all, Sarajevo has rebuilt and is continuing to rebuild itself. The Old Town is now newer than ever, with its numerous cafès and atmospheric houses and mansions, as well as a growing number of backpackers arriving in this magical city. The fantasy-palatial National Library, the most beautiful building in all Bosnia with its exuberant fusion of Austro-Hungarian and Ottoman styles, remained in ruins after the Serbs bombed it on the first day of the war, consigning to history more than 1 million books and manuscripts of 1000 years of Bosnian culture and civilization. It is being rebuilt, like many other monuments in the city. Sarajevo is rising again.

»»»»»

I hopped onto a bus for Mostar, the chief city in the southern region of BiH, known as Herzegovina. Mostar, meaning Keeper of the Bridge, used to be the second most beautiful city of BiH, after Sarajevo. The Old Bridge across the crystal clear waters of the Neretva River, built in 1566 by the genius of a renowned Ottoman architect, was once the crown jewel of the south. Millions of tourists once traveled here to see its slender splendour, curving gracefully like the gentle silhouette of a classical beauty.

Nineteenth-century Western European travellers, who lived in an era that despised anything Ottoman or Islamic, found it difficult to believe that such sophisticated architecture could have been built by the Turks, and instead theorized that it was built by the Romans. But beauty alone could not deter the vandals of war. In November 1993, Bosnian Croat forces fighting against Bosnian Government forces in order to create their own Croatian state in the south of BiH, destroyed this monument of all Mankind.

Today, tourists are coming back in small groups, looking at the empty space where the Bridge used to be. Archaeologists are carefully reassembling its pieces in a prolonged effort to rebuild this treasure. I had tasty Bosnian grill in a small restaurant facing the ruins of the Bridge and the surrounding old town. The ruined Old City is being rebuilt, too. Restaurants and souvenir shops are already opening amidst all the destruction, and groups of day-tripping tourists are arriving from the nearby Croatian tourist cities of Dubrovnik and Split. I wondered about the lost lives, families, time and opportunities. What a march of folly!

Mostar remains a divided city, a Berlin without walls. After chasing out the Serbs in a joint offensive, the Bosniaks and Croats fought each other for a few years, in an episode more ferocious than that fought in Sarajevo. The lack of media coverage relative to that for Sarajevo meant more atrocities and greater destruction. Today, you can see the incredible destruction along the old frontline cutting across what used to be the city centre of Mostar. If you drive into town, you will be confused by signboards proclaiming two city centers, both located in different areas and directions. One is the Bosniak center and the other the Croatian one.

Even today, taxi drivers hesitate to cross the invisible line of death. Bosniaks stay on the eastern side of town and Croats on the western side. If you buy a phone card on the Bosniak side (belonging to BiH Telecom), you can't use it in phones on the western side of town. There you can only use cards sold by the HPT Bosnian Croat Telecom. Of course, you can also forget about using that phone card you bought in Banja Luka, the one issued by Srpske Telecom. The same applies with stamps issued by the post offices of Srpska, BiH and that of the Bosnian Croat Post. A small nation divided into three parts.

»»»»»

I met Miro, my Bosnian contact who works for the EU planning development and reconstruction projects. We clicked immediately and he drove me around the old battlefields of Mostar where the war began, and where the battles were fought, the ruins of the old Serbian Orthodox Church now being rebuilt, the brand new Catholic Church deliberately rebuilt by the Croats to rise well above all Islamic monuments in the City, the offensively huge cross planted on the mountaintop by the Croats, - and the beautiful countryside around Mostar.

Bosnia — so beautiful, so wild and so tragic. As we sped across the timeless countryside of Herzegovina, Miro recited the atrocities that had occurred in the settlements we passed. Town A, two massacres, 100 dead June 1992, 45 dead December 1993; Village B, 233 murdered May 1992; Hamlet C, only one small massacre — five school children killed in a mortar attack. Only five dead in this beautiful village in the meadow. When too many have been killed, the dead become mere statistics.

We visited the old village of Pocitelj, where the Croats ethnically cleansed the inhabitants during the war. A fairytale mediaeval Bosnian fortress perched on the mountaintop overlooking the village which rests on the slopes. We walked into the ruins of the local Mosque, a beautiful Ottoman structure whose bright blue flowery tiles still shone with glory, together with the fantasy strokes of Arabic calligraphy on the inner walls. Outside were cottages once inhabited by artists from around the world, for the tolerant Muslim citizens of Pocitelj opened their village to the creative population of Mother Earth.

This was once a famous artists' colony and Islamic center — no contradiction about it, as most Bosnians would contend. Bosnians have always lived and died defending their multiethnic fabric. The grateful artists gave the village some of their works in return. All these were gone. The war had destroyed it all. I closed my eyes, and tried hard to imagine the old glories of this village. A few new restaurants have opened at the entrance to the village. The villagers are slowly returning. Perhaps one day, the artists would return too, and rebuild this village of eternal tolerance.

Medugorje on the southwest of BiH was hardly heard of by anyone before 1981 but is today a world famous pilgrimage town. On 24 June 1981, six young local Croats were confronted with an apparition of the Virgin Mary — known as Our Lady of Medugorje — and over a number of days, the apparitions of the Virgin Mary appeared to them with messages and secrets to be eventually disclosed to the world. Although the Catholic Church has not formally endorsed these apparitions as miracles, a whole pilgrimage and tourism industry had emerged in Medugorje, even through the war years.

I stood in the grand plaza of Medugorje, where hundreds of pilgrims — Europeans, Latin Americans and Asians — knelt in prayer, the organ music playing from loudspeakers while the sun set over the horizon. I wondered

The beautiful
countryside of
Herzegovina.

Temporary bridge
where the Old
Bridge of Mostar
used to be.

Ruins of
Mostar's old
city centre.

what secrets the Virgin had revealed and if she had predicted the Balkan wars that followed in the 1990s, the ravages of 9/11, and how globalisation would transform the world in which we live today.

» » » » »

Bosnia, beautiful Bosnia, tragic Bosnia. When will its soul recover? The state that is BiH today is a strange monster created by the international community on the ruins of the war. Srpska in the North refuses to acknowledge its presence in a joint state. The South is an uneasy alliance of convenience between the Bosniaks and the Croats. Besides being a supposed federal state in the south (FBiH), that state is subdivided into ten cantons each with its own prime minister ("PM") and cabinet of ministers. BiH today is a nation with 13 PM's and over 200 ministers. A PM for every 300,000 citizens. A bloated bureaucracy supported by the international community.

Srpska is ready to defend its eternal hope for Serbian unity. The South is unhappy with what it sees as a North that got away too easily with its atrocities. Most Bosnians I spoke to are committed to building a multiethnic state. But saying is easier than reality. More than 200,000 Bosniaks and Croats, plus 70,000 Serbs died in this conflict. I choked with shock when I heard a Bosnian officer-guide at the Tunnel Museum say, "If the Serbs want to break away, they can if we kill at least 100,000 of them, and reduce their territory to only 30% of BiH." So much for reconciliation. No wonder the Serbs are hesitating.

As the sun sets over the Neretva Valley, I set off for Split, a sunny city on the Croatian coast. May the Almighty bless this land.

Croatia: Tragedies on Holiday Coast

"I am 56 and my two sons were killed in the war, aged 20 and 26."

That was how Madam Nikolić introduced herself when her sister took me to her house. Both were among the elderly ladies who wait for travellers arriving at the bus station of Dubrovnik, Croatia. Once you get off the bus, they mob you, offering you rooms in their apartments. Since Croatia's independence from Yugoslavia in 1991, (and even after the end of the war in 1995), life has been difficult for many people. Factories have closed down and inflation has reduced many pensions to meaningless numbers.

I did not know why Mdm. Nikolić chose to introduce herself that way. Was it to generate some sympathy so as to mute my protests at the high room rates? I don't know, but at least I was given the spacious living room turned bedroom-for-rental, while Mdm. Nikolić slept in her cramped kitchen, where I spied some pictures of her dead sons — lively, good-looking young men, cannon fodder for the terrible war of 1992–1995.

Over the next few days, I was to realize that Mdm. Nikolić's parents, too, died during the war; not as a direct result of gunfire, but largely due to poor sanitary conditions and lack of medicine for their illness. She also told me about the days spent in the bomb shelter, and that the reason her house was somewhat lower than the surrounding ones was that shelling from the "Orthodox people" had destroyed the top floor. That's how she referred to the Serbs. "Why should they kill us?"

Dubrovnik's spectacular walled city: Besieged during the Balkan War.

But she reserved her bitterest complaints for the political elite of Zagreb. Pointing to the newly resigned Croatian premier on the TV news, she said, "They are all thieves. I lost my sons to the nation but I have nothing today. They have stolen everything. All their Swiss accounts, Mercedes, and holiday houses."

»»»»»

Dubrovnik of Dalmatia, southern Croatia, crown jewel of the Adriatic, is one of the most beautiful cities in the world. Perhaps the most beautiful one on the Mediterranean Sea. Nestled against the barren high cliffs on one side and the azure waters of the Mediterranean on the other, the high walls and bastions of this city had won praises from travellers, poets and writers across the centuries.

Also known as Ragusa, Dubrovnik was once an ancient city-state whose merchant ships sailed throughout the Adriatic. It was a real rival of Venice for many years and its wealth had allowed it to build great churches and palaces within its walls and on the many islands it controlled off the coast. Its fortunes declined with the discovery of the Americas and this glorious republic was finally abolished by Napoleon in 1806.

The 20th century brought new riches — when the age of mass tourism brought tourists in huge numbers to this architectural gem and its many beaches and islands. The good times, however, were interrupted when war broke out in 1991 as Croatia declared its independence. Milosevic, President of Serbia decided that the Dalmatian coast was too good to be given up to the Croats. Immediately the Yugoslav Federal Army and Montenegrin militia blockaded the city. Milosevic and company then cooked up this grand dream of reviving the old Republic of Dubrovnik — and, in what was one of the most comical episodes of modern history, set up a puppet provisional government of the Republic of Dubrovnik in the city's suburb of Cavtat.

Serbian academics rushed to produce tons of scholarly work to prove that the people of Dubrovnik and Dalmatia were not actually Croats, but

Catholic Serbs, that the Dalmatian dialect was closer to Serbian dialects than Croatian ones, etc. The problem with all these theories was that they forgot that the locals disagreed with them.

When the city refused to surrender, the Serbs ravaged the city's suburbs and then surrounded the city with heavy guns and artillery. From October 1991 to May 1992, they laid siege to this ancient city, pounding it with heavy artillery and gunfire — all in the face of the world's media.

The world watched in horror as the old city burned, and smoke rose from the ancient ramparts and cathedrals. Nine grand palaces were burnt to ashes and the rooftops of 70% of the buildings fell to pieces. "Stop the barbaric assault on world heritage," the world shouted. The officers of the Yugoslav Army could hardly have understood that the world had changed since WWII.

In the last decade of the 20th century, we have truly entered the Age of the Mass Media and public opinion does not permit the sort of warfare practiced for centuries to be played out on open TV. If anything, the siege had achieved nothing but a complete public relations disaster for the Serbs.

»»»»»

Mario is the front desk manager of a four-star Dubrovnik hotel now, but eight years ago he was a soldier in the Croatian Army, called-up fresh from university. He drove me around the mountains overlooking the city.

"Look — that's where the Serbs had their artillery. And there, and over there as well." Mario pointed to the old Serbian positions — they occupied all the high points overlooking the city except for the fortress built by Napoleon.

"From these places, they pounded us — the fortress and the city as well — day and night. Day and night! And you hear — whiz...whiz...whiz... missiles flying past, and then you hear huge explosions. It was mad, mad, mad!" Then Mario grinned a boyish smile, "But as a young man, it was sometimes fun too! But this was real war. And many, many people died. It was also really depressing at times, when we thought they might blow all of us up and take this city."

The fortress was pounded so heavily that the first two levels are nothing but ruins today. The nearby TV transmitter was completely destroyed together with the tourist cable car station.

Mario lit a cigarette with one hand, as he continued to steer the car with the other. "Our forces in the fortress were able to communicate with the forces in the city through the 10 underground levels beneath the fortress, all the way down to the Old City level. At nightfall, our commandos came in on speedboats delivering ammunition and food to the besieged citizens and soldiers. Eight months! Eight months in those shitty conditions!"

That was how long it took to lift the terrible siege in stages. Enormous sacrifices were made but the ancient city was saved. I asked Mario what was the worst.

"Snakes, lots of snakes in these hills. I hate them!" Then he burst into loud laughter. "That is a joke, of course. It was the uncertainty. You didn't know whether you would live or die. And you didn't know if you would win the war, or whether all your friends would die in vain."

Since then, international efforts have been made to restore the city. Today as one strolls through its ancient streets, the untrained eye can hardly pick out any war damage, apart from differences in the colours and shades of the roof tiles. Tourism is booming in Croatia. Dubrovnik's hotels are full of tourists again and its streets crowded with souvenir shops, boutiques and restaurants.

Unlike the rest of the former Yugoslav states, Croatia (and Slovenia) is recovering quickly. Tourism is making an impact on local employment and economics. There is tremendous potential. Croatia now attracts 2.5 million tourists, a far cry from the almost 10 million before the war. If you haven't been to these beautiful shores — in my opinion many times more beautiful than the French Riviera — come now before the really massive crowds start pouring in.

Apart from Dubrovnik, I also visited Split, Croatia's second largest city with the famous Palace of Diocletian (a UNESCO World Heritage Site) and the beautiful island of Hvar with its Venetian fortress and fishing villages. Nearby is the island of Korcula, where Marco Polo was born —

the Venetians claim that he was born in Venice, but the Croatians said he was born in Korcula which was then under Venetian control. Off the coast of Dubrovnik is the isle of Lukum, where Franciscan monks coexist with nudist sun-tanners and day-trippers looking for exotic flora and fauna.

»» »» »» »» »»

After sunny Croatia, I decided to go to Montenegro, the junior partner in what remains of the Yugoslav Federation. I took a bus to the tiny strip of common border between Croatia and Montenegro and expected to cross the border without problems. After all, Montenegro has claimed that it is the more liberal of the two republics and wants international support for its desire to achieve independence.

I'd crossed Yugoslav borders before (from Macedonia to Serbia) on this same journey and could obtain a tourist pass on the border, as per Yugoslav Federal regulations. I had also contacted the Montenegro Ministry of Tourism and the Representative (i.e., unofficial ambassador) of the Montenegrin Government in the UK, and confirmed that I could enter the country without a visa.

However, at this godforsaken border amidst great natural beauty — lush green mountains and quaint winding roads — I was refused entry. "This is the Republic of Montenegro, not Yugoslavia," the guards said. They claimed that I needed a visa.

Diocletian's Palace in Split: A UNESCO World Heritage Site.

There I was stuck in the middle of nowhere. It was Saturday morning and I would have to go to Zagreb and wait till Monday to try to get a visa from the Montenegrin Mission there. They might need HQ consultation and more time before the visa was to be granted. More time would be wasted and they might even refuse me a visa on the pretext that I was a non-resident in Croatia.

So I chose Alternative Two — go to Belgrade and try entering Montenegro from there. Serbia and Montenegro are still officially one country and there's less likelihood of a check on their internal border. Even if there were a check, I would have my Yugoslav federal tourist pass to show that I had at least entered the Federation legally. And best of all, I wouldn't waste any time waiting till Monday to try getting a visa in Zagreb.

And so I began my 1,500 km journey in order to get to the other border of a small country only 100-odd km long. I was lucky to be given a 250 km lift to Split by a friendly Russian couple I met on the border — one of whom was a well travelled Arctic scientist — we had a wonderful conversation about travel and all sorts of other things. From Split I hopped onto an overnight bus for Zagreb.

» » » » »

Sometime around midnight, the bus passed through Knin, a city that immediately aroused my attention when I saw it on the bus itinerary. Between 1991 and 1995, this was the capital of the rebel Serbian state, the Serbian Krajina Republic, which had its own postage stamps and banknotes. Krajina is the region of central Croatia bordering Bosnia, where Serbians have lived for 1,000 years. For many years they served as frontier guards for the Austro-Hungarian Empire, defending Western Europe from the Ottoman Turkish Empire.

On the Bosnian side of the border, also known as Krajina, lived another group of Serbs — those of Republika Srpska today — who were frontiersmen for the Turks. The great powers of the past had used Serbs to fight Serbs, but the real Serb knows that his true loyalty is to himself, hence the slogan "Only Unity Will Save the Serbs".

Knin entered world headlines in 1991 when local Serbs declared independence from Croatia following Croatia's own emancipation from Yugoslavia. Determined to remain within Yugoslavia, Knin acquired the massive arms store of the Yugoslav Federal Army. Within a short time, they controlled a quarter of Croatia, and effectively cut the country into two halves by virtue of their control of the centre.

At the height of Knin's power, Krajina Serbs laid siege to the eastern city of Vukovar and reduced the beautiful Austro-Hungarian city to ashes; they surrounded Dubrovnik and horrified the world with the bombing of this World Heritage city; they rained bombs on Zagreb, the Croatian capital, as and when they wished.

Good times did not last. The Croatians recovered from their initial weakness and began rearming. The Krajina Serbs quarreled with Milosevic and supplies slowed to a trickle. The corruption of their own leaders began to affect morale and unity. In August 1995, the Croats launched a sudden attack on Knin. Within 24 hours, Knin fell, and the Krajina Serbian Army fled, together with 150,000 Serbs whose ancestors had lived there for a millennium. In merely a few days, 1,000 years of Serbian settlement had come to an end. So did the Serb Krajina Republic.

The UN has encouraged the Serbs to return, but few have done so. In a recent census, it was revealed that the percentage of Serbs in Croatia has

The Dalmatian island of Hvar: How touristy Marco Polo's alleged birthplace has become.

dropped from 15% before the war to only 4% today. A sad day for global ethnic diversity and racial tolerance.

»»»»»

In a display of sado-masochistic sentiment, I carried a book weighing over a kilogramme around the Balkans. *Black Lamb and Grey Falcon* by Rebecca West is the classic travel narrative of Yugoslavia written by a remarkable American lady about her journey through this ethnically diverse country in the 1930s. Extraordinarily thick and extremely detailed, this book records her observations and analyses of the region and its complex history and political problems, already at boiling point at that stage, as she traveled.

This extract of a review by the *New York Times* in 1941 of this book told as much of 1930's Yugoslavia as of the region today:

> "*The journey here specifically chronicled began with the arrival of Miss West and her husband at Zagreb at Easter time in 1937. They were met by three friends… the Serbian poet Constantine, was an official in the Yugoslav Government; another, the middle-age Croat Gregorievitch, had fought for his people's freedom and found it in union with "their free Slav brothers, the Serbs"; the third, the young Croat scientist Valetta, was a separatist. The meeting crystallizes the book's interest not only in its presentation of the Croatian problem, but in showing the reader with keen understanding that each of these patriots felt and why. And the character of the Yugoslav journey is caught in another way also: if there was much political argument in Zagreb, there was lively intellectual exercise in other talk, too. And Constantine, the poet, who had studied philosophy under Bergson, was the most fascinating talker, as he was also the most poetic and extravagantly individualized of them all… But Constantine… was to show himself stricken by a division worse than the problem of Croatia: his blood was Jewish, his allegiance was Yugoslav, his culture was international; and he had a German wife.*"

»»»»»

I arrived in Zagreb in the early morning. Seven years had passed since I was last here in late May 1995. Now Zagreb was no longer that same drab wartime capital. Every Croat walked around with a cell phone. There was hardly a soldier in sight; bright new advertisements selling cell phones and holidays in the USA, backpackers getting off the train every hour and ATM machines everywhere. President Tudjman, father of modern Croatia, was dead, together with some of his ultra-nationalist theories and authoritarian ideas, some of which had sparked off terrible warfare in Bosnia; others deny the existence of a genocide of Serbians in the Jasenovac WWII camp — a sore point for the Krajina Serbs and a rallying call for their rebellion against the Croatian state.

I hopped onto a train for Belgrade, a line parallel to that famous Highway of Brotherhood and Unity, built in the old Tito days between the capitals of the Federation's two largest republics. The line passed through several landmarks of the past decade of chaos. Novo Gradiska, the small district town which used to be the center of Western Slavonia; and Vinkovci, where passengers get off to go to Vukovar, the city besieged for three months in 1991 and which suffered utter destruction as a result. Vukovar used to be a beautiful place with graceful Austrian buildings and tree lined boulevards. The battle for it shocked the world by its ferocity and the number of atrocities committed.

On the train, I met a pretty Croatian girl going home for a visit from Zagreb. She and her family spent three months in the cellars during the siege, and were lucky to survive when the city fell. They went into exile and only returned in 1998, when the region was returned to Croatian control as part of the UN postwar settlement plan. The Vukovar of today is a sad shell of its past glories. Not only are its historic architectural gems gone, but Serbs and Croats can no longer sit in the same cafés or restaurants. Everything is racially segregated. A tragedy for the city that once used to have the highest percentage of mixed marriages in Yugoslavia.

Crossing the border was easy enough. "Moshe Moshe," the beautiful passport officer with her flashy blonde hair said, "No problem, go ahead."

Wow! Serbia has the most beautiful and friendly people on its borders! Even the male officers were not the fat grouchy type on most Balkan frontiers; a number even looked like male models.

I reached Belgrade at mid afternoon. Good old Belgrade. I love this city! Here I bought a ticket for Bar, a city on the Montenegrin coast. The train was full of young Belgraders going to the coast for summer holidays. As a Singaporean, I was easily the most exotic creature on Earth (or rather on the train), and the center of attention in my cabin. It was impossible to sleep, as wine and snacks were being passed around, together with a thousand questions about my personal life.

And with that, I finally entered Montenegro by its backdoor, after going 1,500km around the former Yugoslavia.

Montenegro: Beach Bums & Mountain Warriors

I arrived in Bar, Montenegro, now Yugoslavia's only port, though perhaps not for much longer. If Montenegro seceded from the federation, Serbia would become a landlocked state. From there I hopped onto a *combi*, or mini-van, to Budva, Montenegro's most fashionable resort city. Upon arrival, I was mobbed by people offering holiday accommodation. Most of them ignored me when they learned that I was staying for only one or two nights. There were plenty of customers staying for one or two weeks, even more, so who cared about a budget-tight backpacker in Budva?

I walked along the waterfront as soon as I had found my lodging (after great difficulty). The place was full of tourists, mostly from Serbia: young Belgraders here during summer school vacations — the fit, healthy and beautiful — stunning golden-haired Serbian girls, and muscular lads with six-packs. This is the Serbian version of Miami Beach and California. Many come here for one to three months, working in bars and restaurants while having a good time.

This is a family place too, with entire families escaping the oppressive heat trapped in the Danubian valleys inland. It seemed as if all Serbia had decamped and moved to the Montenegrin coast. Prices are extraordinarily high by Belgrade standards. In fact a meal can easily cost as much as in

Aspirations of an independent Montenegro.

Greece or Croatia, if not more. Is this really Yugoslavia, the country that has just emerged after a wasted decade of war and stagnation?

Bored, no matter how nice it was looking at bright young things, I got onto a bus to Cetinje, Montenegro's old royal capital in the mountains. OK, who are the Montenegrins? Let me be careful when telling the story, for once again, I am stepping onto a political minefield.

> *Black ridges drew the cloud and brake the storm.*
> *Has breathed a race of mightier mountaineers.*
> —Alfred Lord Tennyson, *Montenegro*, 1877

Montenegro is located on the southwestern coast of Yugoslavia. This is a wild mountainous land between Bosnia and Croatia on the northern side, and Serbia, Kosovo and Albania on the other, scarcely populated (500,000 people) and home to one of the hardiest peoples in Europe. Once led by their prince-bishops, the Montenegrins are a Serbian-speaking people, and the only Balkan nation never to be conquered by the Ottoman Turks, who launched numerous raids but failed to defeat them.

The symbol of this people is the mountaintop mausoleum of their greatest epic poet and ruler, Prince Petar II Petrovic Njegos (1813–1851), on shady Mt. Lovcen, thus this land is known as Montenegro, or "Black Mountain". They were practitioners of ancient codes of honour, which more often than not, demanded the satisfaction of grievances on a tooth-for-a-tooth basis, leading to generations of disastrous blood feuds between clans and tribes. During WWI, Montenegro joined Serbia in her fight against Austro-Hungary but was annexed into Yugoslavia after the war.

During WWII, Montenegrins were formidable fighters in Tito's partisan army, tying divisions of Hitler's army in this harsh land. During the wars in former Yugoslavia in the early 1990's, Montenegrins were known as great warriors and enthusiasts in maintaining the unity of old Yugoslavia. Not only were Montenegrin regiments — formal or irregular ones — among the most ferocious combatants in the sieges around Dubrovnik and Vukovar, but major Serbian leaders like Milosevic and

Karadzic (presidents of Serbia and Republika Srpska respectively) are of Montenegrin descent, as well.

The collapse of the Federation after all these wars, particularly the loss of Kosovo in 1999, has brought a new political idea to the forefront — that of an independent Montenegro. The President of Montenegro, Milo Djukanovic, is a proponent of independence and so is about 40% of the population. However, another 40% of the population fiercely opposes it. Montenegrins are Serbians too, they argue, and the country is too small to be separated from Serbia in any way. The issue threatens to lead to another civil war.

After repeated mediation by the European Union, a temporary measure was decided upon — both Serbia and Montenegro would remain in a loose union for three years, in a new country named Serbia and Montenegro, pending a final solution. Nobody knows what this would lead to — the nationalists see this as an interim measure towards final independence, while latest reports said that the EU had indicated that they would not support an independent Montenegro joining the EU.

In reality, Montenegro already has a de facto independence of sorts. They have denounced the Yugoslav Denars in favour of Euros, and have their own border and passport controls, which are in contravention of federal and international law. They refused to allow me to enter though federal rules would have approved it. They have their own telecommunications and postal network.

Issues of independence aside, Montenegro has amazing scenery. The many pretty coastal groves and hidden beaches, coupled with wild, green mountains, spectacular fjord-like scenery and the occasional sea front castle and fortresses all combine to make this a first class tourism destination. Already, the Russians are jetting in directly from Moscow and St Petersburg, and many of them are snapping up the best seaside locations and villas. Prices are still low but wait till the Western Europeans discover Montenegro as well. Kotor is not too far away from Milan, Vienna or Zurich for a comfortable weekend break. If the independence issue can be resolved, the country may be poised for a takeoff in tourism, which is possibly the best industry to develop in this tiny country with a population too small to sustain a manufacturing economy.

»»»»»

As the old royal capital of the Montenegrin kings, Cetinje is the hotbed of Montenegrin nationalism. Pro-independence posters proclaim support for the cause, something that one hardly sees at prosperous coastal cities like Bar and Budva, which depend a lot on tourism and trade with Serbia. Located in the spectacular highlands above the sunny coastal plains, Cetinje was once the unconquerable fortress of this mountain people.

Today, the capital is in the more comfortable lowland city of Pogodrica (known as Titograd in Tito's days), and Cetinje is but a sleepy (read "boring") provincial town. I visited the sloppy National Museum and walked around looking at old turn of the (19th/20th) century diplomatic missions of European powers and decaying facades of royal palaces and government buildings. Will this be an independent state again? Will it work economically? Will all the Montenegrin people support it? Is independence worth fighting for, especially when half the population does not support the idea?

The beautiful city walls of Kotor, the jewel of Montenegro.

I dropped by the old city of Kotor, a beautiful walled city once controlled by the Venetians. Located at the far end of the deep water Kotor Bay, it is spectacularly stunning with the high cliffs above it surrounding the winding fjord of Kotor Bay. No wonder this is a UNESCO World Heritage site. But will this be the next World Heritage site to suffer the ravages of war?

Not too far away is the tiny magical island of Sveti Stefan, connected to the mainland by only a sand bar. This 15th century former fishing village in the 1960s and 1970s was a getaway-cum-nightclub and casino complex for the rich and famous of the world — people like Elizabeth Taylor, Richard Burton and Claudia Schiffer. The Balkan wars of the 1990s have long since scared away such glamorous visitors. The place looked sleepy though still magical and idyllic nevertheless.

As I watched young Belgraders party day and night on the same beaches where only half the population wanted independence, I wondered if it were all for real. Why can't they all live together in peace and harmony?

I got onto a bus to Ulcinj, the southernmost city of Montenegro, an old Turkish city and slave trading port. About 90% of the population here are ethnic Albanian. Whereas all of Serbia appears to be on the beaches of Budva and resorts further north, Ulcinj is the holiday resort for the similarly inland Kosovar Albanians. Tourism in the Balkans is ethnically based. You go to where your own race goes for vacations. Here, connections are excellent if you are going to Albania, Kosovo and the Albanian-inhabited part of Macedonia.

Here, I got onto another overnight bus, this time Kosovo-bound. Another adventure lay ahead.

Kosovo: There is No Nelson Mandela Here

2002: Fushe Kosovo — the new Albanian name of the historic Kosovo Fields. I stood on its windswept emptiness, with multitudes of blackbirds circling the site. The winds howled while I took refuge in the shadow of the huge monument under which Milosevic made his speech in 1989.

Rubbish littered this holy ground of the Serbs; the interior of the stone tower had been utterly ransacked — I did not know what used to be found within, perhaps an exhibition of the historic events it was built to commemorate, but now there was only rubble to be found. A heavily-armed guard post stood metres away, with sandbags and camouflage net. A bored British soldier was listening to his Discman, while looking out for potential Albanian arsonists.

The United Nations took over Kosovo in 1999, after NATO — which postcards in Belgrade described as the New Antichrist Terrorist Organisation — had inflicted a heavy defeat on what remained of the Yugoslav Federation. Since then, one million Albanian refugees exiled by Milosevic's oppression and genocidal attacks have returned to this troubled land — officially described as a "province" but in reality heading for independence — while most of the 250,000 Serbs have left in haste, like many of their compatriots in what used to be Krajina in Croatia. In his efforts to avert the events of 1389, Milosevic had instead prompted its recurrence. History had come full circle.

I arrived in Kosovo after an overnight bus ride from Montenegro, through the high winding passes of Rugova, into the historic Kosovar city of Peje — it used to be known by its old Serbian name of Peć. Now all the place and road names in Kosovo are being changed. Serbian names had been struck off by vandals, leaving only the Albanian ones. A millennium of Serbian existence in Kosova — the Albanian name for the province, or what the Albanians prefer to call it, the country — is being wiped off books and landscapes.

During the hour-plus bus journey to Prishtina (older Serbian version: Priština), I came across ruins of houses, or even whole ruined villages. The Serbians had destroyed entire communities when NATO bombing began, leading to a mass exodus of ethnic Albanians from Kosovo, in addition to those that had already fled abroad when the Serbs started their campaigns against the guerillas of the Kosovo Liberation Army (UCK).

> *The East End of London would...be lying in ruins if the Balkan Christian powers had not been defeated by the Turks in 1389.*
> — Editors of the *Black Lamb and Grey Falcon*
> by Rebecca West, 1941

After the entry of the UN into Kosovo, the UCK began their revenge attacks on the Serbs, leaving many villages and churches in rubble too — more than 100 had been destroyed since the war ended, and the remaining ones are heavily guarded by KFOR (Kosovo Enforcement Force — a 34-nation contingent force) troops, complete with barbed wire, sandbag bastions and watch towers. One particularly large church still had the top of its bell tower intact, sitting on the rubble of its lower floors. A sad reminder of the ethnic hatred and cycle of vengeance that never seemed to end.

Prishtina used to be a drab town of 300,000 people. Since the end of the war, its population has more than doubled, due to the influx of villagers fleeing the massive destruction in the countryside. The entry of more than 30,000 KFOR troops, plus perhaps an equal number of personnel from UNMIK (UN Mission in Kosovo, the UN ruling body), and the alphabet soup of international organisations and NGO's such as UNICEF, OSCE and EU, meant a boom in the number of fancy restaurants, bars, cybercafés and nightclubs.

On the roads of Kosovo, the UN military presence is never too far away.

Like everywhere else in Kosovo, apart from a few token Serbian signboards on prominent UNMIK buildings, the whole place had been completely Albanianised, with new statues of the Albanian national hero, Skanderbeg; Mother Theresa, the most famous Albanian worldwide; lots of Albanian national flags; and memorials to fallen UCK heroes — the last seen all over Kosovo.

Kosovo is today a very safe place for foreigners, so long as you try to be as non-Serbian as possible. A Bulgarian UN staff member was shot in broad daylight when he spoke Serbian — he was mistaken for a Serb. I tried my best to forget whatever Serbian/Croatian/Bosnian/Macedonian I had learned the past few weeks, although the chances of my being mistaken as a Serb of some sort were negligible.

Even then, I was corrected a few times by locals when I used the more familiar Serbian place names. Even the menu of the Grand Hotel[16], the best in town (which doesn't mean a lot for these state-run enterprises awkwardly taken over by the UNMIK), had the well-known Serbian dishes such as Serbian Salad and Fish Belgrade Style crossed out by hand and renamed 'Albanian Salad and Fish Prishtina Style' instead.

Everywhere I was asked whom I worked for. To most people, the notion of a tourist in Kosovo sounds as ridiculous as going for a skiing holiday in Papua New Guinea. I got tired of trying to explain, and ended up saying I was an economist with UNMIK.

Here I saw a very cosmopolitan mix of foreigners, from Malaysian police to Swedish KFOR troops. Foreigners are treated very well here. They are all regarded as liberators — I have never seen the flags of UN, NATO and the USA flown so widely, from fast food stalls to motels — and the source of the local boom and spending power. I hardly saw any other economic activity. I wondered what would happen when UNMIK's mandate ended.

Perhaps smuggling would remain an important source of income. There were no passport checks whatsoever when I entered Kosovo from Montenegro. No wonder this has become a major centre for the transit of illegal goods, drugs and human cargo.

---

[16] This was the base of renowned journalists during the 1999 war, including Jim Simpson of the BBC.

I jumped onto a local bus to Peje (Serbian: Peć), the number two city of Kosovo. The local bazaar and Islamic quarter were mediocre. Many of the ancient monuments had been destroyed by the Serbian paramilitary and are being rebuilt thanks to funding from Muslim nations like Malaysia and Saudi Arabia. What interested me more were the Serbian monuments — the Peć Patriarchate and the Dečani Monastery, not too far away.

» » » » »

According to Wikipedia:

"In Serbian legend, Prince Lazar is said to have been visited by an angel of God on the night before battle, and offered a choice between an earthly or a Heavenly kingdom, which choice would result in a peaceful capitulation or bloody defeat, respectively, at the Battle of Kosovo."

"...Prophet Elijah then appeared as a gray falcon to Lazar, bearing a letter from the Mother of God that told him the choice was between holding an earthly kingdom and entering the kingdom of heaven..."

Lazar opts for the Heavenly kingdom, which will last "forever and ever" ("Perishable is earthly kingdom, but forever and ever is Kingdom of Heaven!"but he has to perish on the battlefield. "We die with Christ, to live forever", he tells his soldiers. That is Kosovo's destiny and Testament, it is a union which the Serb people made with God — and sealed with martyrs' blood. In Kosovo, Serbs voted with their souls for the Kingdom of Heaven and that was and has been their right destination. Since then all Serbs truthful to that Testament are becoming people of God, Christ's New Testament nation, heavenly Serbia, part of God's New Israel. This is why sometimes Serbs refer to themselves as the people of Heaven."

And so Milosevic marched straight into the many wars of the 1990's, sometimes knowing that almost certain defeat lay ahead. Had an angel appeared before him as well, as did Prince Lazar? Or had Milosevic misguidedly imagined himself to be the martyred prince?[17]

---

[17] Upon Kosovo's declaration of independence, the Serbian government, too, had ignored the possibility of derailing Serbia's efforts to join the European Union, and agitated for the lost cause of Kosovo instead. Is this also reflective of the "Prince Lazar effect"?

Frescoes in Serbian monasteries of Kosovo: These World Heritage treasures are now under threat from Albanian extremists who want to erase centuries of Serbian presence in Kosovo.

Memorial tower at the site of the Battle of Kosovo near Prishtina. Once a rallying point for Serbian nationalism, it is now a lone tower surrounded by barbed wire and guarded by UN troops.

Interior and exterior of Dečani Monastery.

»»»»»

The Peć Patriarchate is the Vatican of the Serbian Orthodox Church. Kosovo at the time of the Battle of 1389 was the heartland of the Serbian people, although it was probably a multiracial land with as many Albanians. Prizren, another major city, was one of the most important Serbian cities between the 14th and 16th centuries.

It was in Peć where the Serbian Church was headquartered that the Serbian kings built numerous churches and monasteries, hence the other Serbian name for the province, Mehotija, or "Church Land". Even today, the official HQ of the Serbian Patriarch (or head of the Serbian church) is in Peć while his cabinet or operational office lies in Belgrade. This explains why the Serbs are so emotional about Kosovo being part of their homeland.

To visit the Peć Patriarchate and Dečani Monastery, one supposedly needs a permit from the KFOR Italian contingent who garrisoned the Peje region. I popped by their HQ at the best hotel in town, Hotel Mehotija, which used to be a four-star establishment, but was surrounded by barbed wire, sandbags and mounted machine guns in downtown Peje. The not-so-eloquent Italian soldier there said, "Just go ahead. No permit required." And so I walked 2km to the Patriarchate, a group of Orthodox-domed buildings surrounded by a mediaeval wall, in the suburbs of the city.

Here I was confronted by a group of monolingual Italian troops, who first aimed their rifles at me, and then agreed to ask their English-speaking officer to deal with me. "You need permits from HQ G5 at KFOR Regional HQ at Hotel Mehotija," he insisted. G5 is a military department that deals with certain security matters. The sort of military designation common to many countries, as I remember from my old army days.

And so I had to return to Hotel Mehotija where I insisted on meeting the Regional Press Officer. Eventually they agreed to get a permit for me while keeping me at a safe distance outside the KFOR security perimeter round the hotel. "Ok, you are now allowed to visit the monasteries," said a burly guy who came out of the building. "But where is the paper permit?" I asked.

The Italians were such a paper-adverse group. They murmured among themselves for a moment, and had yet another phone conversation. Then they told me that G5 and the respective units at the monasteries had my details now and I should just turn up at the monasteries. It was not their policy to issue paper permits, they insisted.

Suspicious but at a loss as to what more to do, I turned up at Peć Patriarchate again. Not surprisingly, no one had my details at all! And they wanted a signed permit on paper. I was firm that the necessary permit had been given and the local officer had yet another chat on the phone. After another 15 minutes, they finally allowed me into the Patriarchate complex.

Black robed nuns fed cows outside while a few lay followers were cleaning the grounds — they had to endure daily jeering by passing Albanian teenagers. At least, the Italian troops at the earlier checkpoint were making sure these passersby did not carry arms. "Dobry Dan," I greeted them in Serbian. "Good Day!" They smiled and took me to the main church building.

There, a friendly English-speaking young man named Nikola greeted me. Nikola was born in Peć, and was forced to flee for his life into the Patriarchate when the Yugoslav Army withdrew from Kosovo. He had been living in this small crowded complex for the past three years! Most of his fellow Serbs had fled to Serbia proper.

Ottoman architecture in the pretty city of Prizren. This was also the capital of the Serbian state in mediaeval times. Today it is almost a purely Albanian city.

He guided me around the complex, where I admired the amazing 12th and 13th century frescoes. Such bright colours and intricate paintings that survived even the Turkish invasion and both world wars — would they survive the latest crisis? It would be tragic if this gem of human civilization were to be destroyed by Albanian extremists, or "terrorists", as the Serbians called them.

The Yugoslav Government has since applied to UNESCO to list the Peć Patriarchate, Dečani Monastery and the Gračanica Church in Kosovo as World Heritage sites, so that they might receive international protection and profiles. I hope they succeed.

I admire people like Nikola, who stay on in this land of their birth, despite overwhelming difficulties, in the hope that better times will come and they can return to their homes. Deep in my heart, however, I wonder if such a day would ever come at all.

After that I hopped onto another local bus for Dečani, though not before meeting two Canadian backpackers — the only ones I had seen in my entire Kosovo stay — who had been refused permission to visit the guarded monasteries. Again, after a long walk through the lonely country road to the Italian KFOR checkpoint, I found that no one had my details — I was not surprised by the Italian lack of organisation though... More waiting time while enquiries were made and finally confirmation received of my permit. An armour-plated landrover came to escort me down the deserted road to the monastery itself.

This monastery was even more impressive, much larger and more monumental than the Peć Patriarchate. It was built by the father of Tsar Dusan the Great of Serbia. More frescoes and works of art. A few monks here spoke English and a Father Stevan guided me around. He, too, had a sad personal history. He had been made a refugee twice! He was born in Krajina, i.e., the Serbian inhabited part of Croatia. He was forced to flee Krajina in 1995, and came here to Kosovo. He served in a church in Priština[18] but was forced to flee again in 1999 after the Serbian defeat by NATO. Now he is under siege in the Dečani Monastery.

---

[18] Here I use the Serbian version without the "h" because that was pre-1999.

On Day Three in Kosovo, I took a local bus to the city of Prizren. This must be the most beautiful city in Kosovo. A kind of mini-Sarajevo, with minarets and church domes and spires set against lush green hills and a winding river. The central attraction is the Mosque of Sinan Pasha, a magical Ottoman building filled with friendly locals who encouraged me to take as many pictures as I liked.

Again, the tragedy of it all was that, unlike Sarajevo which remains multi-ethnic and multi-religious, the Serbs of Prizren, an ancient Serbian capital, had fled, and their churches were surrounded by barbed wire guarded by German KFOR troops. At least these troops could speak English and they seemed a lot better organised. Interestingly, together with Austrian and Swiss KFOR troops, they lived in a camp nearby called Camp Casablanca. Well,

Elderly Albanian man: This land is mine.

Destroyed Serbian churches like this can be seen as one travels across Kosovo.

KFOR troops live in places with fantasy names. The KFOR HQ just outside Prishtina is named Film City because it used to be a Yugoslav film studio.

Back to Prishtina, I decided to jump onto another bus to Gračanica. This is a Serbian village where the local inhabitants have been guarding the ancient royal monastery[19] of the same name for centuries. They remained here even after 1999 and are currently protected by Swedish KFOR troops, i.e., they have become a Serbian enclave surrounded by hostile Albanians, trapped here since 1999, unable or unwilling to leave.

Gračanica is an unusual case different from the earlier two monasteries I visited. It is a living community that lies on the main road between Prishtina and Gjilan, a major city in Kosovo. Up till recently, Albanian buses that go to Gjilan had to pass through Gračanica with a Swedish armoured personnel carrier (APC's) escort, so as to prevent Serbs from attacking the buses, and also to prevent bus passengers from throwing bombs onto the Serbian houses. Now things have settled down but Swedish soldiers still patrol the village on foot — they pass you every ten minutes or so — and APC's roll down the streets to remind everybody of their presence.

I asked the Albanian bus driver to drop me off at Gračanica, a request which provoked a strange look. No problem, he said. And so I got off the bus just outside the Monastery and he quickly sped away in case of trouble, an act which also aroused quite a few eyebrows from the Serbs in a nearby cafe. I walked into the ancient fortified complex — fortunately no permits were required, but I had turned up in shorts — an oversight on my part. The nuns weren't too happy about my lack of modesty and only allowed me to hang around the outer hall of the main church, which had enough frescoes to induce an overdose.

I decided to leave and stroll around the village. The local Serbs were amazed to see an Asian visitor. A magazine kiosk vendor unfolded a black banner with skulls and cross-bones, and the caption in Serbian, "Kosovo is Serbian — Freedom or Death." "Albanish — bad people, they want to kill us," a Serbian teenager said.

---

[19] The monastery was built by Serbian King Milutin in 1321.

I walked over to the Village Hall. The Yugoslav and Serbian flags still flew from there. Serbian signboards everywhere — no Albanian signs anywhere. The people of Gračanica still live under the illusion that Kosovo would return to Serbian rule one day. I wonder what motivated them to stay on. Their irrefutable birthright to this land (as much as the Albanians')? How about job opportunities, or freedom of movement? They could hardly risk travelling outside the village without being lynched. Serbian farmers are still regularly found murdered in post-1999 Kosovo.

Returning to Prishtina was a challenging task. Although many Albanian buses and cars passed through the village, they were all speeding through, as though they were passing some dangerous urban slum and wished to avoid any carjacks of the type one finds in South Africa or Inner City LA.

Two buses passed me without stopping. Perhaps the drivers couldn't imagine why anyone (i.e., any Serb) would want to get on the bus at Gračanica, and so they didn't bother to look at who was at the long-irrelevant bus stop. Eventually, a mini-van stopped when I waved wildly to get some attention; the driver stared hard at me, totally bewildered. I opened the sliding door to find all the passengers gawking at me.

As I got onto the van, the unshaven Albanian guy nearest to me said in Serbian, "Ne Srpski ?" (Not Serbian?). "NE!" I shouted, and the whole van roared with laughter. No laughing matter indeed if you were Serbian. Life is miserable enough in a besieged community like that. Even getting into buses, i.e., Albanian buses (there are no more intercity Serbian buses in the enclaves), might mean a life-threatening adventure if your fellow passengers had family members killed by Milosevic's oppressive forces pre-1999.

Back at my hotel, the receptionist asked, "Where have you been today?" They had become curious about this rare tourist to Kosovo and asked me everyday about my movements. I hesitated but decided to shock him anyway, "Gračanica."

"So, you were visiting those Serbian criminals?" he raised his voice. And then the fifty-plus-year-old chap got a bit emotional, "Do you know they are all criminals? All supporters of Milosevic! They raped women, even grandmothers and children! They shot at us on that main street when

Serbian nun and UN soldier outside Gračanica Monastery.

Signs at the Gračanica Monastery.

Serbian militia banner at Gračanica Village.

UN soldiers on patrol in Gračanica village.

Statue of Albanian national hero, Skanderbeg, at the heart of Prishtina: Ready for the leap into the future

they chased us out of our homes," he pointed at Prishtina's main boulevard just outside the hotel, Mother Theresa Boulevard. "Bang! Bang! Bang! They killed so many! Let's see how long they can last in those villages like Gračanica. One year? Two? Eventually they have to go! We Albanians can afford to wait!"

Suddenly, he became silent for an embarrassing moment. I was a little ashamed at provoking his outburst. The old man then said calmly, smiling a little, "Sorry sir. Nothing. Just to remind you not to be so sympathetic towards these criminals. They use propaganda all the time. I'm sorry. And have a nice evening."

I returned to my room with a heavy heart, my feelings harrowed by the contradictions of the past few days. The walls of Prishtina's public buildings were full of posters with photographs of a handsome young Albanian in military uniform touching the Albanian flag of a double-eagle-on-a-bright-red-field. They called on Albanians to protest against UNMIK, arresting a few Albanian nationalists and ex-UCK guerrillas suspected of killing Albanian collaborators and local Serbs.

On the following day, all these posters would be entirely replaced with new ones showing photos of a Serb extremist in military uniform and dark glasses cutting a young Albanian boy's throat with a sharp knife. Blood streamed down his chest — a very disturbing photo indeed.

This is such a tragic country, and a land of intense hatred. Both ethnic groups have done terrible things to each other. Each has its own story to tell. Serbian extremists under Milosevic committed atrocities and the local Serbs remained silent. After 1999, the local Albanians struck back in bitter vengeance. So many Serbs were killed in equally atrocious circumstances and entire communities forced to flee. One atrocity does not justify another in revenge.

I wondered what was in store for the future. Clearly, Kosovo is heading for independence. It has elected its own President, Prime Minister and Cabinet of Ministers. Officially it is still described by the UN as a Yugoslav Province but everyone apart from the Serbs knows that it is moving towards permanent separation. But will independence solve all issues? Even an independent Republic of Kosovo cannot escape the fact that Serbia will always remain its largest neighbour.

Its supposed motherland, Albania, is the poorest country in Europe bar Moldova, even more backward than Kosovo, which had gone through war and crisis. All the Kosovar Albanians I met admitted that unification was a dream at the moment. In my opinion, difficult as it might be, Kosovo must try to reconcile with Serbia and accept that they are inevitably condemned to be neighbours forever. It is better to be a friend than an enemy.

What are the economic prospects of Kosovo? The country has few viable heavy industries which are independent of its traditional markets in Serbia and Macedonia. Kosovo has coal whose prices have risen in recent times, but transportation costs out of this landlocked state usually blunt its competitiveness. Even its tiny traditional tourism industry is dependent on Serbian skiers[20], although it could try to attract European cultural tourists who might be keen on its ancient Serbian monasteries,

Anti-Serbian poster in Prishtina. The caption reads in English and Albanian, "Don't allow Serbian criminals back into Kosova!" This highly politicised environment disgusted me.

which most ironically its majority Albanian citizens would prefer to forget (and which some would love to see destroyed).

Smaller countries have little choices. Finland and Singapore have learned to live with Russia and Malaysia respectively, even though they would rather relocate wholesale to another part of the world if technology allowed (!) than to live next to their historical "enemy" of sorts. Both nations have succeeded to varying extents to co-exist with their larger neighbour and turn that proximity to their advantage, also partly because both were led by extraordinary leaders (Marshal Mannerheim and Lee Kuan Yew) with the foresight to realise that they could not change their geography.

It is a pity that no great leader capable of transcending such insanity has emerged in Kosovo. There is no Nelson Mandela in Kosovo, or anywhere in much of the Balkans. There is no one capable of extending the olive branch to his former enemy. That, to me, is the greatest tragedy of the Kosovo of today.

With a heavy heart, I left for Albania.

---

[20] Shortly after independence, there was a report that the Serbian government would invest 40 million euros in Kosovar skiing resorts now suffering from the lack of Serbian tourists, in a bizarre move to desmonstrate that it cared for its "rightful" province.

Albania: Land of Teletubbie Bunkers

Viola: What country (friends) is this?
Captain: This is Ilyria Ladie.
Viola: And what should I do in Ilyria?
— William Shakespeare, *Twelfth Night*

Albania, some say, is a dangerous country. Many remember the period in the late 1990's when the country collapsed into anarchy when fraudulent pyramid schemes bankrupted thousands and the nation burst into uprisings. Parts of the country became bandit-land at that time. But Albania has since returned to normality. Even then, this ancient people, descendants of the Illyrians, contemporaries of Alexander the Great and the Romans, attract illogically negative attention from their neighbours.

A few Serbs I met told me when they knew about my Albanian plans, "They are barbarians," or "They will eat you alive!" A Greek taxi driver said after learning that I had just left Albania, "They do not have God there, and so they will murder even for a dollar!" This is a misunderstood people.

Even in the UK where I was living then, an Albanian is synonymous with the darker-skinned gypsies, thieves and perpetrators of petty crimes. Many Roma beggars here claim that they are Albanians. I had never met an Albanian until I went to Skopje at the beginning of my Balkan journey and realised that the Albanians were anything but what I had imagined. Apart from a few minor instances, I experienced nothing but warmth and hospitality during my short stay in this beautiful country.

The Albanians are an Indo-European people, as white as their neighbouring Slavic neighbours, who speak an ancient tongue unlike any other in Europe, i.e., they have their own linguistic group with no close cousins. They once lived across what is today the former Yugoslav republics, but have been pushed back by all their neighbours, into the Republic of Albania, western Macedonia, southern Montenegro and Kosovo. Ruled by the Turks for 600 years, 70% of the Albanians converted to Islam. Even then, the Albanians are hardly dogmatic about religion. It has always been

said, "The only true religion of the Albanians is Albania." Someone told me
— though I am unsure of its truth, that some Albanians go to the mosque
on Fridays, and the church on Sundays.

Two of the greatest heroes of the Albanian people, Skanderbeg and Mother
Theresa, were non-Muslims. Skanderbeg (1405–1468), the national hero,
was the son of a Christian chieftain who converted to Islam when brought to
Istanbul as a Turkish hostage. Subsequently he returned to Albania, returned
to Christianity and raised a rebellion against the Turks. Proclaimed "Athlete
of Christendom" by the Pope for his persistent resistance against the Turks,
he became the eternal hero of his people, even after their conversion to Islam
following the Turkish conquest after his death.

Mother Theresa (1910–1997) born a Christian Albanian in Skopje,
Macedonia, was the greatest living saint of the 20th century and an inspiration
to all. The statues of Skanderbeg occupy the centres of Tirana and Prishtina,
while monuments to Mother Theresa are found in all Albanian lands.

I arrived in Tirana early one morning after a restless overnight journey
across rough mountain roads from Kosovo. I walked into Hotel Kalaja,
which was highly recommended on a website. A young man at the
reception desk took advantage of my pathetic state and charged me US$40,
as against the US$10 mentioned on the site. Later on, when I chatted to
the owner at night, I discovered that it should only have been between
US$15 to US$20. Thereupon, the receptionist stepped into the hall and
heard our conversation. Both had a discussion in Albanian and then they

An idyllic
Albanian village.

told me that US$40 was right and it was a misunderstanding earlier in the chat. The next morning, the receptionist rudely woke me up at 6:30am and wanted me out of the hotel, saying that my 24 hours was up. It was probably his revenge on me for exposing his pocketing of the additional amount I had paid. Well, be warned. Don't stay at this pathetic place.

Tirana is a relatively new city, although like most parts of Albania, it has ancient roots. Capital of Albania since 1920, it was built in the grand functional style of the 1930's with Italian capital and architects, by King Zog, a monarch whose reign was as short as his name. When the Italians invaded in 1939, King Zog was forced to flee to London, together with shiploads of gold and the state treasury, enough for him to rent whole floors of luxury hotels in the city. Given the corrupt governments that have been running the country the past decade, some Albanians are becoming nostalgic about their brief period of monarchy. His son, the pretender King Leka — once an arms trader who grew up in South Africa — is once again actively campaigning for the restoration of the monarchy.

A strange pyramidal marble-and-glass structure rises at the southern fringe of the city centre — this was once the Museum of Enver Hoxha, where the gifts given to this late communist dictator by obscure "working class organisations" round the world were displayed to impress the Albanians of their leader's reputation. Now it is an exhibition centre plus disco, with huge banners of "Vodafone" and "Austrian Airlines" hung across its entrance and outdoor bars on the steps of this once distinguished shrine of the working class. Hoxha must be turning in the grave where his embalmed remains were dumped after the fall of communism in Albania.

I took a bus to the mountainous town of Kruja, where Skanderbeg once held out against the Turks for many years in the citadel which commands a panoramic view of the surrounding countryside. This is Albania's national shrine, where school children learn about their national hero and his struggle for freedom. I bumped into three cute local kids, all eleven years old, and they took me around the village contained within Kruja's citadel.

We rested beside the carpet-covered sarcophagus in the airy domed tekke or shrine of the local Bektashi Sufi sect, with photos and paintings of their babas and dervishes — mainstream Islam doesn't allow human images. I was further plied with Albanian hospitality at the bus station where locals treated me to coffee. I engaged in small talk with the cafe owner and his friends while waiting for the bus to Tirana. And yes, intriguing them with attempts to translate their names into Chinese. In no time at all, they were asking about swear words in Mandarin.

Speaking of Mandarin, I was slightly surprised to come across elderly gentlemen in Albania who greeted me in Mandarin. Yes, phrases like "*Ni Hao*" or "*Zai Jian*" are becoming more common everywhere worldwide but there seemed to be more people in Albania greeting me with them than anywhere else in the world. There is a reason for this. After WWII, Albania turned communist as a result of the communist guerillas' victory in the fight against the Italians and the Germans. It became closely allied with the USSR, but not as a satellite state, as there were no Soviet troops on its soil.

In 1960, after the Soviets demanded for a naval base, Albania broke off relations with them and made China under Mao Zedong its closest ally. During that period, many Chinese advisors were sent to Albania and Albanians went to China for education. Albania even had its own Cultural Revolution during which religion was banned (Albania became the only officially atheistic state in the world) and churches and mosques were destroyed.

Some old books published in the UK and USA during that era inaccurately described Albania as a Chinese satellite in Europe. It was probably during this period that the elderly gentlemen I came across learnt Mandarin. Albania's special friendship with China ended in 1978 when

Bunkers, bunkers everywhere, all over Albania.

China began its market-based economic reforms, a move condemned by the Albanian communists as heretical.

I travelled on yet another local bus — one that smelled of unwashed armpits, fresh cigarettes and stale vodka — to yet another old museum town, Berat, and from there to Fier, where I negotiated for a taxi to get to the Roman city of Apollonia, through rather bad country roads full of potholes the size of bomb craters.

I stood on the hill at Apollonia, next to the ancient columns, and admired the spectacular panorama of the valley beyond: Right in this fertile agricultural countryside whose roadsides were lined with mountains of water melons and vegetable vendors, there were massive nuclear shelters whose tunnel-like holes could probably have accommodated huge trucks and buses at the far end of the valley. The Hoxha regime had vandalized Albania's countryside by building 750,000 bunkers across the nation. Hoxha was paranoid over the prospect of an invasion by the USA, UK, USSR or Yugoslavia, and built bunkers everywhere, especially along the coast. Most of them resembled simple igloos, about the size of a huge wheelbarrow but there were also many, much bigger ones. In a bizarre way, quite a few also looked uncannily like the atrocious abode of our more familiar Teletubbie friends, which I saw more as a plague affecting televisions worldwide. Albania was no exception, it seemed.

Gjirokastra was next. This is a beautiful town six hours by bus from Tirana, down at the deep southern end of the country. This is a region of dusty mountains and rugged slopes. Albania par excellence, the legendary land of ferocious tribes and honourable fighters. The epic land that captured the passion of Lord Byron, and many writers and poets. The mountains here are high, but not significantly taller than those found elsewhere in the Balkans. It was the vigorous tendency of the local tribes to defend their freedom that must have made these mountains seem so much more formidable than they actually were.

This is also the land of blood feuds, where trivial disagreements sometimes lead to terrible cycles of vengeance in which one generation dies for the quarrels of another long past. Generations of men have been forced to stay indoors simply because their forefathers had killed someone from another clan. Many Albanian tribes are bound by a complex code of honour that requires them to avenge deeds done to their ancestors. Only women and children are spared from vengeance, which cannot be carried out in houses. But anywhere else outside the house is open season. As a result, many men grow up as virtual recluses in their fortress-like abodes, away from proper education and interaction with the outside world; yet another cause for the backwardness and criminal legacy of this land.

Gjirokastra itself is a real museum town perched on the side of a rugged mountain and crowned with a citadel. The Drinos River flows through the valley beneath, with rough, barren mountains on the other side of the valley. After I was dumped by the bus off the highway at the lower town, I was promptly "kidnapped" by a taxi driver who wanted to drive me to the upper town, or Old City.

Upon arrival at the square in the picturesque Old City up on the mountain slopes, I was then "snatched" by Mr. Haxhi Kotoni to his famous bed-and-breakfast, the Kotoni B&B. A simple 10-euro room in his authentic traditional Albanian house — windowless on the ground floor, as such houses were built raised above the ground like mini-fortresses during the period of ancient blood feuds — provided a wonderful view of the Old City and the Citadel, but with a balcony where one could admire the sunset and have a sip of great Turkish coffee. Look out for his visitors' book; it's stuffed with wonderful testimonials from people the world over, though mostly international aid workers, diplomats and peacekeepers on R&R from Kosovo.

I decided to leave Albania by direct coach to Ioannina, northern Greece. An unfortunate accident occurred in which three people died in a car that crashed into my bus. It appeared suddenly from a side road and crashed into the massive travel coach like paper against a brick wall. Even in the war-torn and supposedly dangerous Balkans, one forgets everyday hazards because the momentum of living is too great, until like a cheetah sneaking up and then jumping onto an antelope, one is immediately reminded of the ease with which life can be extinguished.

The bus swayed across the highway, and then fell upright into a trench. A brief moment of shock and hesitation — brief images of exploding engines and a burning bus flashed across my mind — and then everyone scrambled off the bus. We discovered the car under the bus, totally flattened, with the driver's head and left arm protruding outside the window; its occupants were almost certainly dead. What mayhem!

A lady ahead of me simply sat down in front of the bus and the crushed car, wailing hysterically. I climbed out of the trench, my right foot scratched by some thorns as I struggled among the bushes. Albanian TV got onto the site quite fast and before long began filming the chaotic scene. If I had been able to watch the Albanian news that evening, I might have seen myself sitting on the ground above the smoking bus, looking dazed.

A sense of panic and hopelessness descended upon me, like the dream of discovering that one was lost in an endless labyrinth of tunnels. For a few moments, I was deeply frightened of the road ahead. Fear has its own devious logic; a way of telling one that the clock could be turned back if one chose the easier road. I searched for the talisman of Guanyin, a Buddhist deity, which was given to me by Mum on my first backpacking trip abroad. There it was, in a side pocket of my daypack.

I have never been religious, worshipping only paychecks and the god of capitalism. But at that moment when I held the talisman tightly in my palm, I realised that I could not turn back. My journey and its outcome should have nothing to do with this terrible accident. The road would go on, despite it all.

And so I proceeded across the border to Greece. A short stay in the magical land of Meteora, where ancient monasteries graced the clear blue skies and strange rock formations. The next morning, I woke up with a big shock, almost falling off the bed. Hoof, I'm still alive! My hands reached out for the Guanyin. I clutched it tightly, more tightly than ever before in my life.

Yemen: Osama's Desert Manhattan (Dec 2007)

KALASHNIKOV & DAGGER. What would you do if you got into a taxi and found that your driver wore a curved dagger and kept a Kalashnikov next to his seat? As Mark Lawson-Statham, a British banker, wrote, just as he had concluded there was little point haggling over the fare in such circumstances, he found the driver chewing *qat*, "an admittedly mild, but nevertheless narcotic plant, [he] abandoned all notions of being in charge of [his] own destiny and succumbed totally to his will[21]."

Yemen is truly a country where time has stood still. As our[22] car sped from the airport to downtown Sana'a, Yemen's capital, I gawked at the sight of Yemeni men walking around in flowing Yemeni-Arab robes with a *jambiya*, the curved traditional dagger, stuck through their intricately embroidered belts. No self-respecting Yemeni man, at least in the northern half of the country, which accounts for 80% of the population, would appear in public without his dagger. Would you? A man without his weapon?

Up till a few years ago, a Kalashnikov slung around the shoulder would have been as de rigueur as the *jambiya*, but the Yemeni government has, from August 2007, begun a phased firearms collection programme. "No firearms are now allowed in cities and firearms will be collected nationwide over time," said Walid, my guide. As I was to notice at a checkpoint outside town, tribesmen now have to deposit their rifles at checkpoints when they enter Sana'a and collect them when they leave the city — the way people elsewhere deposit their belongings when they enter supermarkets.

---

[21] Mark Lawson-Statham, *The Land That Time Forgot, Visitor's Complete Guide to Yemen*, Arab World Tours, 2004.
[22] I traveled to Yemen with Kris and Kelly, whose names also appear in this essay.

I wished the Yemeni authorities luck, for there were 60 million firearms in this country of 20 million inhabitants. Given that 50% of the population is under the age of 15, one can probably deduce that every adult has six guns on average.

》》》》》

GINGERBREAD HOUSES. In Old Sana'a, one of the oldest continuously inhabited cities in the world, ornate mud-brick buildings five or six stories tall with broad white-paint lines that made them almost gingerbread style, still stood as they had for the last 300 to 500 years. Here, craftsmen sold colourful woven baskets in thousand-year-old formerly-Jewish caravanserais and molded *jambiyas* as their families have done for centuries. Children played football and hide-and-seek in the countless cobblestone streets and lanes that form the labyrinth which is Sana'a. This is a photographer's paradise, given the pollution-free, clear blue skies and bright colours associated with crisp highland air.

Men walk around with their *jambiyas* while texting with their fingers on mobile phones. They often have a bulge in their cheeks — an indication that they are chewing *qat*, which Yemenis claim gives them energy and reduces fatigue and stress, though the World Health Organisation classifies it as a narcotic and many countries treat it as a controlled drug.

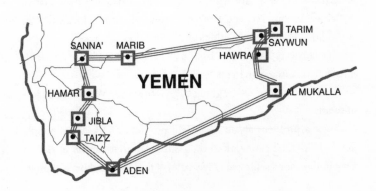

Yemeni women are a conservative lot — they are hardly seen on the streets, and when they do, they hurry around in all-black *burqa* with only their eyes revealed. In fact, dancing between men and women is unheard of — only men dance and amongst themselves, brandishing their *jambiyas* to loud drumbeats. It amazed us when we found stores full of lacy, semi-transparent lingerie and some of the most glittering and sensuous dresses for women, including those that even some western women would be shy to wear on the streets. Well, Yemeni women do wear these, but only at home for their husbands or during ladies parties with other Yemeni women.

Yemeni girls marry young, and many consider 16 to be an appropriate age for women to get married. In parts of the countryside, girls marry at an even younger age. A report said that girls in Hodeidah, Hadramawt and Sayoun, marry at age eight. In Mukalla, they marry at age ten. Yemeni women bear an average of seven children each, which translates into a nation with half its population under 15 years old. Early marriage and lots of children often mean poverty and the inability to get their offspring properly educated and fed.

Another report in the *Yemen Times* said that given the current growth rates, the population would grow from the current 22 million to 30 million in 2015, 43 million in 2025 and 109 million in 2050. Economic growth struggles to keep up with population growth. The poverty rate has increased from 19% in 1992 to 34% in 1999 (and about 50% today).

On the huge square within Old Sana'a just behind the ancient gates of Bab el-Yemen, Kris and I asked a group of curious locals who crowded around us, "How many brothers and sisters do you have?"

The answers were "6", "10", "8", "11" — and "15" came from Ali, a mustached young man in his early 20's.

"But how is your father going to feed them all? Will there be jobs for all of them?"

"Not a problem at all. Allah will provide for us. More people in the family help. One can work in the police. Another can serve chai in a café. One in the shops selling *jambiya*. All will find jobs and have enough to eat," Ali replied.

Yemen ranked 174 out of 184 countries covered in a world survey on human resource development. The present and future look daunting, even disastrous. How is poor mountainous Yemen with limited arable land going to feed more than 100 million people in 2050?

》》》》》

Highlander freedom. We explored villages in the wind-swept plateau and mountains of the central highlands around Sana'a. People still live in defensive towers made of mud bricks — like those in the Caucasus Highlands of Georgia, or remote villages in the Greek Peloponnese — while working on terraced rice fields or herding sheep on mountain slopes. Yemen remains a tribal society where each tribe has a deep-rooted sense of independence and commands the loyalty of the individual Yemeni, even to an extent much greater than the state.

Historically, the Yemeni state hardly has much control over the mountains outside the cities. How could it with millions of firearms in private hands? Heavily-armed soldiers are often found at fortified check points along roads, or cruising around in Toyota pickups equipped with heavy machine guns, and that is what imposes state authority.

View of the Yemeni Highlands.

From time to time, trouble would flare up over land dispute or dissatisfaction over taxes and lack of development. Over the last few decades, tourists have been kidnapped on a number of occasions by unhappy tribes in exchange for government concessions. On most occasions, the kidnapped were treated with great hospitality by their captors and released unharmed. On some occasions where gun battles broke out when the government attempted rescue, tourists have been killed or injured — that is a prospect that continues to adversely affect Yemen's tourism industry, which could otherwise have been developed into a key sector of the economy.

Complicating the picture is the emergence of extremist and fundamentalist Islamic groups that find fertile recruitment ground in a poor country with low literacy rates. The literacy rate is only 50% and underemployment is evident — we saw bored young men sitting around with nothing to do in many towns and villages. However, with the low literacy rate and the Yemeni inclination to chew *qat* all the time, employers often have to recruit literate and more work-conscious foreigners, such as Filipinos and Ethiopians, to get work done.

In 2000, cells of the Al-Qaeda attacked the American warship, *USS Cole*, in Aden, and in July 2007, gunmen attacked a group of tourists in the ruins of Sheba at Marib, killing seven Spanish tourists and two Yemeni guides. The Yemeni Government blamed Al-Qaeda for those attacks. How do you deal with terrorism when the country remains poor and many bored young people cannot feed themselves except with wild ideas of a better afterlife, which they believe to be achievable by bombing and killing innocents indiscriminately?

Conservatism also means most women do not work outside their homes and Yemenia, the national airline, recruits Indonesians as air stewardesses. In any case, Yemeni women have too many children and need to stay at home to look after them.

Whatever the case might be, we experienced nothing but hospitality and warmth from the Yemeni people. We visited ancient homes and shops in godforsaken towns and villages. In many places, we were treated to tea, sweets, snacks and *qat*, despite the lack of sufficient English on their part and our total inability to speak Arabic. We took many pictures of friendly locals, who sometimes put aside any religious reservations they might have had.

Deep in a remote but spectacular canyon in a sub-branch of Wadi Hadramawt is the village of Al-Khoraybah, barely a few kilometers from Ar Ribat, the ancestral hometown of Osama bin Laden. Here, we indulged in small talk with locals while enjoying the many desserts and sweets that a café owner and his friends gave us. For brief moments, we even contemplated setting up a backpacker ghetto in this friendly, cozy village, complete with cybercafés, shisha cafes, backpacker hostels and camel ride and rock-climbing outfits.

» » » » »

Qat. It was Id during our first day in Sana'a (what we call Hari Raya Haji in Singapore). All shops were closed except for the *qat* stalls. Many men were sitting around doing nothing but chewing the notorious drug. Some 80% of all adult Yemeni men chew it on a regular basis. I was given a few leaves to try. It was a fairly bitter stimulant herb but it had no effect on me whatsoever. "You have to chew more than that for it to be effective," said Walid.

I am not sure why the Yemenis love this weed. Some spend 30 to 50% of their income on it. Depending on the quality, *qat* can cost anywhere from about US$3 to US$11 for a small bag. Indeed a bag shown to me cost 5,000 Rials or US$20. According to the *Guardian*, a UK newspaper, "Until the 1960s *qat* chewing was an occasional pastime for the elite. But it is now deeply ingrained, a product, ironically, of the rapid growth of wealth in the 1970s and 1980s."[23]

Some 75% of Yemen's arable land is taken up for *qat* production, and that consumes a lot of water, leaving most of Sana'a devoid of underground water. More and more farmers in this mountainous land are also switching to *qat*, as growing it is more profitable than growing food, even in this era of rising prices. One in seven working Yemenis are involved in the growing, transportation and sale of the plant.

---

[23] Ian Black, The Curse of Yemen, *Guardian*, 12 August 2008

Old Sana'a's fabulous skyline.

Yemen's Grand Canyon:
the spectacular mountains and valleys of Wadi Hadramawt.

More of the amazing Wadi Hadramawt region.

While many Yemenis claim that *qat* keeps them awake throughout the day, I did not find the average Yemeni necessarily more diligent at work. In fact, I have found many Yemeni in a daze in the afternoons. At times, half the country appeared at times to be hopelessly addicted, including the many policemen and soldiers at checkpoints throughout the country. No wonder this is the poorest country in the Middle East and one of the most poverty-ridden worldwide.

The *Yemen Post* revealed that the President had decided to gradually reduce his consumption of *qat*, after medical tests in Germany. It further reported that the President "would also stop attending the *maqil*, or circle of friends devoted to chewing *qat*, in favour of meeting the people and personalities from the political and cultural worlds to hear their opinions on questions of national interest." I suspect more than a mental and social revolution is needed to rid Yemenis of their almost desperate addiction to the noxious weed.

QUEEN OF SHEBA. I went to Marib on a day trip. This is the capital of the ancient kingdom of Sheba — famous for its legendary Queen. The region is in a state of semi-rebellion — it had always been so — and foreigners could only enter the region in a military convoy. During the 1962–1967 North Yemen Civil War, Marib was a major base for the Royalist tribes opposed to the Republican revolutionaries who overthrew the Imam (rulers of the Mutawakkilite dynasty that ruled Yemen from 1918 to 1962) and supported by Abdul Nasser's Egypt. Traditionally, tribal disputes in this area were over resource allocation, but the Government blamed the latest massacre of Spanish tourists in July 2007 on tribes that had teamed up with Al-Qaeda.

Outside Sana'a, the Bedouin tribesmen arm themselves to the teeth — Kalashnikovs, bazookas, ground-to-air anti aircraft missiles, grenades, you name it. Police checkpoints were found every 20 kilometres or so, heavily armed too, often with machine gun-equipped Toyota pickups. I even spied armoured carriers at some spots. At police checkpoints just outside Sana'a, all visitors entering the city border had to deposit their firearms and collect them when they left the capital.

We set off early from Sana'a but had to wait at a checkpoint to the east of the city, for other vehicles to gather and do the journey together as a convoy. When eight vehicles carrying tourists from Germany, Italy, UK, Australia, Poland, Czech Republic, Peru and me (as Singapore's sole representative) arrived, the convoy set off with a military Toyota pickup heading the group.

From time to time, we would stop at military checkpoints where travel permits were examined. The whole venture might have sounded dangerous but the tension certainly wasn't over the top, as before long, the travellers were having fun exchanging travel notes and interacting with the friendly military as well as the Bedouin tribesmen lurking around these stops. Like everywhere else in Yemen, they would ask, "Where are you from?" followed by "Welcome to Yemen." Occasional bundles of *qat* were distributed, and at one particular police fort, we were even invited to join the police in an ad hoc dagger war dance!

The Queen of Sheba was the legendary queen of what the Romans called Arabia Felix, or Happy Arabia. The kingdom controlled the important trade routes for frankincense, spices, rhino horns and other valuable products, in addition to being the key sea route from Egypt to the coast of East Africa and India. The great dam at Marib, an engineering feat built around 700 BC, irrigated the fertile soil of Sheba.

This was the epoch of the great civilizations. The Spring and Autumn period had just begun in China's Yellow River Valley with the mushrooming of city states and feudal principalities, and the first cast iron plough was used around this time in the irrigated plains of Henan, Northern China. The pages of the *Upanishad*, a sacred text of Hinduism, were still fresh. The Etruscans were flourishing in the Italian Peninsula while Rome had just been founded by Romulus and Remus, the legendary twins suckled by a wolf. Greek cities were busy founding colonies in Sicily and North Africa, while they adopted for the first time the alphabet from the Phoenicians. The Assyrian kings were marching across the Middle East sacking cities in Babylonia, Israel, Phoenicia, Egypt and Anatolia, while an Assyrian scribe recorded that Bur-Sagale

An old man in Al Khoraybah, near Ar Ribat, the ancestral hometown of Osama bin Laden.

Man in Aden chewing qat.

Girl in the Haraz Mountains.

Hadramawti women farmers with their distinctive "witch hats".

Yemeni men pose with their weapons.

Ancient alphabet of the Sheba Kingdom on a Marib stone carving.

of Guzana revolted in the city of Assur during the first solar eclipse ever reported in history.

The *Bible* recorded the visit of the rich and wise Queen of Sheba to King Solomon of Israel, while the *Quran* said that the Queen was converted to Islam when she was moved by King Solomon's wisdom (Solomon being an Islamic prophet as well). I found the Ethiopian accounts juicier. According to the Ethiopian version, King Solomon told the Queen that she could not take anything in his palace without seeking his permission. He then served her a very spicy meal but no water. The Queen, unable to resist the spiciness, drank a glass of water without asking for the King's consent. Caught, the King demanded a night's passion as the price of the water. The penalty was duly paid and a son was born from this one-night stand. He was Menelik, legendary first Emperor of Ethiopia and King of Kings, and the first of a line of monarchs that lasted 3,000 years till the overthrow of Emperor Haile Selassie in 1974. Later, as a young man, Menelik was reunited with his father and brought the Ark of the Covenant to Ethiopia.

We visited the ruins of the Great Dam of Marib, whose collapse in 570 AD, the year Prophet Muhammad was born, led to the economic and environmental devastation of Sheba. Today, Marib is a dusty, desolate desert region on the edge of the vast Empty Quarter. We also visited the ruins of Sheba's royal temples with beautiful sand dunes in the distance, as well as the eerie remains of Old Marib village, bombed out during the 1960s' North Yemen Civil War. These were amazing sites, although one needs a bit of imagination and appreciation of the romance of the Queen of Sheba. Whatever it was, it never failed to amaze me that the most enduring image of Yemen in the eyes of the world (if any image of Yemen exists at all)

Seiyun in the
Wadi Hadramawt.

is of a woman who lived three millennia ago, in a country where women have few rights today.

And yes, please do remember to ask for permission when you have a glass of water at someone else's place.

»»»»»

LANGUAGE. Fouad, who drove us around Yemen, spoke mainly Spanish (as he dealt a lot with Spanish tourists) and very little English. I had to dig hard in the depths of my memory for what little Spanish I used to know when I travelled through Latin America during the first half of 2002. On more than one occasion, other tourists watched us communicating in broken Spanish, bewildered by the sight of an East Asian speaking with an Arab in a continental European language.

»»»»»

GRAND CANYON. Wadi Hadramawt — a bright green valley in south-eastern Yemen's rugged desert plateaus and bare mountains. 165km long and between 1km to 12km wide, this is a rare oasis of fertile soil in these godforsaken wastes. Here, lush green vegetable farms, date palm plantations and fields of golden grains flourish. Surrounding the greenery, on virtually all sides stretching as far as one could see, tall vertical cliffs as magnificent as the Grand Canyon mark the limits of the wadi.

The valley's fertility has long been noted in the Bible, Quran and the accounts of early travellers, but what I found extraordinary was that Wadi Hadramawt was one of the major sources of the fabled Arab traders in the Far East. From this landlocked, godforsaken land next to the Empty Quarter, native sons journeyed to the coast on camels, then to Southeast Asia by sea, established trade routes, set up emporiums of spices, silk, craft and exotic fruits and became wealthy landlords in Singapore and Indonesia. At the threshold of World War II, the Hadramawti Arabs were the most important landlords in Singapore[24], after the British Crown itself.

---

[24] Their wealth declined significantly after the war, as a result of government rent control and property acquisition policies.

It is said that most of Singapore's central business district once belonged to the Hadramawti Arabs.

With wealth from the Far East, the Hadramawtis built magnificent palaces and mansions in their hometowns, using the most common and natural material available — mud. This remarkable cosmopolitan era faded with the declining fortunes of the Hadramawti Diaspora and finally ended when former British-controlled South Yemen fell under Marxist rule in 1967. Contacts between the old hometowns and the Diaspora came to a halt and they became assimilated as Singaporeans, Malaysians and Indonesians.

It was amazing that the palaces built from mud did not look-mud-like at all. Their eclectic mixed Arab-European-Oriental architectural styles adopted by their widely travelled owners, continues to stand in this remote valley, although they are fast getting dilapidated. If no action is taken, it won't be long before these monuments disappear completely, washed away by monsoons or withered into nothingness by neglect and plain human indifference.

The gem of Hadramawt has to be Shibam, a small walled city about one square kilometre in area, tightly packed with mud skyscrapers between five and twenty stories tall, built between 300 to 1,000 years ago. Situated at the confluence of five sub-valleys, the city, often nicknamed "Manhattan

Shibam, a UNESCO World Heritage Site, in Wadi Hadramawt.

of the Desert", is surrounded by even higher cliffs and rugged mountains. Not surprisingly, Shibam has been a UNESCO World Heritage Site since 1982. Spectacular beyond words, especially at sunset, this was the highlight of our journey to Wadi Hadramawt.

The view from afar was fantastic, but we discovered a city of slums and rubbish as we walked on Shibam's narrow streets. The open sewers, the lingering smell of rotting rubbish, the countless plastic bags scattered everywhere, the goats and donkeys picking at what few edibles there were among the refuse, the unwashed, barefooted children kicking a football about happily despite the dirt and dust, and bored young men sitting in the city squares on a week day — these are symptoms of poverty and the pathetic lack of economic opportunities.

»»»»»

PRESIDENT. Everywhere in Yemen, one sees the portrait of a mustached, somewhat aloof man, whose eyes stare far ahead as though into nothingness. Typical Third World strongman look-alike, President Ali Abdullah Saleh has been in power since 1978, after the death of the then military leader of North Yemen, Colonel Ahmed ibn Hussein al-Ghashmi, when a bomb in a suitcase carried by an envoy from South Yemen exploded. President Saleh has ruled the country over a dramatic period that saw a border war with South Yemen, unification of North and South Yemen, support for Iraq during the first Gulf War (which led to the expulsion of almost 1 million Yemeni workers in the Gulf), a civil war in which he crushed the rebellious South Yemenis who wanted to secede, the Al-Qaeda attack on USS Cole and other terrorist incidents, and now, what the Yemeni press calls a period of national reconstruction and development.

Despite being supposedly one of the few Arab democracies, the local English press reads like meek party papers (ok, not unlike those in Singapore, to be fair) that congratulate the President, of all people, for Id. Imagine the New York Times congratulating President George W. Bush for Christmas. Sounds somewhat strange to me but that's life in Yemen.

One particular congratulatory message called the President the "Father of Yemen's Development".

Yes, father of development for 29 years of the Middle East's poorest country, where half the population is illiterate and unemployed, where 40% of the water supply is used to irrigate the production of a herb considered by most countries to be an illegal narcotic, and where terrorist incidents occur at a rate of one every six months. A one-term leader might not be blamed for such statistics, but 29 years is a long time.

Guess whom the other most popular figures in Yemen might be? Hint: Who's popular on Arab Street? Yes, Saddam Hussein — way ahead of everybody else in first place, followed by Hezbollah chief, Hassan Nasrallah. Their posters and likenesses can be seen on many cars, shops and public walls, especially those of Saddam. Photos of him in that dark coat firing a rifle, of him holding the Quran in the Court after his arrest by the Americans, and his final moments with the hangman's noose around his neck. Many ordinary Arabs seem to see him as a hero and a martyr. I didn't see any Osama bin Laden posters around but Kris said a Yemeni lady shouted his name when Kris passed by her shop.

>> >> >> >> >>

HONEYMOON. From Wadi Hadramawt, we travelled across Wadi Douan and its many pretty fortified villages and Grand Canyon-like valleys onto a high dusty plateau with few traces of human inhabitation, where we made a turn to a new cliff-side hotel overlooking a confluence of two wadis. Below was a magnificent but unknown village sitting on a citadel that was a little hill in its own right. God knows what its name is — it was in neither the *Lonely Planet* nor the *Bradt Guide* but it was yet another unexpected discovery in this beautiful country.

Al Mukalla, the beautiful coastal city, was next. Once the capital of a powerful tribal sultanate, it is an important fishing port today. Moved by its splendid whitewashed buildings along a curved bay flanked by dark magnificent mountains, a renowned early 20th-century traveller, Freya

Stark, called this a romantic place to have a honeymoon. Yet, Freya Stark never got married, and it was said that "Freya, in her search for marriage was drawn to gay men in the British Foreign Service whom she steadfastly refused to believe were gay.[25]"

» » » » »

The Cuba of the Arabian Peninsula
— Richard Nixon

ADEN IS NO EDEN. We flew Yemenia to Aden, the legendary and strategic city located where the Red Sea meets the Indian Ocean. In the old days of the steamer, ships sailing from Europe to Asia via the Suez Canal had to dock by its yards, overshadowed by the dark extinct volcanoes that form its unusual geography. We stayed at a hotel in Crater, Aden's old Arab commercial district, right next to the souk, where traders from Europe, Arabia, India and China once rubbed shoulders and did business over tea. Great explorers and travellers such as Ibn Battuta, Zhenghe and Vasco da Gama visited Aden, too.

"Ibn Battuta… went to Aden, at the time the largest and richest of all the emporia on the Indian Ocean. 'It is a big city,' he said, 'but no crops, trees or water are found there; during the rainy season water is collected in reservoirs. These lie some distance from the town and the Bedouin often cut the road and prevent the townspeople from reaching them unless they are bribed with money and pieces of cloth … "[26] Has anything changed? Military checkpoints continue to guard the road from Aden to Sana'a, as rebellious and heavily armed tribes are never very far away.

Aden has a chequered modern history. In 1839, the British set up a coaling station here, which became an important supply base linking Britain with India. They were hardly interested in the interior, except to ensure that the inland tribes did not interrupt the supply of food and water. Treaties of friendship were signed by the many sultanates and sheikhdoms in what later became known as South Yemen.

---

25 http://www.amazon.ca/Passionate-Nomad-Life-Freya-Stark/dp/0375757465
26 Paul Launde, *The Traveller, Ian Battuta*, Saudi Aramco World, July/August 2005.

As their colonies worldwide gained independence, the British tried to prepare Aden and its protectorate, as the territory was then known, for self-government. The 22 petty tribal kingdoms, with Ruritanian-sounding names such as Lower Aulaqi, Lower Yafa, Upper Yafa, Maflahi, Shaib, the Upper Aulaqi Sheikhdom and the Upper Aulaqi Sultanate, were grouped together into two pro-western political entities, the Federation of South Arabia and the Protectorate of South Arabia. This was no different from what the UK did in Malaya and the Trucial Coast, i.e., to unite groups of tiny chiefdoms in formerly neglected parts of the empire for independence, so that they would not fall into the hands of the increasingly aggressive Communist Bloc and their Third World supporters.

In the case of Aden, the efforts failed. Before long, a Marxist insurgency broke out. The insurgency spread rapidly and one by one, the sultanates fell. A 1967 *Time Magazine* article entitled "It's No Eden"[27] reported about the hopeless and endless nature of this topic, calling it "an ugly, bloody little war." The writing was on the wall when the UK Government decided to withdraw its forces from all territories east of Suez — overnight, 30% of South Arabia's GDP was washed down the toilet. The Marxists marched into Aden and the communist People's Democratic Republic of Yemen (DPRY), popularly known as South Yemen, was founded. The PDRY was the first and only Marxist state ever to exist in the Middle East.

As a state, the PDRY was poverty-stricken and hardly ever stable politically. Coups and counter-coups, a disastrous civil war, two border wars with North Yemen and a proxy-war with Oman rocked the small nation in the short history of its existence. Soviet subsidies in exchange for docking rights at Aden's port for the Soviet Navy were critical to its survival. When the USSR declined in the late 1980s and with financial support for PDRY shrinking, a decision was taken in 1990 to merge with North Yemen. Differences soon emerged and in 1994, the former Marxists declared South Yemen's secession from the newly-merged Republic of Yemen. Federal forces marched down from Sana'a and crushed the rebellion in nine weeks.

---

[27] It's No Eden, *Time Magazine*, May. 15, 1964

Aden, in 1950, was the world's fourth largest tax-free shipping port. After the chaos of the last few decades, it is a sleepy place today. In spite of its strategic importance at the southern end of the Red Sea, ships no longer call here, be they cargo vessels travelling between Europe and the Far East, or cruise liner tourists and travellers. Not far away Somali pirates now attack ships at will, further scaring away any intrepid tourists who might want to venture here. As Tim Mackintosh-Smith commented in *Yemen — Travels in Dictionary Land* [28], "...in 1992, it still tottered along a narrow divide between quaint and the seedy." If Singapore is not careful, we could potentially end up like Aden, a port whose great potential has been squandered.

South Yemen is no more, but Aden, at least from the surface, looked somewhat different from the conservative north. Whilst South Yemeni women wear the black abbaya as well, most do not cover their faces as their northern cousins do. More women work in public positions and many people in Aden speak English, which is a legacy of British rule. We watched fishermen bring their catch to shore — shark and tuna amongst various fish — and dropped by the flashy new Aden Mall, the only modern mall of its kind in Yemen. Here, few wore the *jambiya* and nobody carried firearms on the streets. What a different Yemen!

» » » » »

THE CHINESE. In 1413, on Admiral Zhenghe's fourth great voyage to the Southern Seas, the great Ming Chinese armada reached Aden. It was said in *The Overall Survey of the Ocean's Shore* (*Ying-yai Sheng-tan*), the journals of Ma Huan, Zhenghe's translator, that the arrival of this great fleet caused so much sensation in the region that nineteen states sent envoys to the fleet with tributes for the Chinese Emperor.

Ma Huan listed the many foodstuffs available in Aden's markets: "Husked and unhusked rice, beans, cereals, barley, wheat, sesame and all kinds of vegetables.... For fruits they have ... Persian dates, pine nuts, almonds, dried

28 Tim Mackintosh-Smith, *Yemen – Travels in Dictionary Land*, 1997, p143

grapes, walnuts, apples, pomegranates, peaches and apricots.[29]" Impressed by the quality of craftsmanship in Aden, Ma Huan said: "All the people in the country who make and inlay fine gold and silver ornaments and other such articles as their occupation produce the most refined and ingenious things, which certainly surpass anything in the world.[30]"

Zhenghe left Yemen with gifts from the ruler of Yemen, al-Malik al-Zahir, "among them two gold belts inlaid with jewels, a letter written on gold leaf and a number of exotic African animals.[31]" The latter included zebras and giraffes[32], which the Chinese had never seen before, and fascinated them a lot. The Chinese called the giraffes "qilin", after one of the four Chinese sacred creatures[33]. The qilin has hooves and magnificent fiery scales, breathes fire and can fly. More importantly, qilins are heavenly creatures that bring good fortune and prosperity.

The Chinese qilin, as depicted in ancient Chinese texts, have much shorter necks than giraffes, which cannot fly. Whatever the case, the Chinese were excited by the strangeness of the giraffes — an account said that the officials "gazed at it and their joy knew no end" — and presented these creatures to the Emperor as tributes from Arabia and Africa. The Emperor, pleased with the latest additions to his collection of unusual objects and exotica, "proclaimed the giraffes magical creatures, whose capture signaled the greatness of his power.[34]" Court painters produced scrolls that depicted these graceful creatures; one such painting is kept today at the National Palace Museum in Taiwan.

»»»»»

TAIZ'Z & EXECUTIONS. Northwards, in dry hilly scrubland, we crossed the old border between North and South Yemen. Where it was once bustling shops serving busy border-crossing traffic, it was now a haunting line of boarded-up shop fronts, windowless two-storied buildings and burnt and blown-up shells of immigration offices and guardhouses.

29, 30, 31, 34 Paul Lunde, *The Admiral Zhenghe*, Saudi Aramco World, July/August 2005.
32 There were other accounts that said that it was the ruler of Mogadishu, or the ruler of Malindi (in today's Kenya) that presented the giraffe to the Ming Emperor.
33 The other three are the dragon, phoenix and tortoise.

Within a few hours, we were in Taiz'z — Yemen's second largest city and one-time capital of imams and kings. Located on the slopes of Mt. Saber, Taiz'z is blessed by a cool climate. This has always been an important inland trading centre and once boasted a Jewish quarter famous for its crafts; silverware, in particular.

Today's Taiz'z is a let down. Potholed streets abound in this city of imams and kings. The street outside our city-centre hotel shut down at mid-afternoon and *qat* addicts took over. They posed no real threat to the passersby, but they slept on the streets, or leaned against the walls with their bulging cheeks full of *qat*. Piles of rubbish were not far away, with flies whirling over them. Nobody would have loved to step over the *qat*-addicts, friendly or not.

We visited the palace of the Muttawakkilite Imams of Yemen, who took over North Yemen after the fall of the Ottoman Empire. We walked into the half-shut museum gates, not sure if the building was open. An ambulance was parked on the driveway and broken plant pots lined the path to the

A small town in
Wadi Hadramawt.

door. The door opened into a dusty room with a damp, musty smell, and three half-sleepy museum staff stared at us as though we had interrupted their afternoon nap.

We walked through the dusty corridors of the palace museum, looking at the huge collection of perfumes and colognes specially ordered by the Imam from the fashion houses of France and Italy, rusty typewriters, moth-eaten curtains and pillowcases, and grotesque period photos of the decapitation and hanging of rebels. This was where Imam Ahmad, who once ruled as governor of Taiz'z, lived before he became Imam, and where he continued to rule the kingdom thereafter.

Imam Ahmad, son of Yayha, founder of the Muttawakkilite Kingdom of Yemen, ruled over what was a mediaeval feudal kingdom, with an iron fist. Four hundred boys were kept as hostages of good behaviour expected from their fathers, who were tribal chiefs from across the country. No matter was too small for the Imam. It was said "it took the Imam's personal signature to get a gasoline permit, authorize a $15 printing job, or order light bulbs for the palace. He clung to every trifle of power.[35]"

Imam Ahmad, who succeeded his father after the latter's assassination in 1948, was himself the target of numerous assassination and coup d'etat attempts, one of which was by his half-brother, Emir Abdullah, in 1955. *Time Magazine* reported[36] on how Colonel Ahmed Thalaya had soldiers surround the Imam's palace and demand that he abdicate. The Imam agreed but demanded that his son Badr succeed him, a proposal that was rejected by the Colonel, who had Emir Abdullah in mind.

The Colonel and Abdullah, confident that the Imam was besieged in the palace with not many troops defending him, went about forming a new government. In the meantime, "the old Imam retired within his palace, broke open the treasury coffers and secretly began buying off the besieging soldiers. Within five days, when the number of besiegers was reduced from 600 to 40, the Imam suddenly burst out of the palace gates flourishing a long

---

[35] Worn Out, *Time Magazine*, Jul. 07 1967
[36] Revolt & Revenge, *Time Magazine*, Apr. 25, 1955
[37] Another conspirator, Qadir Abdulrahman al-Iryani, was also sentenced to be beheaded. Just as the executioner raised his sword, already stained red with the blood of those executed earlier, the Imam suddenly shouted "Stop!" Al-Iryani was released and went on to become the second president of the Yemen Arab Republic in 1967.

scimitar. Before the sentries could get over their shock, he had slashed two of them dead, and scrambled back into the palace. Exchanging the sword for a submachine gun, he led his 150 guards onto the roof of the palace and began a direct attack on the rebels."

As *Time Magazine* reported: "At the end of 28 hours, with 23 rebels and one palace guard dead, Colonel Ahmed Thalaya gave up. Abdullah, guarded by heavily armed slaves, taken for a ride in a jeep in the direction of the rock dungeon of Hajja, was later reported executed.

News leaking from Yemen told of the old Imam leading the defeated colonel into the square in front of the palace and crying to the crowd: "Look at this man. I personally sent him to be educated in Iraq. I made him chief of the army. I trusted him. I even let him use my airplane. And now look how he has repaid me! I leave it to you. If you say 'forgive,' I will let him go. If you say otherwise . . ."

The mob howled for blood; the colonel's hands were bound, and he was forced to kneel in the dust. As the executioner raised his sword, following an old custom, he gave the kneeling man a passing jab in the shoulder, making him jerk forward so that his neck was stretched out tautly for the downcoming stroke. A minute later the mob fell upon the decapitated body and tore it to pieces. The Imam of Yemen was even[37]."

No wonder *Time Magazine* concluded, "If the Imam of Yemen failed to inspire one of Edward Lear's famous limericks, it was only because Lear never heard of him."

A Village in the
Haraz Mountains

Even then, Imam Ahmad lived for another seven years before he died of natural causes. In less than one week after his death, his son, the new Imam, Badr, was overthrown in a coup. Badr fled to safety and with the support of neighbouring Saudi Arabia, rallied the tribes against the Egyptian-backed Yemen Arab Republic. A bitter civil war ensued, which lasted till 1970.

Ultimately, it was realpolitik that mattered. The Arab nations, shocked by the dramatic defeat Israel had wreaked on Egypt, Syria and Jordan in the 1967 war when huge swathes of territories were lost, decided to temporarily put aside their individual disputes and cooperate against Israel. The Yemen Royalists were abandoned by Saudi Arabia in the interests of Arab unity, and Imam Badr went into exile in the countryside of Kent, England.

» » » » »

DANGERS. White clouds changed their shapes in the clear blue skies while we entered and left Dreamland at quarterly intervals. As our car drove through the winding roads of the southern Yemeni Highlands, flocks of predatory birds cruised the skies for prey, while Noah-lookalike farmers worked in the cliff-side terraces of greenery that were qat meadows and vegetables fields.

This is Ibb, a region well known for its terraced fields and much greenery — a microclimate in its own right. In a country better known for barren, dusty hills than lush fertile plains, the people of Ibb learned to build terrace fields to utilise the region's unusually high rainfall. How this reminded me of the Banaue Rice Terraces of Luzon Island, The Philippines, except that here, the black austerity of women in burqa replaced the tropical openness of the Ifugao of Latin Philippines.

Just four decades ago, in 1967, the great modern explorer, Wilfred Thesiger, travelled along this road during the Civil War in the North, between the Republicans and the Royalists. This whole region, according to him, was repeatedly bombed, rocketed and machine-gunned.

In his book, *My Life and Travels*, he recounted his visit to the headquarters of Prince Muhammad al Hussain, Royalist commander of the Southern Front, during which the camp was attacked by Republican warplanes. A shell exploded nearby and a splinter hit him. One of his fellow British travel companions shouted at him in an irritated voice, "Damn it, look what you've done." Blood from his head had soaked a box of cigars which belonged to his companion.

The book noted further: "Two days later the Royalists shot down a Mig and we went to look at the wreckage. The pilot was an unidentifiable mess, but his map and various notes were in Russian. The Egyptians had gone but the Russians had arrived.[38]"

Even today, danger is never too far away in Yemen. We stopped at one anonymous road junction as Kris went for an urgent nature call, with Fouad. Suddenly, a Toyota pickup came to a screeching stop 10 metres from us, and five men with rifles and machine guns jumped off the vehicle. They stopped all passing vehicles and stared hard at the drivers and passengers as though searching for an enemy.

One of them, a rather fierce-looking young man with bloodshot eyes and a pointed turban walked up to our car. I opened my door, "*Salaam aleikum*." I uttered the standard Muslim greeting, but instead of getting the usual reciprocal friendliness, he waved his arm and shouted angrily, "Go, go!" Then he turned his back on me and returned to his companions.

At this point, a sixth man stepped out of the Toyota with what looked like a mini bazooka. Another Toyota — fully mounted with three machine-guns — raced to an abrupt halt and four more men hopped out and joined those already there. Something was obviously very wrong. These men were looking for an enemy, or, more likely, a group of enemies — perhaps a rival tribe, and fully intended to eliminate them from the face of this planet. Looking at the arsenal of weaponry they had with them, they seemed prepared for a ferocious battle.

Just as I was half expecting a hailstorm of bullets and half-a-dozen missile launches, Kris and Fouad returned to the car, oblivious to what was happening. I shouted, "Let's go, let's go!" Fouad saw the armed crowd, started the engine, and raced as fast as he could, out of what might shortly have become a violent battleground.

[38] Wilfred Thesiger, *My Life and Travels*, 2002, p253-6.

»»»»»

QUEEN & COFFEE. We headed for nearby Jibla, a small dusty town on the gentle upper slopes of a mountain, which suddenly falls into a deep gully beneath. This was once the capital of Queen Arwa, one of the greatest of Yemeni regional rulers. Born in 1048, the year Oslo was founded by Harald III Hadrada[39], Arwa ruled Yemen alone for over 50 years (excluding an initial period of co-rule with her two husbands). She was renowned for her courage, beauty, intelligence, artistic talent as well as learnedness in the Quran. She had to rule over the kingdom because her husband, the rightful king, was too sick. She lured the murderer of her husband's father to his death by laying a cunning trap for him, thus killing the greatest warlord in the region and avenging her father-in-law's demise.

After her husband's death, Saba ibn Ahmad, another powerful regional leader and cousin of her late husband, sent an army to demand her kingdom and her hand. She refused, and raised an army to fight the impending battle. At this juncture, the Egyptian-Fatimid Caliph al-Mustansir, supreme overlord of the Islamic Empire, commanded her to marry Saba ibn Ahmad. She did so reluctantly and staged a warm welcome for Saba ibn Ahmad, but requested that the marriage be unconsummated. Saba ibn Ahmad was impressed by the welcome staged, as well as her intelligence and talents. He

Terraced fields in the Ibb region.

left her and her kingdom unmolested and from then on, assisted her from time to time.

Today, what remains of Queen Arwa's legacy are the many shops in Jibla named after her, and the huge mosque built by and named after her. This is also where her tomb is located. We walked through the narrow lanes of Jibla, sharing them with street vendors, donkeys and school children.

Ahmad, a religious teacher who teaches in the children's madressa attached to the Queen Arwa Mosque, invited us to his 600-year-old fortified mud-brick home, in a dark dirt lane behind the mosque. As we raced up the spiral staircase with his two sons, soft afternoon light crept through the metal grill windows, projecting shadows onto the dusty floor. In a room at the highest floor of Ahmad's tower house, he served us exceedingly sweet local dates and tea, and asked if we wanted coffee as well.

Yemen, after all, is one of the two countries that claim to be the original homeland of coffee.[40] Not too far away is the port of Al-Mokha on the Red Sea, after which Mocha coffee is named. These acidic coffee beans, renowned for their strong chocolate flavour when properly roasted and processed, are actually grown in the terraced plantations in Yemen's western highlands but were first noticed by Portuguese sailors in the 17th century at the small port of Al-Mokha. From Al-Mokha, these beans were shipped to Europe — an export trade that turned this small village into a wealthy city. The city, however, has declined since the 19th century, when plantations elsewhere in the world began growing these beans as well[41].

The portrait of Saddam Hussein, who would have looked like a kind grandfather to anyone unaware of his deeds, smiled benevolently from the high central wall normally reserved for family patriarchs. A clock with an image of the Kaaba hung on the adjacent wall, while a small model of the Dome of the Rock in Jerusalem sat on a little dressing table by the side.

---

[39] King Harold III Hadrada of Norway, last of the great Viking kings, was killed at the Battle of Stamford Bridge, Yorkshire, in 1066 when he battled the forces of King Harold Godwinson of England, before the latter was himself killed at the Battle of Hastings less than three weeks later.

[40] The other is Ethiopia just across the Red Sea. Both countries also claim to be the land of the Queen of Sheba, which is not surprising given their common historical heritage before the coming of Islam. Yemen became Muslim while Ethiopia has remained Christian.

[41] Interestingly, according to Wikipedia, Al-Mokha "is the ancestral home of Alyan Muhammad Ali al-Wa'eli, a Yemeni terrorist accused of participating in the 2000 USS Cole attack in the Gulf of Aden."

"Allahu Akbar, Allahu Akbar. Allahu Akbar, Allahu Akbar. Ashadu An La Illaha Illallah. Ashadu An La Illaha Illallah. Ashadu Anna Muhammad-ar-Rasool-ul-Allah.[42]" The loudspeaker outside went heavy-duty as the muezzin called for prayer. But there in the room, I was mesmerized by the Mocca and the many anonymous sweets laid on the table. Kris played chess with Ahmad's daughter, Fatima, aged eight, on the intricately-sewn though well-faded carpet, while Kelly examined an English-Arabic textbook which Ahmad's eldest son, Sherif (or "sword" in Arabic), aged 15, was reading. The setting sun had now penetrated the room through a strategically-placed stained glass, turning my corner into an amazing kaleidoscope of colours. Wasn't that a most magical moment?

---

[42] Translation: "Allah is the greatest, Allah is the greatest. Allah is the greatest, Allah is the greatest. I declare that there is no god but Allah. I witness that there is no god but Allah. I witness that Muhammad is prophet of Allah."

Libya: Revolutionary in the Sahara (April–May 2008)

Libya, one of the largest but least populous countries in Africa, has long been a hot destination for travellers interested in unique political regimes, in particular, those once identified by the US Government as a member of the Axis of Evil or state sponsors of terrorism.

The public face of Libya has long been its enigmatic leader, Colonel Gaddafi, who has ruled the country since 1 September 1969, when he, as a 28-year-old army officer, launched a coup d'etat and overthrew King Idris Sanusi. Gaddafi sees himself as the quintessential Arab socialist revolutionary and philosopher king. He expelled foreign troops, nationalized the economy, and proclaimed support for the Palestinians, liberation movements across Africa and a whole host of rebel movements all over the world.

His idol was Abdul Nasser, former president and revolutionary leader of Egypt, who also overthrew a pro-western monarchy, and provoked western ire by nationalizing the Suez Canal. In fact, as noted in a 1971 issue of *Time Magazine*:[43]

"You know," Egypt's Gamal Abdel Nasser mused during an Arab meeting in Cairo shortly before his death last year, "I rather like Gaddafi. He reminds me of myself when I was that age." Not even the young Nasser, however, was a hell raiser to compare with Muammar Gaddafi, who at 28 is leader of the revolutionary council that rules oil-rich Libya."

Gaddafi proclaimed Libya the world's first "Jamahiriya", broadly translated as "state of the masses", in which the people supposedly govern themselves without any government. And Libya became officially known

---

[43] *Time Magazine*, 2 August 1971

as the Socialist People's Libyan Arab Jamahiriya — what a mouthful of grammatically awkward English.

His radical rhetoric and support for various anti-western causes earned him the wrath of America and the West. He was accused of sponsoring terrorism — specifically for the 1985 bombings in Berlin and the destruction in 1988 of Pan Am flight 103 over the Scottish town of Lockerbie in which 270 people were killed. In 1986, the US bombed Libya, killing more than 100 people, including Gaddafi's adopted daughter, Hanna, and injured, among others, two of his sons.

In defiance, Gaddafi sent submarines to bomb a tiny Italian island, proclaiming victory by declaring that Libya had destroyed five US warplanes. The word "Great" was added to Libya's official name, hence its current official name, Great Socialist People's Libyan Arab Jamahiriya, or "Great Libyan Jamahiriya" in short.

The West demanded that Libya hand over two bombing suspects and when this was refused, sanctions were imposed on Libya, which lasted seven years, during which the Libyan economy shrank and 21,000 Libyans died because they could not go overseas for medical treatment. US$30 billion of revenue was lost during the same period.

A deal was struck in 1999 where Libya handed over the suspects for international trial in The Hague, and UN sanctions were accordingly suspended. In 2003, Libya gave up its nuclear, chemical and biological weapons programmes and opened the sites for international inspections. In 2006, the US removed Libya from its list of states sponsoring terrorism. Economic reforms began to be implemented. Officially, the socialist ideas of Gaddafi's *Green Book* remain, but in reality, capitalism is in full swing.

»»»»»

Together with my friends from Singapore, Gary and Kenneth, I arrived in a Libya in the midst of rapid change and drastic if not confusing economic reforms. From there, we began our journey through its ancient Greek and Roman cities, as well as an expedition into the Sahara.

These are exciting times for Libya as the country rushes to refurbish its ageing and under-maintained infrastructure, and marches towards modern capitalism. A stock exchange was even established in Tripoli in 2007. Foreign investors and businessmen are dropping by to exploit the new opportunities. It was during our visit that the Singapore government sent a business delegation headed by Senior Minister Goh Chok Tong.

Libya remains wary of the world. The nation continues to apply archaic rules to foreigners wanting to visit the country. Its visa application process is outrageously complicated and bureaucratic, even when compared to North Korea. We went through a lot of trouble to get our passports translated into Arabic and then to get the translations duly endorsed by our passport issuing authority, as required by Libyan regulations.

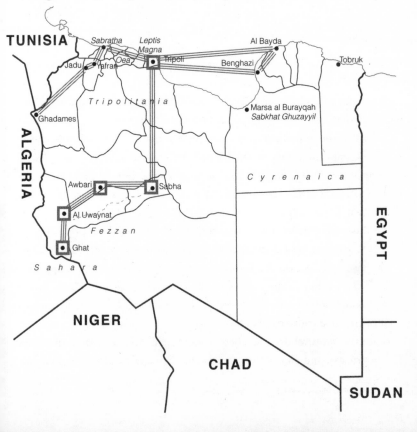

This rule had been in force for a long time, abolished a few years ago, and then suddenly re-imposed in November 2007 after Colonel Gaddafi was allegedly angered by French refusal to allow all his bodyguards to accompany him on his visit to France. No notice was given for the implementation of the rule, and it was reported that at least two plane loads of French tourists and one cruise ship were turned back at Libya's airport and port respectively for not having the required Arabic translations, notwithstanding that the rule was only announced less than 24 hours prior to their arrival.

We had complied with the translation rule and had a tiring exchange of emails before getting a version of our visa approval letter emailed to us so that we could board the plane for Libya. We thought that everything would be all right upon arrival. We were very wrong.

》》》》》

This must be one of our most nightmarish bureaucratic experiences ever. I got my visa upon arrival at Tripoli airport after an hour's wait (though there was a 1.5 hour tussle with Nairobi Airport[44] officials due to a silly translation error in the visa approval letter). Gary, however, was in deep trouble through no fault of his own. Whilst the Libyans had evidence of our visa approval, they could not find the original copy (i.e., they had a copy but not the original) of Gary's visa invitation letter in their file records. As a result, they refused to grant Gary a visa and we spent five hours at Tripoli airport dealing with the problem.

Basically, a government department had misplaced the original copy of the visa approval document and although everyone had evidence of the visa approval (in the form of copies made of the original approval as well as notice to the airlines to allow us to fly into Libya), the actual visa could not be issued if the original approval could not be found and properly filed with a copy of the actual visa to be issued at the airport. But since the approval itself had been complicated, no one wanted to restart the process, and clearly the officials who had approved the original visa

---

[44] I had set off for Libya from Kenya on a pan-African journey.

could not re-approve something they had previously already approved. Hence we got stuck in the middle as no one wanted to compromise or do anything about it.

In a poor corrupt country, one could just slip some green bills into an envelope and all problems would be resolved within an hour. But not in Libya. It is an oil-rich state still (or at least trying to appear to be) living in the 1960's radical fervor of its revolutionary leader. Clearly, in a country blessed with record oil revenues, few officials were concerned about the predicament of potential foreign investors or tourists. Everybody was probably more concerned about making sure rules were strictly followed and his own turf guarded.

We couldn't resolve the issue on our first day in Tripoli. A special pass was issued to Gary so that he could leave the airport but had to return to resolve the issue the next day. Our original itinerary, which involved setting off for the Sahara immediately the next day, had to be set aside as a result of this fiasco. Gary would eventually have to return to the airport on the second and the third days.

It was only on the third day after our arrival, after interminable paper-shuffling, discussions among government departments (all of which was in Arabic and hence we had no idea whatsoever of the proceedings), and many phone calls to our local contacts that they agreed to issue the visa to Gary. We still have no idea what transpired but the approval itself was cause for celebration. Allahu Akbar! Allah is Great!

»»»»»

> Izzy: O'Connell, if you give me that gold stick there, you can shave my
>   head, wax my legs, and use me for a surfboard.
> Rick: Didn't we do that in Tripoli?
>   — The Mummy Returns, movie (2001):

TRIPOLI. A city with the old and new; myriad small lanes in the Old City; tall office blocks; billboards of Colonel Gaddafi everywhere in his characteristic dark glasses and clasped-fist Chinese congratulatious pose; kebab stalls at every corner. The weather was surprisingly cold even with the sunny Mediterranean sun. The waterfront could have been Cannes or Marseilles, with swaying palm trees and couples sharing secrets on benches.

Very few people spoke English here but everyone was genuinely friendly and tried to communicate with us in a bizarre mix of Arabic, French and Italian. There were few English signboards — virtually all signs were in Arabic, the outcome of Colonel Gaddafi's famous Arab-language policy.

We walked through the Old City, visited the Roman Arch of Marcus Aurelius, one of the symbols of ancient Tripoli. This city was once known as Oea, whose ruins and foundations now lie beneath modern Tripoli. We also visited the Green Square, where Colonel Gaddafi gave speeches and presided over military parades and so-called million-men rallies.

In Libyan supermarkets, we found many products from Tunisia, Egypt and the United Arab Emirates. Things were surprisingly cheap and affordable here. I was to discover that even at the airport in Sabha in the Sahara, one could find packs of biscuits for only 2 or 3 dinars (1 Libyan dinar was about US$0.70), which implied an efficient transportation and delivery network even to remote, sparsely populated areas, hence keeping prices low. But of course, the cheap fuel helped.

We had a good time strolling along the fine sandy beaches of West Tripoli — Libya clearly has a future if it decides to develop a beach tourism industry like Egypt, Morocco or Tunisia. However, the country will need to simplify entry requirements and visa rules so that casual tourists can come whenever they want, with a minimum of fuss; and a transformation of their cultural mindset, difficult though it might be, so that more liberal forms of international beach practices become acceptable in this country.

Later, Kenneth's Libyan friend Abdalla took us to the seafood market where we had very fresh seafood and a good chat about many aspects of life in Libya. This is a country with enormous potential though one very misunderstood by most parts of the world due to the events of the last few decades. Abdalla had spoken about Libya at seminars in Europe and met many cynics who highlighted all sorts of perceived problems in Libya, to which Abdalla responded jokingly that he would be very afraid to return to Libya if what they said were indeed true.

» » » » »

Colonel Gaddafi, who came to power through the coup of 1 September 1969, is mentioned everywhere in Libyan newspapers but hardly quoted by name. He is always "Leader of the Revolution". Gigantic billboards bearing his likeness, or those with the number "38" (the number of years since his revolution) or "1969/9/1" (the date of the revolution) are everywhere. Every year, these billboards are replaced with newer ones with an additional year added to the previous figure.

His quotations from the *Green Book*, in which he espoused his "Third Universal Theory" (supposedly after the first two, capitalism and Marxism), are quoted on banners and monuments everywhere in Libya. Here are some of his catchy slogans and core beliefs:

    a. Partners, not wage-workers

    b. Democracy with popular congresses everywhere

    c. The problem of democracy in the world is finally solved!
        (of course, by the *Green Book*)

    d. Political struggle that results in the victory of a candidate
        with 51% of the votes leads to a dictatorial governing body

Gaddafi billboard: 38 represents the 38th anniversary of his Revolution.

disguised as a false democracy, since 49% of the electorate is ruled by an instrument of governing they did not vote for, but had imposed upon them. This is dictatorship.

e. Sport is a public activity that must be practiced rather than watched."

f. An individual has the right to express himself or herself even if he or she behaves irrationally to demonstrate his or her insanity.

g. Black people will prevail in the world

Gaddafi proposes that all governments should be abolished and replaced by popular committees and congresses everywhere. There will be no inter-party squabbling common in democracies and instead everyone in a country will work together as one singular party to select their representatives who do not have selfish personal or partisan interests. There are no governments, presidents or governors, as all decisions are undertaken by the people through committees. In fact, all government departments in Libya are known as "General Committees" and embassies abroad are called "People's Bureau". Gaddafi is a mere Leader, or as one of our guides called "Advisor to the Revolution".

One sometimes find billboards depicting people of the world admiring the Green Book (which reminded me of similar propaganda about North Korea's Kim Il Sung and his Juche Theory), or Africans cheering Gaddafi, or

Roman mosaic at the Jamahiriya Museum.

billboards bearing the numbers 1999/9/9, the date Gaddafi announced his plan for the formation of the United States of Africa, a supranational union on the same basis as the European Union. Gaddafi considers himself the chief advocate and father of African unity. Interestingly, Afriqayah Airways of Libya has adopted the numbers 9.9.99 as its logo.

» » » » »

Libya is an African country. May Allah help the Arabs and keep them away from us. We don't want anything to do with them. They did not fight with us against the Italians, and they did not fight with us against the Americans. They did not lift the sanctions and siege from us....I won't be a party to a conspiracy to mobilize the Arabs against the Persians. Only the forces of colonialism benefit from such a conspiracy. I won't be a party to a conspiracy that splits Islam into two - Shiite Islam and Sunni Islam – mobilizing Sunni Islam against Shiite Islam.

— *Colonel Gaddafi*[52]

Many of the Old City's inhabitants are black Africans, whereas people in other parts of Tripoli have fair or a typically brownish Mediterranean complexion. Could it be that middle class Libyans have moved out of the Old City into the suburbs, leaving the congested and dilapidated old dwellings with antiquated or non-existent plumbing to the poor African illegal migrants from the south? Call it the 'ghettoisation' of the inner city — a process long-crystalised in most large Western cities.

Walking through the many shops blaring flamboyant English and French rap, I suspect that these people had only recently been living in the shantytowns of Ibadan and Ouagadougou, and are dreaming of moving on to the bright lights of Milan and Paris. Thousands drown every year in their attempts to reach Europe from Africa in small rickety boats, that is, if they succeed in crossing the hot merciless Sahara first.

---

[52] http://www.memritv.org/clip_transcript/en/1421.htm, "Libyan Leader Mu'ammar Al-Qadhafi: The Arab Nation's Time Is Up; I Love the Black American Secretary of State of African Origin Leezza Very Much", an interview aired on Al-Jazeera TV on 27 March, 2007

An issue of the *Tripoli Post* carried a statement from the Libyan General People's Committee for Public Security declaring that Libya would no longer be obliged to protect Italian coasts from illegal immigration so long as Italy does not provide the necessary support. The Libyans have a point here. Libya is a large country with a small population. Why should it incur heavy costs to guard the Italian coast if Italy does little on its part? After all, the continuing stream of illegals provides manpower-scarce Libya with a constant source of low-cost manual labour necessary for the country's development.

≫ ≫ ≫ ≫ ≫

We visited the Jamahiriya Museum, a huge depository of Libya's national treasures in Tripoli's Red Castle. This is a fantastic place with lots of Greek and Roman sculptures and mosaics. The Roman sculptures were particularly erotic. Gaddafi's cars were also exhibited, together with amusing captions in rather bad English propaganda that betrayed an imitation of the Soviet-style English once articulated by TASS and Novosti Press Agency. The jeep in which Gaddafi stormed to power in the 1969 coup had this caption: "This car is the apparent witness of the historical penetration and courageous swoop on the aurora of the morning 01/09/1969…which carried the leader [Gaddafi]…on the obvious victory procession with his battlefield uniform risking one's soul for Libya, Arabism, Islam and Humanity altogether." I guess, as a member of humanity, I have to thank this vehicle for carrying the Leader to victory. Perhaps I should tremble with awe, too.

A Volkswagen that used to carry Gaddafi around the country for his clandestine revolutionary activities was captioned: "…it has embodied the simplicity in confronting the Mercedes Benz car, which has incarnated clamor, haltingness and false arrogance. There were great differences between the two cars while the Volkswagen was rolling up time and distances to bring closer the salvation day, the Mercedes was moving between night clubs, gambling halls and military bases driven by agents of the Italians, Americans and British in the defunct regime. All paid from the Libyan people's wealth.

The people were suffering from poverty, oppression, sleeping on the ground, and protecting themselves from heat and cold by zinc panels under the yoke of an agent regime that had lost sovereignty, will and legitimacy, whereas it infiltrated to the country from abroad in the darkness under the cover of charlatanism, heresy."

》》》》》

There is no state with a democracy except Libya on the whole planet
— Colonel Gadaffi, live satellite conference with an
audience at New York's Columbia University[46]

We did a fair bit of shopping for clothing in Tripoli. Libyan (and Turkish) businessmen went to Italy to seek (in reality, to steal) designs, especially the Italian-style t-shirts and jeans, and got them custom-made in China. They were all on sale in Tripoli for between 15 to 20 dinars (about US$12 to US$17). Very good prices. You cannot find similar Italian-style designs in China or Thailand. I bought 5 pieces! We all agreed that Tripoli was a most unexpected fashion paradise. Gary even said that it was better than the Chatuchak Market or the MBK Shopping Mall in Bangkok.

》》》》》

We flew more than 1,000 kilometres south to the desert garrison town of Sabha, where Gaddafi spent his formative teenage years in a secondary school. There were probably more Gaddafi billboards here than any other Libyan town we visited. At the airport, we were picked up by Musa, our guide, Baraka, our cook, and Muhammad, our driver. Musa and Baraka were both Tuareg; they were born in Niger's Agadez region but have lived in Libya for many years.

We were to discover that the entire tourism industry in the Libyan Sahara, from guides to drivers and souvenir stall keepers, seemed to be

---

[46] Gaddafi gives lesson on democracy, BBC. http://news.bbc.co.uk/2/hi/africa/4839670.stm

manned and run by Tuaregs from Niger, who speak a mixture of Tamashek, their ancient tongue, and French, the language of their ex-colonisers and of their successor regimes in Tunis, Algiers, Rabat, Bamako, Niamey and N'djamena, the capitals of modern nation-states that rule the Tuareg lands today. Perhaps, Arabs from the Libyan Mediterranean coast are too comfortable with the urban lifestyle, preferring to leave the Sahara to the Tuaregs, whether or not the latter are Libyan citizens.

Gaddafi himself, though an Arab of Bedouin descent, has long cultivated the Tuaregs and often praised their nomadic and independent way of life. By cultivating this ethnic group whose kin straddle the territories of Libya, Tunisia, Algeria, Morocco, Mali, Niger and Chad[47], Gaddafi hoped to consolidate his efforts to unify Africa and perhaps even lay claim to huge swaths of Tuareg-inhabited Sahelian Africa. For people such as Musa, who had no Libyan citizenship despite having lived here for many years and married a Libyan citizen, his loyalty, as he confided to me, always lay with the tribe rather than the state.

Niger, to the south of Libya, is the poorest country in the world. Niger has one of the world's richest uranium deposits but that wealth probably goes straight into its leaders' Swiss bank accounts. The Tuaregs, who live in the northeastern swath of the Nigèrien[48] Sahara around the ancient caravan town of Agadez, are up in arms against the government, and this insurgency is gradually spreading across to the Tuareg-inhabited part of neighbouring Mali. Niamey, the Nigèrien capital which I also visited, was a nervous garrison town at the edge of the insurgency. The instability is causing many Nigèrien Tuaregs to move to Libya, by crossing the desert in a 60-day camel ride.

Libya, after all, has lots of oil. Since 1969, Colonel Gaddafi has been using the nation's oil revenue to finance his many adventures to "liberate" other lands and lavish diplomatic gifts around the world. His efforts have long been in vain, as many are interested in his cash, not his ideas. Over the years, Gaddafi had made protégées not only among revolutionaries such as

---

[47] Over the years, Gaddafi had signed unification agreements with most of his neighbours but none of these unions ever materialized.
[48] This refers to the part of the Sahara which lies within the borders of the French-speaking Republic of Niger, which is to the north of the English-speaking country of the Federal Republic of Nigeria.

Nelson Mandela and Thomas Sankara of Burkina Faso, but also bloodthirsty tyrants and villains such as Idi Amin and Charles Taylor.

»»»»»

Libya is one of the largest African nations by surface area, but it has only 6 million inhabitants of which 2 million are expatriate workers. This is one of the world's most sparsely populated nations. Most of its inhabitants live along a narrow coastal strip whereas the rest of the country is the hot, arid desert of the Sahara. We sped southwards deeper into the Sahara, initially on paved highways at a comfortable speed of 160km per hour, then went off-road onto a dirt track. Before long, we were deep in the Sahara — gigantic sand dunes, strange rock formations shaped by millions of years of wind, erosion and friction, and fields of rocks and boulders around us, sometimes all at the same time.

There were no road signs, vegetation or landmarks of any kind, just tracks from previous vehicles and occasional piles of stones left as road markers by two millennia of caravans passing through these regions. But it all looked the same to me. We were, for lack of a better description, in the middle of nowhere. It was the sort of place where if you wanted to take a leak, no convenient bushes or shelter could be found.

The Tuaregs: Masters of the Sahara.

Sahara adventure: An amazing natural arch in the Acacus region.

Spectacular sand dunes like this are found in many parts of the Libyan Sahara.

Um Al Ma, or Mother of Water, one of the prettiest of the salt lakes in the Ubari Sand Sea.

Ancient carvings at Wadi Methkandonsh.

Ancient prehistoric wall paintings at Jebel Acacus.

Landscape on the way to Ghadames, near the Algerian border.

In this wide expanse of near-nothingness, I felt a sense of helplessness. My survival lay in the hands of these Tuaregs whom I trust probably knew this land like the back of their palms. In 1999, the Tuaregs that took me into the Moroccan Sahara for an evening of camel rides told me that they relied on the stars, but here we were penetrating the desert to its deepest in broad daylight.

Muhammad drove like a contestant in the Paris–Dakar cross-country rally, testing the suspension of our vehicle to the limit and kicking up a trail of dust wherever we went. Our hardy 4WD rocked and shook as it negotiated the rugged terrain, sometimes making sharp 45-degree descents down the sides of sand dunes.

Many a time I prayed silently to Guanyin, Allah and all the almighties for our vehicle and our safety, for we had broken the cardinal rule of desert travel — always travel in groups of at least two vehicles. Any breakdown in the desert is potentially deadly. One dies within days either from exposure or lack of water.

Over the next few days, we passed by the famed prehistoric rock carvings and paintings of Wadi Methkandonsh and Jebel Acacus. Between 10,000 to 18,000 years ago, ancient men, mostly hunter-gatherers and pioneer pastoralists, drew or carved these images of daily life, celebrations and a wide range of animals including giraffes, cattle, elephants, hippopotami, crocodiles, dogs and big cats. Obviously, the Sahara was then a different land altogether. The desert used to be a fertile plain of huge lakes and long rivers supporting lots of vegetation and wild creatures. Climatic changes over the millennia had long driven its creatures either to extinction or to move to places with more hospitable climates further south. This ancient rock art is today a World Heritage Site.

We spent nights in the open, among the huge sand dunes of Wan Caza and the Ubari Sand Sea. Endless crests of rolling dunes of soft fine sand, some well-shaped like the firm breasts of a young lady. We climbed up the high dunes on several occasions, hoping to witness the famous Sahara sunset. Unfortunately, at the critical moment, the skies were always cloudy. This was the season when the hot Harmattan whirlwinds of the Sahel met the cold Mediterranean from the north, creating no less than a mini-revolt in the skies and opaque clouds that obstructed what could have been spectacular sunsets over the Sahara.

At night, we could hear whispers from afar, for the desert breeze carries conversations far beyond, in a phenomena that sometimes tempts the unwary to wander out to investigate, only to get lost in the sand sea.

Every evening, we looked forward to Baraka's 'Soup de Tuareg', a delightful mixture of salted dried beef and vegetables, stirred with cumin powder, coriander, chili and, somewhat disappointingly, Maggi soup cubes. I wondered if the soup was genuinely delicious, or whether it was our desperation for something hearty, warm and mildly spicy after a day in the wilderness. Meals were inevitably followed by tea Libyan style which involved green tea prepared from leaves imported from China into Niger, and packed and labeled there with a local-sounding brand name. The tea was poured from one cup to another so that bubbles formed. This was very much like our *teh tarik* ('pulled' tea) though the main difference is that Libyans use green tea for this, whereas Singaporeans and Malaysians use red. Had we discovered the origins of *teh tarik*?

》》》》》

The 50 million Muslims of Europe will turn it into a Muslim continent within a few decades. Europe is in a predicament, and so is America. They should agree to become Islamic in the course of time, or else declare war on the Muslims.

— *Colonel Gaddafi*[49]

Jebel Acacus has one of the most spectacular landscapes I have ever seen in my life. This is a region of small mountains and weird black rocks towering above sand dunes for as far as the horizon. Sculpted by wind and erosion, the pinnacles and rocks formed the most unlikely of shapes and together they resulted in a landscape that reminded me of Mars and scenes from *Planet of the Apes*.

---

[49] http://www.memritv.org/clip_transcript/en/1121.htm, "Libyan Leader Mu'ammar Al-Qadhafi: Europe and the U.S. Should Agree to Become Islamic or Declare War on the Muslims", speech aired on Al-Jazeera TV on 10 April 2006.

We drove towards the ancient caravan town of Ghat, once a great trading centre in the middle of the Sahara. Today it is a sleepy backwater with a decaying, abandoned, old centre of mud bricks, linked to the rest of Libya by a road from Sabha. The old caravan road was cut off from the town after an incursion of Algerian troops into a wadi 10 kilometres south of the town, a few years ago.

The weather was rapidly changing — hot, still, oppressive air was enveloping the land with a shroud of trapped heat. Mosquitoes were everywhere. The only comfort was that they moved about slowly and were easy targets for the human hand. In that respect, they seemed as slow as their normal prey, the locals, some of whom took life easy and seemed to take forever to perform simple tasks.

It was near Ghat that we came by the towering peaks of Kaj Ajnoun, the Devil's Mountain, which cast a dark shadow over the plains and beyond, like Dracula's Castle transported whole to the sand dunes of the Sahara. Located in the deepest Sahara of southern Libya, this 1281-metre high rocky massif rises almost vertically above the desert plains and sand dunes where the Libyan Sahara kisses the Algerian border. Its massive silhouette looks like an impregnable citadel; its pinnacles the watchtowers and the protruding boulders, steps on magical ladders.

The Tuaregs, master navigators and nomads of the Sahara, have numerous tales about the mountain and the powerful *jinns* (genies) that

One of the courtyards in the beautiful town of Ghadames.

gather here from thousands of miles around. They say that on windy nights, one sees the lights of *jinns* in conference shining from the peaks, and hears their drums and the celebratory firing of their powerful guns. Those who challenge the legends by climbing the mountain will suffer for the deed. As such, traditional Tuaregs, brave warriors though they be, give Kaf Ajnoun a wide berth.

I had no intention of challenging the ancient myths, but seeing the Devil's Mountain from afar probably did one no harm. Among the many Tuareg legends associated with Kaj Ajnoun was one about a Ghadames merchant who met a red-haired *jinn* here on his way to Algeria. The *jinn* passed him a piece of paper with strange symbols and unknown writing, to be handled over to a black dog which would meet him at a specific place in Tuat, Algeria. The merchant headed for that place in Tuat and was, indeed, met by a black dog that gave him a lifetime of wondrous riches.

A few explorers attempted to climb Kaj Ajnoun and some of them suffered badly from illness soon after. One, Heinrich Barth, became sick and unwell soon after the climb, and lost his way while descending the mountain. Dehydrated and thirsty, he cut a vein to drink his own blood. Almost unconscious, down with high fever and close to death from exposure, he was saved by passing Tuaregs. A holiday need not be so dramatic, so we merely took a few pictures at the foot of the cursed mountain and pressed on with our journey.

» » » » »

Do we share a culture with Europe? Absolutely not. We each have our own culture. Our cultures are completely different. In Scandinavia, people walk around naked. Can you walk around naked in Tunisia, Algeria, Egypt, or Libya? They would stone you and throw you into a mental hospital. But in Scandinavia, it is common to see people walk around naked. That's their culture. Is it conceivable for a union to be formed between somebody naked and somebody who considers this to be crazy?

> *The capital [of the union] would be Brussels. If I told my people*
> *that Brussels would be the capital, they would stone me. If I told them*
> *that I went and formed a union with the Israelis, with the North Pole,*
> *and with the whole wide world, and that its capital would be Brussels*
> *— would they applaud me? No, they would boo me.*
>
> — *Colonel Gaddafi[50]*

»»»»»

Day four in the Sahara and we were finally getting restless with the usual green salads, Tuareg soup and spaghetti. The vegetables were no longer fresh; we had new concerns over Baraka's casual handling of the meat and greens with his bare hands; the four-day-old bread now had a much-hardened crust and its stale interior was covered, like all of us and everything else, with a thin layer of fine golden sand.

Another three hours' drive saw us past a range of desolate table-mountains, a Repsol oil installation (the nation's oilfields lie here), a huge car junkyard, a dumping ground for plastic bags and a few new model towns to which Colonel Gaddafi had moved the formerly nomadic people.

Finally, we arrived at Germa, where we visited the ruins of the capital of the Garamantian Empire, which once fought against the Romans for supremacy in the interior of North Africa, before disappearing mysteriously around 500AD. Some historians believe that the Garamantians had declined due to the depletion of water and natural resources, the result of over-population and wastage. Will modern Libya go the same way if the Great Man-Made River project of Gaddafi, which diverted underground water from the Sahara to the coast, used up all the water available?

The Garamantian ruins were little more than piles of collapsed mud brick. The setting was eerie, with strong winds beating against the walls and the plains. A huge field full of the trunks of dead palm trees with decapitated tops, stood beyond the ancient walls.

---

50 http://www.memritv.org/clip_transcript/en/1809.htm, "Libyan Leader Mu'ammar Al-Qadhafi Explains His Objection to the Union for the Mediterranean: Libyans Cannot Form a Union with Europeans Who Walk around Naked", Speech made by Libyan Leader Mu'ammar Al-Qadhafi, which aired on Al-Jazeera TV on July 9, 2008.

»»»»»

We explored the salt lakes of the Ubari Sand Sea. Slivers of silver surrounded by palm trees, papyrus reeds and the curves and crests of huge sand dunes. Visitors jumped into these salty lakes, floating like they would in the famous salt waters of the Dead Sea. Was this the proverbial Garden of Eden? Gentle breezes covered us with a thin layer of sand. Even as I went to the toilet for my own bombardment of ancient Germa, I discovered a mysterious layer of sand even on my bum. No idea how that came about, but I had had enough of sand by this Day Five in the Sahara. I would have liked a nice hot shower, clean toilets, soft beds, the Internet and better choices of food for my meals; whether or not I got to see beautiful lakes in the sand dunes, (yet-to-be-discovered) glorious Sahara sunsets, lost civilizations in the desert, mysterious rock paintings, and heaven- or hell-inspired natural rock formations.

»»»»»

Our final day in the Sahara: We woke up to find ourselves amidst glorious sand dunes and the best of clear blue skies. Perfect for photo shots. We took the best sand dune photos of the entire trip so far. I even got Baraka, our cook, to pose like a Tuareg warrior. Even though most of the time Baraka had behaved like a self-proclaimed joker who brought out the loudest laughter from everyone, I managed to get him to pose in all seriousness, in his blue-and-green turban and robes, gazing afar into the horizon, with sand dunes in the background. Thank Allah for the invention of the digital camera!

»»»»»

Back at Tripoli, we explored the ancient Roman cities of Leptis Magna and Sabratha. The first urban settlements on the northern coast of Libya were built by the Phoenicians from ancient Lebanon, which ruled these cities from Carthage in what is today Tunisia. The Phoenicians sacrificed their first born to the gods and huge amphorae containing the charred bones of their victims have been found in the sacred places of these ancient Carthaginian cities. Enriched by trade and the riches of Africa, Spain and the Mediterranean islands, the Carthaginian (also known as the Punic) Empire was once one of the greatest powers of the Mediterranean, until their rivalry and eventual defeat by the Romans.

Carthage itself was destroyed but cities such as Leptis Magna, Sabratha and Oea, collectively known as Tripoli ("Three Cities"), gained autonomy and prosperity as self-governing city states in the Roman Empire. They embraced Roman culture and religion with enthusiasm and their status was further enhanced with later grants of status as Roman colonies.

Leptis Magna, in particular, became one of the empire's greatest cities when a local boy founded the Severan dynasty that ruled Rome for a few glorious decades. Grand theatres, amphitheatres, forums and temples were built in the city that was the capital of the province of Libya which was at that time the granary of the Empire. Sabratha, a smaller city, was similarly prosperous, and was bestowed with grand public structures with intricate carvings and magnificent mosaics. Today, even in a ruined state, Leptis Magna and Sabratha continue to impress visitors with Libya's glorious Roman past.

»»»»»

Leptis Magna: Once one of the richest cities in the Roman Empire.

We headed inland to the Berber towns of Jebel Nafusa. Located on top of Jebel Nafusa near the border with Tunisia, Nalut is an important cultural centre for the Berber people, the original inhabitants of North Africa, many of who have fair complexions and blue or green eyes. One can find signboards in the very symbol-like alphabet of the Berber language here. We visited Nalut Castle with its amazing claustrophobic, closely built rooms. Here one also finds many Tunisian vehicles loading up on cheap Libyan petrol, which costs US$0.10 per litre, to sell across the border in Tunisia.

The Berbers, who are more numerous in Morocco and Algeria, are a people immensely proud of their cultural heritage and their non-Arabic identity. Increasingly, Berber cultural monuments such as the Qasr al Haj, a huge fortified granary once home to hundreds of Berbers, and various dammus, which are traditional underground cave dwellings, are preserved and opened to visitors as museums and showcases of Berber heritage.

From Nalut, we drove to the ancient caravan town of Ghadames. The landscape en route was bleak and dry. Not quite the sand dunes of Fezzan but the high plateau, arid plains and bone-dry wadis here were equally eerie and dead silent. In fact, the Berbers like the Tuaregs of the region, still tell tales of the *jinns* that live in these parts.

Ghadames, located near the tri-border region of Libya, Tunisia and Algeria, was once a major caravan-trading town. Settled Tuaregs built a city of palm gardens with a sophisticated water distribution system and a natural air ventilation system that still allows its inhabitants to enjoy a naturally air-conditioned environment much welcomed in a desert where temperatures often rise into the 45–50°C range during the hot season. (The world's hottest temperature ever recorded was 53°C in a location south of Tripoli in the 1960s). Ghadames' labyrinthine sheltered streets and whitewashed walls were amazing, and evoked images of Darth Vader and Luke Skywalker's *Star Wars* locale. In fact, the movie was filmed at nearby towns in southern Tunisia, which bears a similar kind of local architecture.

»»»»»

We believe America is practicing all kinds of terrorism against Libya.
Even the accusation that we are involved in terrorism is in itself an act
of terrorism.

— *Colonel Gaddafi[51], 1981*

We flew to Benghazi, Libya's second largest city and historically the
metropolis of Libya's eastern half known as Cyrenacia. We were guests of our
Libyan friend, Abdalla, whose family hails from Al Bayda, a city to the east
of Benghazi. We were driven around Benghazi's landmarks. Much of the city
was destroyed during WWII and hence there were few old buildings. Even
then, we stumbled upon a nice Roman Catholic church — where we met
the Papal Ambassador to Libya, who is Maltese — and the Libyan Society
of Architects' building which is a nice Moorish-Andalusian style mansion
with nice carvings and exhibits on Libya's heritage.

From Benghazi, we headed for Al Bayda, which is located in the beautiful
Green Mountains. Up in the highlands, Al Bayda enjoys a year-round
temperate climate, with snowfall in winter and cool comfortable weather in
summer. The ample rainfall here has allowed the city and the surrounding
region to develop an agricultural economy not found elsewhere in dry, arid
Libya. Al Bayda is also the base to visit the ancient Greek cities of Cyrene
and Apollonia, both are within 30km from the city radius.

With Abdalla and his family and friends, we experienced Libyan
hospitality at its best. Even though he was busy with the affairs of his family's
business holdings and the engagement of one of his younger brothers (the
engagement ceremonies and parties would involve their entire tribe, which
included thousands of people), Abdalla still spent a lot of time with us,
driving us around the various ancient Greek, Roman and Byzantine sites of
Cyrenacia. We also met many of his friends, and had lots of tea and smoked
the shisha with them.

We visited the Friday market. The climate was cool and it even drizzled
a little — what a contrast with the Fezzan where it rained only a few times

---

[51] Interview with Time Magazine, June 8, 1981 http://www.time.com/time/magazine/article/0,9171,922551-2,00.
html.

a year, or even not at all some years. No wonder the Green Mountains produce so many vegetables.

We dropped by Cyrene, once the largest Greek city outside Greece and the granary of Ancient Greece, founded in 630BC by Battus I, an adventurer from the island of Thera, who arrived here based on advice from the Oracle of Delphi. It was the time when the feudal Zhou princes of China had begun to fight each other for supremacy in the North while political philosophers were traveling across the states preaching good governance and strategy in a chaotic era. In the Middle East, the city-states of Mesopotamia were continuing to battle each other and smaller tribal kingdoms in Judea and Anatolia. Metal coins were used for the first time by Lydians in what is today Turkey. Sappho, one of the nine great Greek classical 'lyric poets', was born on the Aegean island of Lesbos, and her works on love, infatuations and passion were, according to some, what eventually led to the use of the word 'lesbian' to denote same-sex love among women.

Cyrene became a powerful city-state and at one time even tried to invade Egypt. Today, the ruins of Cyrene are located on an enormous site spread across sloping hillsides from the high fertile plateau of the Green Mountains to a lower plain also full of greenery and farms. From this lower plain, the plateau fell 200 meters to a coastal strip by the Mediterranean. It was also along this coastal strip that ancient Apollonia, the port of Cyrene, was located. Compared to the grid-like streets and organized patterns of the Roman cities of Leptis and Sabratha, Cyrene was more disorderly, with crooked lanes and a labyrinth of alleys.

We were told about the local belief that powerful *jinns* lived in these hills and the many caves and crannies that dot these cliff sides and slopes. There are many legends and even modern day tales about treasure hunters and troublemakers who disturbed the peace of the ruins and got punished by the *jinns*.

We also visited Susa, the gateway town to Appollonia. Susa became home to many Cretan Muslims who fled here after the Cretan War between

---

[52] Omar-Al-Mukhtar was also the hero portrayed in the movie *Lion of the Desert* (1981) starring Anthony Quinn as the elderly guerrilla fighter. He began fighting against the Italians who invaded Ottoman Libya in 1912, till his arrest and execution in 1931. A large percentage of Cyrenacia's population died as a result of Italian suppression of Libyan resistance.

the Turks and Greeks in the 1890s. A few Cretans were pointed out to me and they had very fair complexions. The mother of Abdalla's good friend, Ahmat, is a Cretan and that could explain his European looks.

The centre of Susa looked deserted. We were told that many people moved out during the last two years after a powerful *jinn* named Abdul Kadir got upset with treasure hunters digging around Apollonia and started "creating trouble" for people who hung around the area after dark. It was interesting that the belief in *jinns* seemed strong in Libya. I don't recall people telling me about *jinns* in my travels across the Middle East over the years. In fact, someone also told me about spiritual men who poked spikes through their cheeks in honour of *jinns* and local deities. That hardly sounded Islamic. In fact, there were many similarities with the ancient shamanistic practices of Southeast and East Asia.

Apollonia is quite small and has little more than a few groups of columns. Most of the city, like Leptis Magna, Sabratha and Cyrene, was destroyed in the great earthquake and tsunami of 365AD, which also devastated much of Greece, Sicily and the Nile delta of Egypt, including the great city of Alexandria. We drove to picturesque Ras al-Hillal — a verdant grove where a small stream flowed down from a pool formed from a waterfall plunging down the Green Mountains. The nearby coast and mountains combine to form a symphony of nature and geography. Abdalla commented that we were privileged to see the Ras al-Hillal before

Omar–Al–Mukhtar University of Al Bayda, named after the leader of Libya's resistance movement against Italian invaders[52]. This billboard depicts Gaddafi with the Libyan national hero. Don't all politicians like to be compared to past heroes?

development took off there. Indeed, a few villas had already been built nearby, not to mention a huge house and marina at a nearby bay owned by relatives of the powers of the land.

The beautiful coast was full of rocky coves and forests of low bushes. Crystal clear azure waters, glaring sun and blue skies. This could have been the Cote d-Azur or Provence, except for the absence of vehicles, luxury villas and settlements of any reasonable size. There was definitely much potential for tourism development, but Libya would need to cut the red tape and even learn to accept the habits of more open-minded foreigners.

There was a stretch of coast covered by low young forest, which grew after the ancient groves were burned down in the 1990s by the government in order to flush out some anti-government rebels. Beneath the calm there was always some undercurrent of unhappiness and the potential for violence. This has invariably been the case in the volatile Middle East.

We went to Abdalla's family farm where lots of grapes and fruits of all sorts were grown. Abdalla personally prepared lamb in the traditional manner for us — a hole was dug in the ground, a fire lit in it and the lamb placed inside to be cooked after the hole had been covered over with mud and soil. He had to collect firewood and mix mud and water to prepare the earthen oven. The lamb tasted fantastic, but it was the friendship and hospitality that meant so much more.

»»»»»

Libya is a country blessed with great historical cities and spectacular natural scenery and landscapes, much of which remains unknown to most people outside the country. Politically, Libya has long been a pariah state, hugely misunderstood by others. It is now opening up and exciting developments are taking place. The stock market is new and small, with only four listed companies. Interesting opportunities abound and I shall be keeping a close watch.

The Sudan: Pyramids & the War Zone (May 2008)

Khartoum was… rebuilt by Kitchener in 1889. He laid it out — with what magisterial self-righteousness and confidence! — in the shape of a Union Jack.

— John Gunther, *Inside Africa*, 1955

The Sudan[53] for a holiday? Hasn't this country been plagued by civil war and coups since independence in 1956? For many years, Sudan seemed to be synonymous with famine, war, genocide and slavery. In short, it was a failed state. First, it was the Christian south that wanted to break away from the Islamic north. Then, just as the south signed a peace agreement with the north, the Darfur crisis broke out.

But Sudan, land of the blacks, as the name means in Arabic, is an ancient land with a history dating back more than 4,000 years. At 2.5 million sq km, it is the largest country in Africa and about one quarter the size of the United States. The ancient land of Nubia, once the southern frontier land of the ancient Egyptian civilization, is today part of southern Egypt and northern Sudan. Nubia was an ethnic melting pot, where African tribes faded into Egypt. This was the land of the tropical trade, where merchants from the deep African south supplied slaves, elephants, giraffes, lions and other exotic goods to the pharaohs' courts.

Political and military control switched back and forth between the Egyptians and the native Nubians, who by then had adapted Egyptian culture and added African elements of their own. The Kush-Nubian kings

---

[53] Sudan is always correctly called "The Sudan"; its official name is The Republic of the Sudan. For simplicity, however, most writers call the country Sudan.

built pyramids and great temples where they worshipped Egyptian gods as well as their own, mummified their dead rulers and developed their own writing system which evolved from Egyptian hieroglyphics. The Nubian kings even conquered and ruled Egypt in 1550 BC.

Later, after the Kushites, as the Nubians were then known, were defeated by the Assyrians from what is today Iraq, they retreated south to Meroe, 300km north of Khartoum, where they built more pyramids and great temples. Here they practiced Egyptian religion and customs with a vengeance and lasted much longer than the Egyptian civilization itself.

In the meantime, the Greeks of Alexander the Great conquered Egypt, followed by the Romans, whose Greek and Roman gods replaced the ancient Egyptian ones. Even the Roman gods were eventually replaced by the monotheistic Christian faith (and later the Islamic religion). The Meroe kingdom survived with all its hybrid African-Egyptian culture, until 350AD when it was destroyed by invading Axumites from Ethiopia.

Today, the ancient pyramids of Nubia and Meroe still stand timelessly in the bare wind-swept deserts of northern Sudan. Unfortunately, just like Ethiopia's ancient and glorious past was overshadowed by the famines and wars of recent decades, hardly anyone outside Sudan has heard of its relatively obscure though once cosmopolitan civilization. The news elsewhere spoke of nothing but mayhem and crisis.

» » » »

I arrived in a Sudan hot in more ways than one. Firstly, this was the height of the Sudanese summer. I landed at 4:45am from Cairo and the temperature was 33°C. Daytime temperatures would rise above 50°C by noon.

Secondly, just four days before, Khartoum, capital of Sudan, was attacked by rebels from the province of Darfur, where a bitter conflict had been waged for the last few years. Although the Sudan had seen insurgency since 1956, Khartoum had never been attacked from the outside. Apart from a few coups, the city has always been an oasis of peace. It shocked everyone that the rebels could travel 700km from faraway Darfur undetected by the government troops, and suddenly attack the heart of the Sudanese state.

The rebels were crushed after two to three days of street fighting in Omdurman, Khartoum's twin city in its western suburbs. I had heard about the fighting while in Libya, and contemplated aborting the trip. But I cast the die to come here while in Cairo, when I heard that the fighting had ceased, flights had resumed to Khartoum and that the Sudanese embassy in Cairo could grant me a visa that same day.

The Egyptair Boeing was completely full, mostly with Sudanese stranded abroad when Khartoum airport was closed for a few days during the rebel attack; there were a few European members of UN agencies and NGOs based in Khartoum. Yes, the UN and NGOs — I had seen so many of them across Africa's conflict zones past and present. The Cote d'Ivoire, Liberia, Sierra Leone, Somaliland, Ethiopia, Eritrea, Rwanda — just to name a few. In Sudan, the UN presence is so big that it has become the largest operator of domestic flights within the country.

In many countries, when conflicts break out — and even for many years after the end of the fighting — the UN and assorted NGOs would provide

Dusty downtown Khartoum. A new modern Khartoum of skyscrapers is being built with oil money.

employment not only for a number of locals, but also a large number of very highly paid international civil servants, whose tax-free income would no doubt stimulate the economy through the appearance of expensive restaurants, night clubs, bars, supermarkets with flashy imported goods and luxuries of every kind imaginable. It is an extraordinary opportunity for the entrepreneur and those with the right connections to profit from such situations. This, however, also leads to high inflation and the appearance of a sex industry.

I had an interesting chat with a Dutch NGO couple on the flight. They had spent the last two decades in various troubled spots in Africa — Congo, Rwanda, Chad, etc, plus Kurdistan. Now they work in Khartoum and South Sudan, the latter currently ruled by former rebels of the Sudan People's Liberation Movement (SPLM).

The leader of the SPLM is also the President of the Government of South Sudan (GOSS) and Vice President of all Sudan. A referendum will be held in 2010 to decide if oil-rich South Sudan should become independent[54]. The Dutch said that if I wanted to go to South Sudan, I should have entered from Kenya or Uganda, as nobody needed a visa when entering from the south, where they run their own immigration.

On the day the Darfur rebels attacked Omdurman, the couple heard gunshots and saw smoke rising from Omdurman. They simply walked to the airport — no taxis were available because no one wanted to drive out given the trouble and conflicting news — and took the last, yet-to-be-cancelled Egyptair flight out to Cairo, where they went on a shopping spree while waiting for the fighting to cease.

Over the next few days, I spoke to the locals about the fighting. The friendly Sudanese would smile and say the fighting was no big deal. In an understated way, they would add, "Only a few were killed" though foreign reports indicated a few hundred dead. Some of them did admit that maybe it was serious after all, but the Sudanese were so used to conflicts that they simply stayed at home and waited for the battle to finish.

»»»»»

---

[54] Many predict that war might break out again at that time, as it seems almost certain that the South Sudanese, embittered by years of brutal rule from the north, would vote for independence.

Khartoum is a city of great contrasts. The airport is very modern and there were chic mobile ads everywhere; I heard an even newer airport is being built for US$500 million. There were free Internet terminals and wireless Internet (WIFI) at the airport. For a country with a longstanding civil conflict, immigration clearance was surprisingly fast and efficient. No questions asked. I changed money and found a booth belonging to Zain Celtel, the pan-African mobile operator. I saluted globalisation as I added value to my Celtel Uganda mobile phone which worked in a total of 12 African countries including Sudan.

Interestingly, most of the airport's workers were either Filipinos or Indians. This might be a bit surprising given Sudan's high unemployment, but I suppose these expat workers were also the reason why this airport was run so well, not to mention the WIFI, the presence of a never-ceasing cleaning crew and English-speaking Filipino counter-staff everywhere. The Sudanese, with all due respect, were a lot more relaxed about time; few of them could speak English; and even fewer had been educated beyond a a stint in the village Quranic school where the main (and sometimes sole) goal was to enable the student to take part in rote-reading of the *Quran* and participation in the annual district *Quran* recital competition.

» » » » »

Friendly Sudanese at the market near Souk Arabiya, Khartoum.

I checked into the very basic Hotel Al Nakhil right at the heart of Souk Arabiya. It had bed sheets that looked like they hadn't been washed for 20 years; broken furniture with sharp uneven angles; exposed wires across the entire wall, one thick cable that ran across my room, and a squatting toilet (no toilet paper provided) whose poorly angled flush was so strong that it spurted water not only out of the toilet bowl but into the room, across its uneven floor — like a flash flood gushing into a dry riverbed in a desert — then under the door into the corridor.

When I caused the first major flood of the day shortly after checking in, the Nubian cleaning ladies knocked on my door to point out the resulting collateral damage, and then indicated by sign language that I should use the tap and hose instead of the flush. The naughty boy in me lowered his eye brows and pretended nothing had happened. Even then, over the next four days, the advice would slip my mind and three more deluges would occur. I was more worried about the likelihood of an electrical short-circuit from that strange cable on the floor and wondered if I would be electrocuted.

》》》》》

My hotel was located in the middle of the city-centre souk, Souk Arabiya — Arabian Market in English. Loud African rap mixed with classical Egyptian music could be heard. That was not surprising, as Sudan, Land of the Blacks in the Arabic language, after all, is where the Arab World becomes African. In Sudan, you still have to bargain to buy things, but people are more reasonable than in Egypt. Many people had heard of Singapore and said that many of their products came from Singapore, although I hadn't seen any. Maybe many products used to come from Singapore at one time, before the factories all moved to China.

》》》》》

I forget how many days we passed in the "Sudd", where there is nothing in ken but "green beds of growing rushes where no leaf blooms or blushes." ...

There was a story that Lady Cromer's maid on the third or fourth day of this had said to her mistress, "How long, my Lady, must we tarry in this shrubbery?" but as I was told afterwards that Lady Cromer had never been in the Sudd, it must have been someone else's maid.
                                          — Edward Marsh, *A Number of People*, 1908

Khartoum has long been reported, whether in the early 20th century or today — sometimes by people who have never been there — to be nothing more than a shithole and a temple of doom, but the reality is a lot more complicated than that.

Khartoum is a very dusty and sandy city full of one or two storey buildings. But great changes are taking place. The huge oil revenue that came in the last two years, courtesy of sanction-busting Mainland Chinese, Indian and Malaysian oil companies, meant a suddenly hugely enriched upper class with lots of cash floating around, seeking all the good things in life.

Whilst many roads remain unpaved, huge blocks in the centre are being torn down for redevelopment. Skyscrapers and shopping malls are being built in Khartoum and its suburbs, and huge billboards advertise developments with fanciful names reminding one of those in the Riviera, Dubai and Long Beach. Some went so far as to call Khartoum the new Dubai of the Nile.

With sanctions in place, Westerners are hardly on the scene, at least not openly except as employees of UN agencies or NGOs, and a few assorted mobile companies. Khartoum is the playground of the Chinese, Indians and

The sailboat-like hotel is Burj al Fatah built by the Libyans along the Blue Nile. It has become one of the city's key landmarks.

Malaysians. I was to pass the huge refineries of the China National Petroleum Corporation (CNPC) outside Khartoum, together with several large billboards proclaiming eternal Sino-Sudanese friendship in the Chinese and Arabic languages; and every few hundred meters on Khartoum's streets, locals greeted me with "*Ni hao*". The Chinese have also invested in at least one major Sudanese mineral water company. The labels had Chinese words praising the water quality. Many petrol stations belonging to Petronas, Malaysia's national oil company, were found across Khartoum and one of the two five-star hotels in the city was the Malaysian-owned Holiday Villas Hotel which charged US$250 per night.

» » » » »

I was very cautious during my first few hours in Khartoum. The normally camera-happy me took few photos that day. According to Sudanese law, tourists have to register with the police's Aliens Registration Office (ARO); those who want to take photos must get photography permits from the Ministry of Tourism; and those heading south of Khartoum need travel permits from the Ministry of Humanitarian Affairs. I had arrived on a Friday and none of these offices were open.

But things were not right even as I walked around Khartoum's sandy streets. They were full of troops, given the failed rebel attack over the last weekend. The soldiers were found at many street corners and junctions, often in armoured Toyota pickups with machine guns and anti-aircraft guns mounted as well. Some government offices even had sand bags and barbwire. That made it impossible for me to take photos of any large building or public square in Khartoum. A photo of a national flag was always something I took wherever I went, but I have done Sudan without a single photo of the Sudanese flag, since they were inevitably flown from public buildings heavily guarded by the military.

Whenever I took out my camera, stern-looking plainclothes secret police would run over, shouting "No, no!" There were many secret policemen around. They tended to wear nicely-ironed shirts, stood around street corners, and observed passers-by with rather stern looks that betrayed their presence. You noticed them immediately. Unconfirmed foreign press reports said that these secret policemen were now busy arresting people from Darfur province who resided in Khartoum, some of whom were suspected by the authorities to be the "Fifth Column" and might have assisted the provincial rebels in attacking the capital. You wouldn't want to end up in a Sudanese jail, even for one night.

Sudanese soldiers tended to sit under trees taking shelter from the heat, often looking very bored and some indulged in small talk with me (How are you? Where are you from? What is your name? Do you like Sudan?). Some were amused that I was there as a tourist and most were friendly. With hindsight, I had to consider myself lucky not to have been arrested as a suspected spy — but whom could I have been spying for? Certainly not tiny, faraway Singapore? Maybe for the Chinese — not a problem for them as China was the Sudanese government's favourite ally. A few soldiers even asked me to come by to chat with them. It is such boredom that often plagues soldiers in guerilla wars. Rebels often take advantage of a seemingly prolonged lull to strike again. Thank goodness they did not do so while I was in swinging Khartoum.

I also spoke to three young security guards outside an office block. Two were law undergraduates at a Khartoum university and the third had graduated from law school the year before. They were friendly guys anxious to practise their English. There were no better jobs here for them. The sole graduate among them said his law degree was useless. Despite the apparent boom, no one would hire them. All of them wanted to go somewhere — the Gulf States, Europe, the US, anywhere.

Ironically, while I was unable to take photos of buildings, many Sudanese, including women, loved to have their photos taken. As I walked through the souks (markets) and Oudurman's Hamed el Nil, many people asked me to take their photos. They really enjoyed posing (often too sternly) and then looking at the pictures taken with my digital camera.

Oh, I love the spiced Sudanese coffee, or *jabanna*. It's like the coffee version of the Indian masala tea, with the excitement of spices infused into traditional coffee. Fresh fruit juice was great too. The fantastic fresh mango juice costs only half a Sudanese Pound (US$0.25). I was a little worried about the small ice cubes inside the glass but I guess my stomach was getting acclimatized to the local water and bacteria. I was less happy about the food however. In the city centre, there wasn't anything more than street kebabs or grilled chicken sold from stalls whose hygiene I considered suspicious. Desperate for real food, I was to head for the expats' suburbs, and a minor fiasco I will describe later.

I passed by the huge offices of CNPC and Petronas, the oil companies of China and Malaysia respectively, by the Blue Nile, just north of central Khartoum very near to the presidential palace. (Petronas took up a large part of the Holiday Villa Hotel as their local HQ). BP or Shell would have taken up posh offices here in this breezy prime location if it were the British who were the proconsuls of Sudan.

Nearby was the futuristic hotel, Burj al Fatah, which with its sailing yacht shape, looked like a carbon copy of the world renowned Burj al Arab of Dubai. The Sudanese version is financed by Colonel Gaddafi of Libya, and guarded by a bunch of very fierce soldiers. Although photos of the building had appeared in articles and brochures on Khartoum (I guess promoters of Khartoum love the seemingly progressive linkage with Dubai, albeit it was a

Despite an austere Islamic image portrayed to the outside world, Sudanese people are fairly open-minded. In Khartoum's market, even local women encouraged me to take their photos, something inconceivable in many parts of the Islamic world.

massive unlicensed copycat version), these soldiers screamed at me when I raised my camera. I half expected them to shoot at me at any moment. It was only two days later that I managed to find a safe angle a few hundred meters away to take my well-deserved shot.

>> >> >> >> >>

The Nubian is interesting in his appearance and character; his figure is tall, thin, sinewy, and graceful, possessing what would be called in civilized life an uncommon degree of gentility; his face is rather dark, though far removed from African blackness; his features are long and aquiline, decidedly resembling the Roman; the expression of his face mild, amiable, and approaching to melancholy.
— John Lloyd Stephens, *Incidents of Travel in Egypt, etc.,* 1837

I crossed the Nile over to Oudurman, Khartoum's twin city, founded in the 19th century as the capital by the Mahdi, an Islamic teacher who proclaimed himself the holy saviour and resolved to chase out the corrupt Anglo-Egyptian regime that had conquered Sudan not long before and transformed Khartoum into a prosperous slave-trading centre (despite that the official reason for colonizing this region was to eliminate slavery).

He raised an army which defeated the Anglo-Egyptian army under General Charles Gordon. Gordon himself, then a British war hero, was killed during the fall of Khartoum — he was also known as "Chinese Gordon", for his leadership of the British Army that invaded China and defeated and humiliated the Son of Heaven. Chinese historical literature described General Gordon as a bloodthirsty imperialist who massacred countless innocent Chinese civilians and destroyed palaces, temples and other Chinese cultural monuments.

Today's Chinese and Sudanese political literature proclaim solidarity in their common hatred for Gordon, their eternal villain in a struggle against a West they see as a historical and perhaps, current and future enemy. Chinese visitors to Khartoum are often taken to where Gordon fell, where they would duly declare to their Sudanese friends how glad they were that the Sudanese had avenged Chinese grievances against their hated enemy.

But the history of the world has always been more complicated than governments would like it to be. Not only is a hero to one side often a villain to another, but many heroes also have complicated double-sided personalities and histories. Charles Gordon was one such personality and a rather extraordinary one at that.

In 1860, at the age of 27, young Captain Charles Gordon was sent to China in the middle of the Second Opium War. He arrived just as Anglo-French forces were looting and burning the Summer Palace in Beijing — the Chinese equivalent of the French Versailles — as a punishment for the Qing emperor's torture and killing of over 20 British, French and Indian captives.

But Gordon sounded remorseful about his tour of duty. He wrote: "We went out, and, after pillaging it, burned the whole place, destroying in a vandal-like manner most valuable property…You can scarcely imagine the beauty and magnificence of the places we burnt. It made one's heart sore to burn them… It was wretchedly demoralizing work for an army."

The war was soon over with the total defeat and surrender of China upon humiliating terms, which included the cessation of Kowloon Peninsula in Hong Kong to the British. Gordon remained in China, however, and went on to Shanghai, China's emerging port city with a huge international community. The city was at that time threatened by rebels who had declared the formation of the Taiping Heavenly Kingdom. The Taiping rebellion

Mobile phone
advertisement
in Khartoum:
Your weight in gold?

was launched by a Hakka former Christian convert from southern China named Hong Xiuquan, who claimed to be the younger brother of Jesus. Hong wanted to overthrow the Qing dynasty and spread his bizarre mix of Christianity and traditional folk beliefs through out the land. His rebellion began in 1850 and by 1860 he controlled huge parts of central and southern China, and ruled over more than 30 million people.

The Qing emperor, much weakened by the Second Opium War, prolonged civil conflict and natural disasters, could not put up an effective resistance against him, using traditional battle technology. Instead, a European mercenary force was quickly put together by foreign merchants in Shanghai, which through the efficient use of machine guns and the latest weaponry technology of the times, successfully defended Shanghai. After the death of Ward, founder of the force, Gordon took over and soon won a series of victories on behalf of the Qing Court. A fearsome reputation emerged which was further fanned after the force was renamed "Chang Sheng Jun" or "Ever Victorious Army". Some historians called this force the first Chinese army organised along Western lines. It was with the victories of the Ever Victorious Army that the Qing reconquest of Taiping-occupied lands began and gained momentum.

Whatever modern-day Chinese historians and politicians love to say about Gordon, it was the Battle of Suzhou that defined Gordon as a principled character. Suzhou, a city famous among the Chinese for its arts, culture and architecture, was also a major strategic garrison for the Taipings. In 1863, the Qing Army, together with Gordon's Ever Victorious Army, arrived at the walls of Suzhou. The Taiping front commander, Gao Yunguan, was unhappy with the Taiping leadership over promotion and sharing of spoils, and was tempted to defect to the Qing. Secret negotiations took place between Gordon and Gao, during which Gordon guaranteed Gao safety as well as riches for him and his men if they surrendered.

Gao agreed, slaughtered his chief commander, opened the gates of Suzhou, and surrendered the entire Taiping garrison without a fight. As Gordon entered the city, Qing forces under Li Hongzhang, Governor of Jiangsu Province (and later, a prominent senior statesman) suddenly detained Gordon on account of safety, for one hour. It was during that one hour that Gao and over two thousand officers and men of the surrendered Taiping forces were beheaded despite earlier promises made by Gordon. Gordon was furious at the betrayal of his personal honour, and almost shot Li when he confronted him over the betrayal. He protested to the Emperor and wanted to resign. Li was ordered to mourn Gao and the executed Taiping soldiers in a public ceremony, but it was only after the Emperor's grant of public honours and much silver, that Gordon was finally placated.

This episode formed the basis of the movie *The Warlords* (2007) directed by Peter Chan and starring Asian superstars Jet Li, Andy Lau and Takeshi Kaneshiro. Andy Lau played a "Gordon-like" character who negotiated the surrender of Suzhou but was betrayed by his blood-brother general. It is simply politically incorrect in modern-day China to have a white man portrayed as a righteous but betrayed protagonist. And so the Gordon character became Chinese instead.

By 1864, the Taiping Rebellion was crushed and Hong had killed himself. The Ever Victorious Army was disbanded and Gordon left China. From China, Gordon went on to win other glories for the British Empire, negotiate peace and settle uncertain frontiers with allies and enemies. Crimea, Sudan, Ethiopia, Congo and other wild lands followed. "Chinese" Gordon became the hero of the Empire.

The Hamed el Nil Mosque where sufi performances are held every Friday.

In public, Gordon was also a fanatical Christian who never hesitated to invoke God and hellfire, often asking God to carry him into eternal paradise. Privately, he was almost certainly a homosexual[56]. He was known to delight in the company of handsome boys and youths, and young, dashing officers near him were almost certain to receive more than a reasonably comfortable degree of personal attention.

In 1884, when Sudan was threatened by the Mahdist rebellion, Gordon was rushed to Khartoum to evacuate the garrison, where his legendary exploits in China had preceded him. Even before his arrival, he telegrammed the local garrison: "You are men, not women. Be not afraid; I am coming." But evacuation was not Gordon's style. He believed that the Mahdists must be defeated or Egypt — key to the British Empire — would be threatened. He rallied the defenders of Khartoum who almost became convinced of his invincibility. "Khartoum is as safe as Kensington Gardens," he proclaimed.

But Khartoum became a Kensington Gardens under siege instead, and a rather pathetic one too. As the months passed, food ran out and no relief force was in sight. As noted in *Chinese Gordon: The Story of a Hero* by Lawrence and Elisabeth Hanson: "Gordon ordered all dogs and cats and donkeys to be killed and eaten, rats to be caught and eaten... The gentle Gordon changed into an old man, white-haired... kicking, shouting, punishing."

On 26 January 1885, more than 10 months into the siege, taking advantage of the Nile's low level, 50,000 Mahdist troops stormed into Khartoum. The city burned and its inhabitants and garrison were massacred. Lawrence and Elisabeth Hanson described the scene of Gordon's death:

> *The screams of dying citizens rang in Gordon's ears as he stood unarmed at the top of the palace steps. A party of Arabs, their "bloodstained white robes [swinging] brightly in the dim light," swept up to him and halted.*
> *"Where is the Mahdi?" demanded Gordon. They made no reply.*
> *"Where is the Mahdi?" he asked again.*
> *This time, the leading sheik answered with a shrill scream: "Oh cursed one, your time is come!" and drove his spear through Gordon's body.*

---

[56] Interestingly, Lord Kitchener, Field Marshal, reconqueror of Sudan in 1898 and one of the greatest military leaders of the British Empire in the late 19th century and early 20th century, was also homosexual.

It was believed that Gordon was beheaded and then hacked to pieces, despite the Mahdi's specific prohibition against it — the Mahdi had preferred to keep him alive and convert him to Islam — that would have been seen by most Muslims as a great achievement. According to Lytton Strachey in the book *Eminent Victorians* (1918), "When Gordon's head was unwrapped at the Mahdi's feet, he ordered the head transfixed between the branches of a tree where all who passed it could look in disdain, children could throw stones at it and the hawks of the desert could sweep and circle above." It was only two days later that relief troops arrived.

Gordon's death led to the downfall of long-time Prime Minister, William Gladstone, and it was only in 1898 that the British recaptured Sudan. The Mahdi's shrine was destroyed, his ashes disinterred and thrown unceremoniously into the Nile. No one knew where Gordon's remains were.

»»»»»

In May 2008, however, Oudurman once again entered world headlines when the Darfur rebels attacked and almost took over this Khartoum suburb. I was there a week later, not so much to look for burnt-out buildings, vehicles or bodies, but to attend the weekly ceremony of the whirling dervishes. Under the grand greenish domes of the Hamed el Nil Mosque, built to commemorate a Muslim sufi (or mystic) buried here, I had a good time watching the whirling dervishes dance around in trance, proclaiming their love for Allah.

The dervishes were joined by a few hundred spectators holding hands around them in a big circle, singing sacred songs, interspersed with choruses that included "Allah" repeated again and again. Members of the religious orders marched with green and red banners, chanting "*La illaha illallah*" ("The is no God but Allah"). By chanting many of Allah's names and key Islamic phases, and singing and dancing at the same time, they believed that they would be able to enter a state of ecstatic communication with Allah.

I had imagined that the session would resemble the well-choreographed order of Turkey's famous sufis which I had seen on video. Instead, the

Sudanese version was more spontaneous, rowdy, and involved mass audience participation. It also contained what seemed to me a vigorous African beat, with lots of hip swinging and swaggering. There was some whirling around by individual sufis, most of whom were dressed in red and green robes. They certainly did not whirl around in the "synchronized" Turkish fashion. Some of the sufis were dancing around in semi-trance, perhaps in a form of ecstasy while proclaiming their love for Allah, and certainly without the possessed looks found among tanki-shaman priests in Singapore.

Everyone I met was friendly. "Welcome, welcome," many exclaimed when they saw me. "Take any photo you want. Make yourself at home. We Sudanese are your friends." I was treated to tea, coffee and assorted snacks. "Stand there, or here," they said, "for better view." Or "Come meet our sheikh", or "Meet the big man".

I spoke to the locals about the rebel attacks. They said many of the rebels were young people in their late teens, who were very tactical when driving more than 700km from Darfur to Oudurman, but did not quite know their way once in Greater Khartoum. They did not harm civilians, merely asking people the way to either the air base, broadcasting station, strategic bridges or presidential palace. Eventually, they were all decimated by government soldiers without any great effort. It was all about politics, and ordinary civilians just wanted to get on with life without getting involved. Who knew what devil these rebels represented. After all, the current regime, brutal and

A whirling sufi
at Hamed el Nil,
Oudurman.

nasty though it might have been, had ruled for 18 years, and was the devil that everyone knew.

»»»»»

On Day Two in Khartoum, I had a frustrating wild goose chase trying to get the alien registration required of all foreigners within three days of arrival in Sudan. My hotel seemed clueless and gave me neither the requisite letters nor pointers. I followed *Lonely Planet's* instructions, going to an office near the Blue Nile. But upon reaching there, no one seemed to know where the office was, and asked me to go to another office on the next street.

Over at that office, people were perplexed and they asked me to go to yet another place, this time far from the city centre, at a place called "Buri". They got me into a taxi and told the driver to take me there. At Buri, they said the place was for long-stay visitors or those who needed to extend visas. They told me to get the hotel's official letter certifying I was staying there and go to another office downtown near the US Embassy. I was very frustrated. I felt like a headless chicken not knowing what to do or where to do the necessary.

I returned to the hotel asking for the requisite official letter and they told me to return in a few hours' time for the letter. When I came back at the appointed time, they got me the required letter and I managed to get them to send a junior staff member to go with me to the Aliens Registration Office. We walked in 50°C heat, but unfortunately, the office was closing for the day when we arrived there at 1pm. They insisted that I submit the registration the next day, as the cashier was out. I felt like grabbing the machine gun from the soldier guarding the place, and sending all of them to meet Allah as martyrs of a mad idol-worshipper from the Far East.

»»»»»

I walked around Khartoum centre, checking out some souvenir shops — nothing special, mostly the generic trashy pyramids and pharaohnic trinkets one finds in Egypt at one fifth the price, and lots of crocodile skins and figurines made from ivory, the latter of which are illegal in accordance with the Convention on International Trade on Endangered Species ("CITES") and Interpol. Of course, wildlife conventions do not matter that much if the government has already been accused of genocide, massacres and encouraging the slavery of minority tribes.

I also passed by some hotels, all of which had very expensive rooms with some including all meals in the price — something very useful to a journalist covering dangerous places where coups and riots can mean that restaurants are suddenly shut without warning. These hotels can do the alien registration for the busy guest, but charge US$60 for work that would cost only US$44 if one appeared at the ARO himself, like I did.

I wanted to visit the National Museum, Ethnographical Museum and the Republican Palace Museum, but they were all closed, for reasons not entirely clear. I suspected it had something to do with the strategic locations of these museums which became critical in a crisis or war situation. In fact, the soldiers at the Republican Palace Museum were very nasty and shouted angrily at me, demanding that I return to the other side of the road. The museum, which appeared to be housed in a decommissioned Anglican cathedral, was just next to the presidential palace and perhaps they were nervous about a rebel attack.

Egyptian-style statues of Nubian kings at the National Museum.

Once again, I spoke to a few friendly private security guards who were graduates or undergraduates. I suspect the Filipino counter-staff I saw at Khartoum Airport got paid more than these uni-grad security guards but I bet these guards might need a mind-bogglingly massive change of cultural outlook and attitude towards work and life in order to provide the same level of service at the airport.

A Christian South Sudanese lad — whose skin was so dark that it shone — chatted to me while I walked around the city centre and he whispered about his access to liquor — Johnny Walker, Vodka, French Reds and Whites, maybe champagnes as well. Sudan is officially a dry country. Its leaders had come to power 18 years ago on the banner of upholding Islam and imposing Sharia law on all, thus provoking the escalation of the campaign by the Christian south to break away. But becoming dry, saving my liver and restoring my health was one of my reasons for leaving my previous job, and I was not about to risk getting stoned or whipped in public for transgression of this local law.

»»»»»

For a country of its size, it is not surprising that many of the ethnic groups outside Khartoum cannot identify with this modern day creation called The Sudan. In 1965, *Time Magazine*[57] wrote about the diversity of Sudan in an article about the rebellion that broke out among the southern tribes:

"To its 9th century invaders, it was Bilad al-Sudan—Land of the Blacks. To the 4,000,000 blacks who live on its southern flood plains, the name is a mockery. Ruled by harsh Arab masters for most of the past 200 years, the Sudanese Negroes are little more than primitive prisoners in their own land. Political rights have been denied them, education withheld, and they have managed to preserve their dignity only by clinging to their past. The tall, naked Dinkas still worship animal spirits and fear the evil eye. The fierce Nuer herdsmen still subsist on milk, termites and the blood of cattle. The stately Shilluks still spear lion and crocodile, still stand for hours, cranelike, on one foot."

---

[57] Bad Medicine, *Time Magazine*, 30 Jul 1965.

The conflict was brutal right from its beginning, as *Time* continued:

"... The Juba rebels ambushed a lone sergeant out for an evening stroll, sawed off the top of his head, emasculated him, and stuck the amputated part in his mouth. The Arab garrison went berserk. Its troops exploded into the street, firing wildly at everything that moved. They cordoned off the black districts along the Nile, sent four-man assassination parties down every street, setting fire to the thatched native huts and shooting down their occupants as they emerged. Many residents, caught between the advancing vengeance squads and the army cordon, threw themselves in panic into the Nile and were drowned. Unofficial death toll: 1,400.

The waves of reciprocal terrorism were just what the rebels had been waiting for. As thousands of black refugees fled the Sudan, leaders of the two southern parties showed up in Kenya and Uganda to try to line up all of black Africa against the Arabs. Charging that "the Khartoum government has embarked on deliberate genocide, "they demanded intervention by the U.N., the Red Cross and the Organization of African Unity to free the south from "foreign domination.""

Has anything changed?

» » » » »

To prove that I was a true-blue shopping-loving Singaporean, I headed for the Afra Mall, Sudan's only modern shopping mall, near the airport. (The Filipino receptionist at my hotel warned me not to expect too much). OK, I was also desperate for some decent food after days of oily hamburgers and kebabs in central Khartoum. A stretch near the airport had many restaurants indeed but they seemed to be serving fast food as well, though in a classier environment than the roadside eateries around Souk Arabiya.

I walked around the Turkish-run mall. Strange that they switched off the air-conditioning whereas I had imagined people would want to come here because of it. A case of potential business failure? The food court served overpriced food — US$10 to US$20 for a paper-box of sweet and sour pork or fried noodle. I refused to eat the same rubbishy fast food here at Singapore restaurant prices and with no functioning air-conditioning to boot.

Somewhat desperate for Chinese food, however, I hopped into a *bajaj* (a three-wheeled vehicle similar to a Thai tuk-tuk) asking for the Chinese Panda Restaurant, which I heard from Holiday Villa staff, was at the Amarat area. The *bajaj* driver, in order to grab my business, not only said that he knew the place but also that it cost only 5 Sudanese pounds (SDG 5, about US$2.25) which sounded fair if it were indeed nearby as what I was told.

However, he drove round and round a residential area not knowing where to go, and eventually drove me to a Mainland Chinese-run hospital. He asked me to ask the Chinese working there where Panda Restaurant was. I was very upset at not only the waste of time but also the unpleasantness of having to step into a huge hospital, not a place to hang around if one were merely looking for dinner. The Chinese staff and nurses here were not familiar with Khartoum. After all, this was perceived as a hardship posting where they aimed to make as much money as possible, and then return home. They would save money by cooking for themselves rather than eating out at pricey places meant for businessmen, diplomats and the Sudanese upper class. The instructions they gave were vague, and the driver had a hard time but eventually found the place.

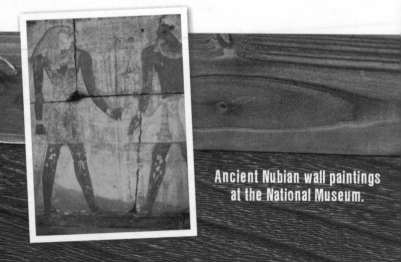

Ancient Nubian wall paintings at the National Museum.

I wanted to give him SDG5 as agreed but he demanded fifty instead. I was fired into anger by what seemed to be a ridiculous demand. I said the most I would give him was SDG10 because he had not only said earlier that he knew the place but that it cost SDG5. In fact, he had spoiled my mood by not only wasting a lot of time but also taking me to a hospital, which most traditional Chinese (oh, I'm beginning to think like a traditional Chinese — must be a sign of ageing) would find quite inauspicious. He was upset but could only fume away in Arabic. I had encountered too many of these Sudanese who either tried to cheat on fares, or genuinely couldn't understand my suggested fares in English and nodded even when they couldn't understand a word.

I wanted him to get into a pharmacy nearby with me so that I could find an English speaker — I thought pharmacists were probably better educated. He refused and we had a big quarrel in the street — arguing in our own languages and not understanding each other. A local who worked in the pharmacy came out and listened to both of us. He asked me to hand over SDG10 and he added SDG5 of his own, and the driver walked away with it. Problem resolved? This, however, also made me wonder if the driver had mispronounced earlier — perhaps he had asked for SDG15 but mispronounced it as SDG50, which really provoked and upset me.

I walked into the very pricey Chinese Panda restaurant and spent SDG33 for rather mediocre fried rice and beef with bamboo shoots and mushrooms. As I left the restaurant, I couldn't help but wonder if the unhappy taxi driver would be waiting for me outside with his friends, ready to take revenge. Not surprising at all, in a country full of guns, machetes and all sorts of dodgy, well-armed people. Maybe I shouldn't have argued over those amounts. Fortunately, nothing worse occurred. I hopped into a SDG10 taxi back to the hotel where I created yet another major inundation in the Al Nakhil Hotel. Strangely, like a flash flood in the desert, it happened quickly at night but the floor was dry as a bone by morning.

»»»»»

Day Three in Sudan and the deadline for alien registration was approaching. If I could not register by then, I would be in technical breach of Sudanese law. God knows what penalties there would be. Would it be caning or stoning by Sharia law? Or a sentence of 30 years in a Sudanese prison? Exile as an army labourer in Darfur? A bond-slave in an upper-class Khartoum household? Hmm…the last was probably less likely for they were probably used to the physically much stronger South Sudanese and Darfuris occasionally captured by the Arab pro-government janjaweed militias for sale in the underground slave market some said to be still operating in Khartoum today.

I set off for the Aliens Registration Office with the reception boy at 9am. The sun was very hot. Unfortunately, when we reached there, we couldn't submit the registration as the staff told us that they wanted a photocopy of the ID of the hotel owner, whose name appeared on the hotel's official letter. So we had to walk back to the hotel where at my insistence, they rang the owner to ask him to come to deal with the matter immediately.

I waited for a while and had to pester the hotel staff repeatedly before the hotel owner turned up. We went to the ARO again. After a confusing Arabic conversation between the hotel owner and stodgy-faced ARO bureaucrats, I was told that they didn't really need the ID copy but they wanted the hotel letter to be redrafted with the wordings required. Bloody

Early Christian wall frescoes of Nubia, National Museum.

bureaucrats who either didn't know what they were doing, or they wanted to test one's patience, or both! One of the junior officers even shrugged and admitted very honestly that, "in Sudan, different officials have different rules." We returned to the hotel. Can you believe it? They didn't have any computer at the hotel. The owner had to draft the letter with a pen, and then asked the reception guy to bring it to a nearby "business centre" to get it typed and printed.

By coincidence, a Yemeni businessman staying at the hotel also needed to get registered. So we went to the ARO again — my third time that morning. This time we managed to submit our applications. I was asked to return at 3pm to get the registration sticker to be pasted onto the passport to indicate due registration and pay the cashier (now out for lunch) SDG88 as registration fee. (This amount, about US$44, was on top of the US$100 visa fee I paid to the Sudanese Embassy in Cairo).

I returned to the ARO at 3pm and by 3:30pm got my registration sticker on my passport. Hurrah! Halleluiah! Allahu Akbar! Huat La! Huat La!

» » » » »

I went to the amazing National Museum, a wonderful depository of artifacts from 5,000 years of Sudanese history; was very inspiring after three days of visits to the distinguished Alien Registration Office. Here, huge reassembled Egyptian-Nubian-Meroe temples greeted the visitor in the museum courtyard. The ground floor of the main building was full of carvings, pottery, grave objects, mummy cases and all sorts of things from the old Sudanese-Egyptian kingdoms, while the second floor was devoted to old Nubian-Christian fresco art. After the collapse of the Meroe Empire in 370AD, it split into smaller states which became Christian. The heart of these kingdoms was in Nubia in what is today northern Sudan. During its Christian period (before it became Muslim in the 7th century after the Arab conquest), the Nubian Church, which was linked to the Egyptian Coptic Church, produced many great pieces of art, which can be found in the National Museum. Whilst Nubian artists were painting the walls of desert cathedrals and palaces, much of Europe was a region of economic and political chaos — the Roman Empire had just collapsed, barbarian tribes were on the march across the continent and Christian monks were having a hard time persuading European tribes to give up human sacrifice and pray to an unfamiliar monotheistic god. What a different world it was then.

In the evening, a local contact invited me to a private party in an expatriate's house in Khartoum 2, a district near the airport popular with foreigners. (In conflict zones, foreigners tend to live near the airport so that they can organize a speedy evacuation if a crisis breaks out). The party was very international. There were a group of Egyptian/Brazilian/Lebanese telecommunications engineers, a Pakistani banker together with his family and Filipino maid, a Dutch diplomat, a group of South African aircraft engineers and Syrian business executives, among others. It reminded me of the London parties among expats there, with soft drinks, BBQ and finger food. It was earlier whispered that there could be wine and liquor as well, though I did not see any. There were even a few very westernized Sudanese ladies who dressed like the party girls one sees on Lebanese or Egyptian MTVs. A number of partygoers danced the salsa as well. This was no big deal anywhere else in the world, but seemed scandalously wild by my perceptions of what the Middle East was like. An eye-opener indeed.

Everyone I spoke to was amazed that I was a tourist. Khartoum might not be like Iraq today or Saigon in 1975, but flying in a few days after the last rebel attack was something notable. Some of them probably thought that I was a spy, or a purveyor of fine guns, rockets or even chemical weapons, as we did joke about it. Who knows, some of them might really have been, too. I told them that I spent half of the last three days getting my alien registration and I would be leaving in 24 hours. My most vivid image of Sudan was the ARO.

A few of those present at the party convinced me that I should visit Meroe. I rang a local contact, and negotiated for a car and a driver for US$250 excluding four entrance fees of US$10 each. In a country where car owners could rent vehicles to UN agencies and NGOs for limitless amounts, especially during a crisis, the lone tourist like me had little bargaining power.

»»»»»

Day Four and my final full day in Sudan. Sherif, my driver for the day, turned up at my hotel. He would drive me to three major archeological sites in Sudan — Naga, Musawarat and Meroe. Naga's avenue of rams in front of its ancient temple and Musawarat's Temple of Lions were interesting though not wildly exciting. They were located near wells and there were nomads around them, which made them all the more picturesque. But anyone who had been to Egypt would have seen many grander structures and carvings. The two sites were also located off the asphalt road and it would be quite an effort to get there without one's own transport (which would also have been very expensive).

Meroe, however, was amazing. A valley of over 30 pyramids in the desert, totally deserted, with me as the only visitor for the day. The Egyptian pyramids were much grander but one would have had to share them with thousands of tourists, an army of souvenir touts and assorted conmen and tricksters. The wind-swept valley that is Meroe felt eerie. I could almost imagine the ghosts of ancient Sudanese-Egyptian pharaohs, priests and court attendants around me.

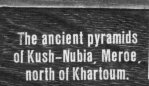

The ancient pyramids of Kush–Nubia, Meroe, north of Khartoum.

Sand dunes were everywhere, even pressing the modern wooden doors of the pyramids (installed by the Sudanese Government some years ago) tight. I managed to push one open and found myself staring at amazing carvings of an Egyptian jackal-headed god mummifying a king, plus those of various ancient deities and scenes of everyday life.

Could you imagine the sense of excitement and awe as I stood there staring at the carvings, almost frozen with amazement, with a kind of Indiana-Jones-feel about the whole place? Yet my goose bumps suddenly stood up and my instinct told me I had to leave the dead and the gods to their peace. After all, the 50-plus degree heat was simply too much. Although I had considered staying till 7pm for sunset, we decided to leave at 5:30pm for Khartoum instead.

As the sun set over the fine desert dunes, gathering winds began to howl across the arid plains nearby. The dying light blanketed the monuments and mounds of stones with a soft, yellow glow, which soon turned orange and then magenta, before a sharp descent into deep dull brown and darkness. I could, or I imagined that I could, still make out the shadows of the corpses of a long-gone empire, even as we sped towards Khartoum.

Iran: Many Lands (May 2008)

Iran of Ancient Kings of Kings

"The Great God is Ahura Mazda, who created this earth, who created yonder sky, who created man, who created happiness for man, who made Xerxes king, the one king of many, the one master of many. I am Xerxes, the Great King, King of Kings, King on this great earth even far off King Darius' son, an Achaemenid. Proclaims Xerxes, the King: By the will of Ahura Mazda, this Gateway of All Nations I built. Much other beautiful was made within this Persepolis, which I constructed and which my father constructed. Whatever is beautiful, all that we built by the will of Ahura Mazda ... may Ahura Mazda protect me, my kingdom, and what was built by me, and what was built by my father."[58]

The inscriptions proclaiming the ancient king's greatness in three ancient languages — Old Persian, Elamite[59] and Babylonian, were chiseled high above the huge statues of man-bulls — mythological creatures with the head of a stern bearded warrior wearing a Persian horned feather-cap and the muscular body of a bull. For 2,500 years, these statues have stood guard at the Gateway of All Nations, the entrance leading to the magnificent Apadana Palace of the Kings of the Persian Empire, at the royal city of Persepolis.

It was through these gates that ambassadors from numerous subject nations came to pay tribute to the Great King Xerxes, whose name meant "ruler of heroes", who was the reunifier of the first world empire history

---

[58] Heidemarie Kokh, *Persepolis and its Surroundings*, 2006, p 25.
[59] The Elamites were an ancient race which once dominated what is today Iran, before the Persians conquered the land.

had ever known (it was originally established by his great uncle, Cyrus the Great). Mind you, this was not the sadistic, body-piercing god-king leading a monstrously, evil and cruel horde (as portrayed in Hollywood's *300*) against a band of three hundred brave and chivalrous Spartans; but the just ruler of an empire, a re-unifier, a rigorous enforcer of law and justice, crusher of Egyptian and Babylonian rebels (though he could not crush the rebellious Greeks led by the Spartans), a patron of civilization, architecture and the arts, and the great builder of Persepolis.

> *No, Persia wasn't all depressing. Beautiful Isfahan and Shiraz. Wicked, pompous, oily British. Nervous, cunning, corrupt and delightful Persian bloody bastards. Opium no good. Persian vodka made of beetroot, like stimulating sockjuice, very enjoyable. Beer full of glycerine and pips. Women veiled or unveiled ugly, or beautiful and entirely inaccessible, or hungry. The lovely camels who sit on their necks and smile.*
> — Dylan Thomas, Letter to J.M. Brinnin, 12 April 1951

There are many Irans. There is Iran, the land of ancient civilizations, centre of the first world empire stretching from Greece and Egypt in the west to the Indus River and the gates of China in the east, cradle of Persian culture, and land of great poets — Ferdosi, Omar Khayyam, Hafez and Sa'di — who wrote of wine, heroes and their women. There is another Iran: The Iran of the Ayatollahs, of *chador* and *hejab*, the kill-joy state that bans singing, dancing, dating and tea-houses, of *jihad* and religious martyrs, the alleged state-sponsor of terrorism and a US-declared member of the Axis of Evil. Which is the Iran you know?

I wanted to find out for myself, and so I flew into Teheran in late May 2008. As I have heard from many friends and would confirm for myself, Iran, I dare say, is one of my favourite countries in the world. The Iranian people are incredibly hospitable and would probably win first prize if a contest of the world's friendliest people were ever held.

IKA, Imam Khomeini International Airport, named after Iran's late leader of the Islamic Revolution of 1978, is very modern. Built by a Turkish-

Austrian consortium not too long ago, it has a chequered history. The Iranian Defence Ministry, citing national security, refused to let planes land. The consortium was eventually forced to hand the airport over to the Iranian Defence Ministry despite a binding contract signed with the Iranian Government.

The 30-km journey to the suburbs of Tehran took only 20–30 minutes by car but the next 30 minutes was spent stuck in Tehran's notorious traffic congestion. Tehran is a metropolis of 12 million people — some say as many as 20 million — nobody really knows, but the city is an enormous urban sprawl as far as the eye can see.

I walked around the surrounding areas, had a quick late lunch at a kebab place. The weather was nice and cool. The high Alborz Mountains, which provide Tehran with plenty of water and a pleasant climate in this largely dry, desert land, still had traces of snow on its summit.

People seemed friendly. Strangers greeted me with a simple "Hello", or "Welcome to Iran!" The unfortunate thing was, few people spoke English, perhaps the result of prolonged international isolation. Ironically, it was the older generation who had lived through the Shah's pro-American days who could speak better English than the younger ones. Inevitably, conversations were short and limited to "How are you?" and "Where are you from?" Some teenagers were so intrigued to see me that they took photos of me with their mobile phones.

Whatever it was, at least Iran had not followed Libya, which according to sources, now requires those in school to learn African languages such as Swahili and Hausa, in line with Gaddafi's African Unity Policy. I wonder what that would do to the Libyans' linguistic ability in 20 years' time.

I walked towards central Tehran to investigate flights to the south, and within minutes, booked a flight to Kerman in southeast Iran. Domestic flights in Iran are dirt cheap — only about US$43 for this 1-hour flight across 1,300km of this large country.

The Iranian government subsidizes fuel costs, which is why plane tickets as well as gasoline are so cheap. Although among the top oil producers in the world, Iran had not benefited from the oil bonanza. Iran had under-invested in petroleum and oil refining industries over the last 30 years (since the Islamic Revolution). It did not have the capacity to refine the oil it produced and had to export it and then import refined fuel at a much higher price — 40% of its domestic consumption had to be imported.

Worse, the Iranian government had been subsidizing domestic consumption of fuel — gasoline in this country costs only US$0.08 per liter whereas mineral water costs US$0.11 per liter. With the huge jump in oil price, the total amount of subsidies the Iranian government had committed to has surged to unimaginable amounts. Given that very little had been invested in non-oil sectors, there is simply no other source of revenue to offset the huge increase in government deficit. Inflation had already risen to significant levels — unofficial estimates were at well above 20% per year — and popular discontent would further increase if the government increased fuel prices. In fact, when fuel rationing was announced in 2007, riots and arson broke out immediately across the country.

» » » »

Kerman could not be more different from Tehran. With only 300,000 inhabitants, Kerman is a sleepy provincial centre in the southeast desert waste of Iran. Many people here wear the *shawar kameez*, the traditional dress of Afghans and Pakistanis — not surprising, as Kerman is not too far away from the borders with Afghanistan and Pakistan.

Kerman and the lands further east are considered by some to be the wild east of Iran. The press reported about police skirmishes with bandits in which many people were killed, and the kidnapping of foreigners by local drug lords and Baluchi tribals unhappy with the government. But the streets looked peaceful and perfectly normal. In fact, Kerman is growing in importance as a regional centre, and with that, the appearance of many cars, flashy shop-fronts and tacky new buildings. It is a very decent and normal-looking "wild east" — if the term still remains appropriate.

I visited Kerman's bazaar which is not quite the kind of labyrinth typical of large Middle Eastern cities. I felt really good here after the mess that was Sudan. I also visited the Masjid Jamee (Friday Mosque) where I was a little apprehensive about taking photos especially in presence of worshippers, but people were so friendly. Many said, "Welcome to Iran. Thank you."

Billboards like this are found across Iran. The government continues to try to rally the population through patriotic images of the Iran–Iraq War, which ended in 1988.

After a few months in the Middle East, I have concluded that Libyan guys, with their keen Italian dress sense and penchant for fine cutting, are the best-dressed Middle Easterners. No matter how well the Gulf Arabs dress, their oversized bellies spoil it all. As for Egyptian and Iranian men, they appear to be stuck firmly in the Elvis era.

In Iran, women are required by law to abide by the *hejab* dress code, which means that they must never reveal their hair, shoulders, body and limbs. In many places such as shrines, they must wear the *chador* which is an all-encompassing black robe. Foreign women must also comply with such laws or risk scrutiny or even arrest by the police. But 30 years after the Revolution, Iranian girls are constantly testing the *hejab* limits in various ways. Many wore finely cut pants with elements of the latest Parisian designs. Yes, designer *hejabs*. I was told that wearing black jeans was now the in-thing and I noticed many of these. Till the next crackdown, *inshallah*.

At every street corner were huge billboards showing the faces of young men. These were the war dead from the bitter Iran-Iraq War of 1980–1988. Proclaimed as martyrs, their portraits could be found across the cities, towns and villages of Iran. Two decades might have lapsed since the war ended but the government continues to remind the people constantly of this terrible conflict, and some wonder if this is to boost the legitimacy of its rule.

»»»»»

The people at my hotel reception were intrigued about my adventures in Sudan: not so much about the places I visited or about the war and politics there, but more about any adventure of a sexual nature. "How are Sudanese women in bed?" they asked. I tried to divert their prurience by saying something lamely unrelated, "Iranian women are beautiful and self-confident." The reception guy shook his head and said, "But Iranian women are very difficult." He raised his pointed finger to his throat and did the universal throat-cutting sign. "You could lose your life if you were not careful." A few years ago, a German businessman was sentenced to death for having sex with an Iranian woman, though in the wake of international shock and protests, he was fined and deported.

»»»»»

I got onto a bus for a five-hour journey across dramatic but bleak, dry desert landscape flanked by bare peaks, to the city of Yazd, west of Kerman. The bus played a video of what appeared to be a ghost movie. A fellow Iranian passenger pointed to the handsome, charming actor and said, "That's Iran's best actor, Muhammad Reza Golzar." Previously a musician, Golzar is now the Brad Pitt of Iran. An Iranian girl later told me, "He is cute, talented and has stolen the hearts of many Iranian girls. Who cares about acting alone?" The world is the same all over, even in this aspect.

Upon arrival in Yazd, I went to the Silk Road Hotel recommended by Singaporean friends. This was a nice traditional house with a courtyard where travelers hung around. Unfortunately, the hotel was full but they asked me to go to the Oriental Hotel on the opposite side of the road (it was run by the same people.) The Oriental, too, had a great courtyard and it was full as well. The reception guy here took me to the Oasis Hotel 50 meters down the road, (the same people were in-charge there, too) and had a similar layout. Wonderful, so far so good.

I returned to the Oriental to have a late lunch at the rooftop restaurant. It had a wonderful view of the skyline of Yazd — amazing blue domes

The current Supreme Leader, Ayatollah Khamenei, with Ayatollah Khomeini. The current leadership attempts to draw parallels with a more idealistic era.

with intricate geometric patterns, slander phallic-looking minarets soaring to the skies; strange-looking wind towers that provide ventilation to the houses of this otherwise oppressively hot oasis town; and tall, hauntingly bare khaki-coloured mountains flanking the edge of this UNESCO-listed world heritage city.

The Oriental served great food, much more than kebab, kebab and kebab, which was the usual choice in most Iranian eating-places — and they prepared the food quickly, too — all within 15 minutes. They knew the norm elsewhere in the world and what tourists loved to see. Many places in the Middle East and Africa take at least half an hour for the food to arrive; that includes the time needed to buy the ingredients required (sorry, no refrigerator to keep food bought in advance, or because the power does not work half the time), and prepare the food, apart from actually cooking it. Restaurants in most of these places simply have neither the customer volume to justify preparing food in advance nor the experience to understand what travelers want.

The Oriental was also a great place to meet cool people on long-term travel. A few were travelling for as long as three years. Here I met, among others, a German couple who had driven from Germany to India and were now making the return journey; and a Brazilian couple on a three-year road trip round the world — yes, they had driven here all the way from Brazil, albeit hopping onto a few cargo boats between continents.

I also met Raj, a London lawyer of Indian descent. An Oxford graduate, he was a linguist who went on to law school and had worked in major City law firms dealing with capital market transactions before moving on to a large American outfit. He spoke many languages, among them Hindi, Gujarati, French, German, Russian, Mandarin (after half a year in Hangzhou, he writes better Chinese than I do), and Spanish, in addition to English. For this two-week holiday, he spent a week studying Farsi. Over the next few days, I would be amazed at how fluently he communicated in Farsi and the attention he received from Iranians as a result.

I explored the old town of Yazd and its narrow streets. I visited Alexander's Prison, a depression within an ancient madressa where Alexander the Great had supposedly founded a prison. Here, I met rather brave Iranian girls who, despite oppressive gender rules forbidding socializing with the opposite sex, chatted with me and allowed me to take their pictures.

Despite the various restrictions the Islamic Republic imposed on Iranian women, such as the cruel requirement to wear the *hejab* which is one of the most impracticable and crippling forms of clothing ever invented, and various social restrictions that limited Iranian women's social circles (for instance, they were not allowed to be in the company of an unrelated male without the presence of other people), I have found Iranian women rather daring when approaching and talking to me on the streets. Some of them spoke fairly good English and allowed me to take photos of them. I attributed this to the self-confidence and independence acquired through education. There were more women than men in Iranian universities and the long-standing emphasis on education among the Iranians had probably brushed aside what religious inhibitions might have existed.

In contrast, Arab women in the other Middle East countries, despite not having major legal restrictions on social behavior or dressing, were a lot more meek and wary of foreigners. Few had the confidence to even greet or engage in small talk with foreigners. Fewer Arab women go to higher education and the social conservatism that prevailed prevented them from displaying any significant degree of independence.

Walking along Iranian streets, I sometimes found people staring at me, and occasionally even exchanging eye signals. I wandered if this was due to curiosity about foreigners after years of isolation, or something more carnal in nature. One should always be careful with respect to the latter. I mentioned earlier the German sentenced to death and later deported for sexual relations with an Iranian woman. Last year, images of the public hanging of two teenagers for their homosexuality shocked the world — it is unbelievable that such atrocities could still happen in the 21st century.

»»»»»

In Yazd, I met Hamid, a 19-year-old Afghan refugee. Tall, talkative and handsome with short, brown-dyed hair, Hamid was born in Iran of Afghani Tajik parents. In fact, his parents were born in Tajikistan, taken over to Afghanistan and then on to Iran as children when the Soviets invaded Afghanistan in 1979.

Despite having lived in Iran all his life, Hamid, like most Afghans in a similar situation, remains an Afghan citizen. With no Iranian citizenship, these Afghans are often at the mercy of Iranian police and bureaucrats; they cannot go to Iranian universities without paying exorbitant school fees and they cannot be employed at many jobs.

Hamid has had a tough life, yet he has learned to speak English, French and a bit of German, all from tourists who frequent the handicraft shop where he occasionally worked. Iran might be the darling of travelers, but Hamid could not wait to get out of Iran — he had been offered a scholarship to study in Germany and was waiting for his visa. Hamid was even arrested by the police once and badly beaten for uttering negative things about Iran. The visa he was waiting for was his chance to get out and reinvent himself. I wished him luck.

Hamid was the first of many Afghans I was to meet in Iran. Every one of them probably had a heart-rending tale to tell. I cannot help but feel fortunate about my own circumstances whenever I hear such stories.

» » » » »

On a few occasions, I came across people who had oriental features. I realized who they were when someone asked if I were a Hazara, a Shia tribe in Afghanistan who were supposedly descendants of Genghis Khan's Mongol army. The Hazara have East Asian looks and live in Bamiyan Valley in Afghanistan's Hazarajat region where the giant Buddhas used to be before the Taleban destroyed them. From then on, I occasionally told people I was Afghani-Hazara.

» » » » »

From Yazd, I went on a day trip to two Zoroastrian sites — Chak Chak and the Tower of Silence near Cham in the suburbs of Yazd.

Zoroastrianism is the ancient religion of Iran. Founded 2,500 years ago by Zoroaster, this was one of the first religions of the world that proposed the concept of a single god, a concept later adopted by Judaism, Christianity and Islam. Zoroastrians worship fire as the symbol of their god, Ahura Mazda, and an eternal flame is always kept burning in their temples, sometimes known as fire temples. Many Zoroastrians would tell you that the flame in their temple had been burning for 2,500 years, since the days of the great Persian Empire, and passed from temple to temple, till today.

The religion is often represented by layers on the wings of a bird, which symbolise purity of thought, word and action. They believe in the purity of elements, hence the dead must never pollute the sacred soil or the atmosphere. As a result, they neither bury nor cremate their dead. Instead, the dead were brought to "towers of silence" where they were eaten by vultures, an ancient practice that makes sound theological sense but sends shivers down most other people's spines. In the 20th century, however, this practice became illegal in Iran and the towers were no longer used. Most Zoroastrians bury their dead today, in graves lined with concrete, to prevent contamination of the soil.

Zoroastrianism was the state religion of Iran until the Islamic armies of Arabia conquered the region. Today, 150,000 people continue to practise this ancient religion, of which a small number still reside in Iran

Zoroastrian wall hanging, with images of the sacred flame and the prophets.

(mostly around Yazd). Over half of the other followers live in Mumbai, India, where they call themselves Parsees. A few Parsee families live in Singapore where they are wealthy businessmen. The Parsees are descendants of Zoroastrian refugees who fled Iran for India when the Arabs invaded Iran, bringing Islam along with them. Today, the Parsees face the formidable challenge of reversing a drastic decline in their numbers, the result of their ancient rules of marriage, which discourages marriage with non-Parsees.

Chak Chak is an important Zoroastrian shrine 50km northwest of Yazd. Located in the mountains bordering the Dasht-e Lut Desert, the setting of the shrine and its surrounding desert plains was spectacularly breathtaking. It is certainly a location that inspires the religious with thoughts of the creations of the omnipotent almighty.

Cham is a small Zoroastrian farming village located about 15km outside Yazd. Whilst Zoroastrian women conform to the *hejab* dress code of the Islamic Republic, they never wear *chadors*. Instead they wear embroidered scarves of different colours which come closest to the colourful vibrancy of their ancestors who were the elite of ancient Persia.

The ruins of the ancient towers of silence and associated religious and ceremonial buildings continue to stand in Yazd and its surrounding areas, often in the most dramatic landscapes and setting. The towers often resemble citadels perched on cliff sides or small hills, overlooking the plains beyond, silent witnesses to the endlessness and omnipresence of the almighty.

Picturesque in their eroded state, these eerie towers were often built on the foundations of earlier Zoroastrian buildings and one could almost imagine the kings, priests and soldiers of ancient Persia still wandering amongst these ruins.

» » » » »

From Yazd, Raj and I got on a bus to Shiraz, during which we passed some amazing landscapes. Iran is a huge and beautiful country, with a diversity of geographical features and landscapes. Whilst large parts of the country are covered by the desert, the presence of wetter microclimatic regions, high mountains, natural underground water reservoirs and a whole network of ancient man-made underground irrigation canals that harness what nature has provided, allow the country to have enough water for its many fertile river valleys and oases.

Ultimately, it is Iran's huge and flourishing agricultural sector that supports an unusually large population of 75 million inhabitants. On the bus journey, we passed through many wonderfully fertile oases and valleys, flanked by the shocking contrasts of bare dry mountain ranges and merciless brown desert plateaus.

We reached Shiraz at 6pm, as correctly predicted by the bus company. Iranian bus companies are probably among the most honest in the developing world at telling their customers how long their journeys would take — perhaps even more so than those doing the Singapore-Malaysia route!

Located in southern Iran, Shiraz is a busy, bustling city of more than a million inhabitants. Its streets were crowded with vehicles, people and

Friendly Iranians
in a mosque.

merchandise that spilled over from the city's many shops. Like all large Iranian cities, it was almost perilous crossing the streets. There was the usual suicide bomber traffic — cars that increased their speed when they saw pedestrians attempting to cross. They would only slow down when it looked as though they were about to run down the pedestrians. But if one did not attempt to step forward, there was no way these cars would even slow down at all.

Some Iranians boasted that Iranians were the world's best drivers because they could drive in such wild traffic. I have heard the same nonsense from drivers in China, Egypt and Libya — typical third-world excuses for bad driving and lousy road ethics. (Singaporean drivers are awful but not quite as suicidal) During my stay in Iran, I saw numerous accidents and wreckages. Countries like this have appalling accident rates and unless they change their attitude and increase police supervision, nothing will improve.

»»»»»

The Persians are the Asiatic Frenchmen. They are good poets, courteous, and of tolerably refined taste. They are not rigorous followers of Islam; and they allow their own voluptuous tendencies a pretty latitudinarian interpretation of the Koran.

—Thomas de Quincey, Translation of Kant on *National Character in Relation to the Sense of the Sublime and Beautiful,* 1824

Shiraz is one of Iran's greatest and most famous classical cities (but of course, Esfahan is the most famous one). From the time of the Arab conquest, through the Mongol and Timurid periods followed by the 18th century Zand dynasty during which Shiraz was the capital, the city flourished under the patronage of great foreign and local rulers. Shiraz became known as the cradle and heartland of ancient and mediaeval Persian culture.

In fact, the word "Persian" came from the word "Fars", which is the name of the province of which Shiraz is the capital today. The Iranians also use the word "Pars" or "Parsian" to mean Fars and Farsian — the latter which

I initially thought was "Parisian" misspelled. But given the sophistication of Persian classical and mediaeval culture, Parisian might well have been an appropriate word.

During its golden age, Shiraz was renowned as the city of wine and poets. The shiraz, which fills wine cellars all over the world, came from here. European merchants have long stayed in this city, exporting this wonderful grape and the wine produced from it, to the world over. Unfortunately, wine has been forbidden in Iran since the Islamic Revolution. A long heritage of wine growing and appreciation dating back to the days of the Persian Empire more than 2,500 years ago was washed down the drain.

Wine was the object of appreciation for many great poets; among them, two of old Persia's greatest, Hafez (1324–1389) and Sa'di (1207–1291), who lived here. Wine, women and the good things of life — these appear in the many works of these two poets, and their tombs in Shiraz are popular places of reverence and outings for ordinary Iranians. The Farsi language (aka Persian or the "language of Fars") is a poetic and romantic one — an image somehow inconsistent with the cold, heartless image of a fundamentalist Iran known to much of the world today.

At the tomb of Hafez, we saw Iranian families crowding around the grave of their revered poet: a father holding his young daughter's hand, touching the flamboyantly carved calligraphy on the tomb's surface as if the wisdom and creativity of the mediaeval poet that resided in those words would somehow come alive; a young couple stood nearby, almost certainly married or else they would have been in breach of the laws of the Islamic Republic since dating without the presence of other relatives is strictly forbidden — their hands locked together most lovingly, their eyes melted in each other's stares, drawing inspiration from the poet's Divan. Raj could not help but recite a line from a copy of the *Divan-e Hafez* he bought at the bookshop here. He should definitely hold a monthly public recital of Persian Poetry in London after the trip.

We looked for the teahouse mentioned in *Lonely Planet*, but unfortunately found it closed. We were told that many teahouses have been closed in recent years by the henchmen of the Islamic Republic, for teahouses were alleged to be meeting places for unmarried men and women, and thus places where scandalous and sacrilegious pursuits took place. Besides, too many men smoked waterpipes in these "*chaykhunehs*", instead of devoting more time to the study of the *Quran*. Such idle pleasures could not be allowed to take place and together with them, other idle and un-Islamic activities such as dancing and singing.

We visited the Citadel of Shiraz, which has an interesting exhibition of old photos of the city and municipal life. It was remarkable how similar the costumes and headdresses of the 19th/early 20th century were to those of townsmen in the old Central Asian khanates and cities of Kokand, Khiva, Bukhara and Samarkand in the same period. This, together with the obvious Persian architecture (especially the intricate and elaborate rectangular gateways of mosques) of these great cities and the fact that these cities used to speak Persian (instead of Uzbek as claimed by the modern-day government of Uzbekistan), is further evidence of the extent of the Persian cultural sphere in most of Central Asia.

We explored the labyrinth that is old Shiraz, as well as the many grand old mosques including the Masjed-e Vakil (the Regent's Mosque) and Emamzadeh-ye Ebne-e Hamze, the mausoleum of the nephew of the seventh Shiite imam. The latter was magnificent, for it had a huge dome resembling a tulip bulb, complete with intricate geometric patterns, and its interior was a treasure house of glasswork — its inner walls were covered with thousands of small mirrors, reflecting light at different angles

The wind towers of Yazd, the amazing oasis city in the desert.

and intensity. The devout might well think he was at the gateway of Allah's promised paradise.

The entrance of the main buildings contained a long account of the story of the imam's nephew, who settled here with his followers and lived anonymously and most virtuously to escape the persecution of the Sunnis. They were discovered one day and massacred to the last man. When beheaded, the head of the imam's nephew fell onto his outstretched palms. The head shouted *"Allahu Akbar"* (God is great), and the headless torso walked a few steps before collapsing to the ground. Today, his tomb has become a shrine where the devout pray and hope for their prayers to be answered.

≫ ≫ ≫ ≫

Darius the Great King, King of Kings, King of Lands, the son of Hystaspes, an Achaemenid. Proclaims Darius, the King: This kingdom which I hold, from the Scythians who are beyond Sogdiana, from there as far as Ethiopia, from India, from there as far as Lydia, Ahura Mazda the greatest of the gods bestowed upon me. Me may Ahura Mazda protect and my royal house.

— Inscription, Apadana Palace, Persepolis[60]

The first great empire in what is today Iran was that of the Elamites who lived in the southwest where they fought constantly against the Babylonians and Assyrians. Next came the nomadic early Persians who gradually replaced the Elamites as masters of the land.

However, it was during the reign of Cyrus the Great that the great Persian Empire was established, when he conquered territories ranging from Greece in the west to the Indus River (in today's Pakistan) to the east[61].

---

[60] Heidemarie Kokh, *Persepolis and its Surroundings*, 2006, p 31.
[61] Cyrus was eventually killed fighting the Massagetae, a tribe in what is today southern Kazakhstan. According to the great Roman historian, Herodotus, Cyrus invaded the territory of the fiercely nomadic Massagetaes after their queen, Tomyris, rejected Cyrus' offer of marriage. When he learnt that the Massagetaes were not familiar with wine and its intoxicating effects, he tricked them into capturing a camp full of wine. The Massagetaes drank themselves silly, whereupon Cyrus launched a sudden attack which led to the death of Spargapises, son of Tomyris. The queen vowed vengeance, and defeated the Persians in a massive battle in which Cyrus was killed. Tomyris then decapitated Cyrus and dipped his head in a vessel of blood as a sacrifice to her son.

The great empire-builder became king in 559 BC — four years after the birth of Siddhartha Gautama, later known as the Buddha, in a palace in what is southern Nepal today, near the Indian border; three years after the death of Nebuchadnezzar II, king of Babylon, builder of the famous Gardens and the conqueror of Jerusalem who sent the Jews to exile for the first time; and eight years before the birth of Confucius, China's greatest sage

He established his capital in Shush, the old capital of the Elamites, but also stayed at the old Median capital of Ecbatana (today's Hamadan), and later built a new capital at Pasargadae where his tomb now lies (though his remains are no longer there, probably scattered by the vengeful troops of Alexander the Great who conquered the Persian Empire).

The empire was in disarray by the time of Cyrus' grand son, Darius the Great, who defeated the pretenders to the throne, rebel princes and states, reunited the country and established a new ceremonial capital at Persepolis

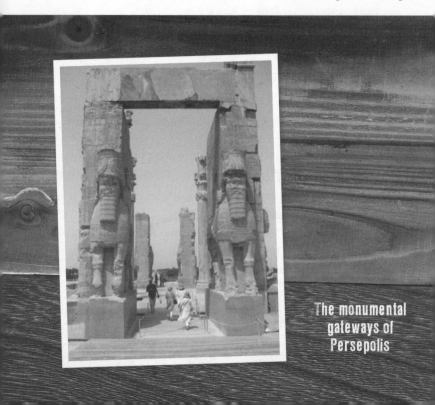

The monumental gateways of Persepolis

near Shiraz in 512 BC. Darius' son, Xerxes, expanded Persepolis hugely and adorned it with monumental palaces and buildings.

In the wind-swept basin that was Persepolis, a huge terrace or raised platform was built, and on it, grand halls where the rulers of subject nations were received as well as many monumental palaces and administrative buildings where taxes due from faraway lands were computed. Huge sculptures of real and mythological creatures were raised, together with symbols of vigor and power, such as that of a fierce lion with its jaws on a bull — projecting the image of imperial power and strength.

On the famous Apadana Staircase were carvings of the ambassadors, soldiers and servants of more than 20 subject nations, among them Egypt, India, Arabia, Parthia, Armenia and Greece, arriving at the court of the Persian king, bringing tributes and exotic products from their lands. The grandeur of that era could be imagined from these carvings as well as the many columns that have remained standing.

All these came to an end in 330 BC, during a visit by Alexander the Great, the Macedonian empire builder who had earlier conquered the Persian Empire. After a night of drunken frenzy, the whole city complex was destroyed and burned to the ground. Some said it was an accident; others insist it was in revenge for the destruction of Athens by the Persian king Xerxes 150 years before that; some blamed it on Alexander's sadness after the death of his favourite lover-general.

During the day, we also visited other great Persian ruins, such as the amazing royal necropolis at Naqsh-e-Rostam, with amazing sculptures of great Persian kings, their battles against rival-claimants to the throne, rebels and the Romans, as well as their investiture by gods; and Cyrus the Great's capital and tomb at Pasargadae — all UNESCO World Heritage Sites. Pasargadae is located on the windswept plain where Cyrus defeated his enemies, reunited his father's empire and built his capital. Not much remains of Cyrus the Great's capital except a few columns scattered across the plain. It must be great to be here early in the morning, before the tourist hordes arrive, and when it is still misty, with the silhouette of distant hills forming the backdrop for these lonely columns.

What was irritating was the crowd which overwhelmed what could have been a pretty picturesque scene. There was a group of army conscripts, all fascinated by our presence. I must have been the most exotic foreigner there and many mobbed me for a photo with or of me. Maybe this could be a second career for me, being photographed by Iranians curious about foreigners. Cyrus would have been puzzled. In his day, no one would have blinked an eye when the subjects of a hundred nations came here to pay tribute to the god-king.

With this, I left Shiraz and leaped more than a millennium across history, to Esfahan, the city that was for the longest period, the capital of Persia. Esfahan, with its magnificent monuments, palaces, mosques and gardens, is the epitome of the architectural brilliance and rich artistic heritage of the golden age of mediaeval Iran, an era during which Persia was at the heart of the Silk Road, enriched by the trade and commerce that passed its territory.

Iran of Poets, Wine & Women

Here sits the enchanted prince, solemn, dignified… he comes to meet you as you enter, his house is yours, his garden is yours, better still his tea and fruit are yours… Your magnificence sits down and spends ten minutes in brandying florid compliments through an interpreter while ices are served and coffee, after which you ride home refreshed, charmed, and with many blessings on your fortunate head. And all the time your host was probably a perfect stranger into whose privacy you had forced yourself in this unblushing way.

— Gertrude Bell, Letter to Horace Marshall, 18 June 1892

I got onto the 9am bus to Esfahan, whose inhabitants called it "Half the World", on account of its grand monuments and aesthetic urban design. Once again, the bus travelled through more than 400km of wild, dramatic landscapes which included the dry ranges of the Zagros Mountains, desert wastes, dry grasslands and fertile oases and river valleys.

I arrived in Esfahan's southern Soffeh Bus Terminal punctually at 4pm. I got onto a local taxi to the Persia Hotel on the main thoroughfare, Chahar Bagh Abbasi Street. The taxi skirted around a huge chunk of this enormous modern city to get to my destination. A modern ring road and expressway system helped to manage traffic flow — needless to say, I was suitably impressed.

The amazing glories of classical Persian architecture.

I loved the tree-lined streets of Esfahan and the many shops on both sides of Chahar Bagh Abbasi St. Esfahan also seemed to get a lot of domestic tourists — one must not forget Iran has 75 million inhabitants; hence domestic tourism is huge for this middle-income country (Iran's GDP per capita of US$12,000 on a Purchasing Power Parity basis is just below Malaysia's).

Singapore is not unknown to Iranians. In Iran, I came across quite a few people who had either been to Singapore or had family who had. They seemed to like the orderliness and cleanliness but complained about the high cost of visiting Singapore. I also met at least two retired sailors who had sailed to Singapore a number of times.

I visited the magnificent Imam Khomeini Square. It was huge and beautiful, and I would return a more few times during my stay in Esfahan, to look at the changing light and evolving colours. Thursday evening was when families came to picnic on the square's grassy patch ahead of Friday's rest day. Friendly Esfahanis invited me to join them and I did join one particular family — mainly ladies in *hejab*. They could not speak a lot of English but we managed anyway. They fed me with bread-cheese rolls, sweets, desserts and endless cups of tea. There were also others who beckoned to me to join them for small talk. The hospitality was overwhelming. One could just walk around and get fed by random people. Indeed, over the next few days during my four-day stay in Esfahan, I would be invited to endless cups of tea by Iranians on this spectacular square.

»»»»»

If, as Iran says, this program is for peaceful purposes, why oppose it? It has the right to develop its program... Besides, there is the supervision of the IAEA, which was established, I'm sad to say, for the weak countries. I once asked Al-Baradei: "Do you monitor the nuclear programs of the US, Britain, Russia, or China?" He said: "No way! They don't recognize us. We cannot monitor their programs, and ask them how many bombs they have, and how they store them, and whether they destroy them or

not. That's impossible. We are only good for wretches like you." That's
the truth. That's what is happening now. If the program is for peaceful
purposes it must not be opposed. If they are concerned that the program
will become nuclear, let it be subject to international supervision, and I
believe that it is subject to the supervision of Al-Baradei. This is generally
speaking. But if we take it to an extreme, Iran or any other country...
People may say: How come America produces nuclear bombs, and so
do China and India, but we cannot?

— Colonel Gaddafi[62]

》》》》》

I walked into a five-star hotel to check out a bookshop, only to be invited
by the banquet manager for snacks, tea and desserts even though he knew I
wasn't a guest and that I was staying at a US$16 place. He showed me around
the hotel's panoramic rooftop and the garden teahouse, and we chatted for a
good hour and a half.

At the rooftop restaurant, he showed me the banquet hall, divided
into two for the different sexes which by law were not allowed to interact.
Interestingly, the men's section had large tables whilst ladies had to content
themselves with small side tables probably with enough space only for
snacks and desserts. He also showed me the men's pool — here, women
were segregated, too. Men swam in an open pool while ladies had an indoor
pool so that no men could see them. What a waste of resources!

On the historic Si-o-She bridge across the Zayandeh River, I got to
know Maryam, an Iranian girl who had just completed her masters degree
and was planning to go abroad for a PhD. What was an even more amazing
coincidence was that she was the same person Raj had mentioned a few
days ago. He had told me how intelligent and hospitable she was. We had a
long chat and she walked me around half of Esfahan.

---

[62] http://www.memritv.org/clip_transcript/en/1421.htm, "Libyan Leader Mu'ammar Al-Qadhafi: The Arab Nation's Time Is Up; I Love the Black American Secretary of State of African Origin Leezza Very Much", an interview aired on Al-Jazeera TV on 27 March, 2007

»»»»»

Singaporeans get 15 days' visa-free entry into Iran. I had intended to stay 18 days in Iran and needed a three-day extension from the Foreign Affairs Department in Esfahan. When I reached the location indicated in my guidebook, I could not find it. As I walked around the vicinity in search of the office, a man in a car parked nearby asked what I was after. He then offered to drive me around to search for the office.

Hamid was an air force pilot waiting for his wife to finish her exams at the university premises nearby. We drove round the area but could not find the place. We then came across an old man who said that the department had moved to another location at the other end of town. So we drove across town to the new office of the Foreign Affairs office and Hamid dropped me there after providing me with his contact details in case I needed further help. Could you find such kindness anywhere else in the world?

Unfortunately, the Foreign Affairs officers there told me they only had authority to extend issued visas, not visa-free entry. They asked me to go to Tehran to extend my stay. This was really strange as I had Singapore friends who had extended their visa-free entry in other cities without problems. The situation was not ideal, as there were only two working days left before the following week's long holidays started in Iran. Originally, there were to be two holidays the following week — the anniversaries of Khomeini's death and that of Khomeini's denunciation of the Shah — but the government decreed a few more days of holiday so that the people could more properly mourn Khomeini who died 19 years ago, together with Fatima, the Prophet's daughter, who had passed away more than 1,000 years before.

My guidebook specifically warned about the slowness and confusion that reigned in the Teheran visa office, where any form of visa extension might take as many as five days to process. If I were to rush to Teheran that night to try get the visa-free extension before the holiday week began, I would have missed seeing all the sights I had yet to visit in Esfahan and would probably have to endure two more days of hassle in Teheran trying to get a three-day extension. Not worth the effort at all.

Hence I decided to stay in Iran till my final visa expiry date, and then leave on Gulf Air from Tehran to Beirut via Bahrain at 23:55 on 4 June, five minutes before my visa-free stay expired. Iran Air, Jazeera Airways and Air Arabia flights out of Iran were all fully booked — it was holiday week and all those who could afford it were travelling either within or outside the country.

Many provincials were also travelling to Teheran on pilgrimage to Khomeini's tomb, officially known as The Imam Khomeini Holy Shrine. I contemplated visiting Ahwaz in the southwest to see the ancient fortress-pyramids of Mesopotamia but flights there and back to Teheran were full too. So I had to give up going to Ahwaz. I bought a seven-hour bus ticket to Teheran three days in advance instead — in case the bus tickets also ran out during the holiday season!

»»»»»

In the evening, I met Maryam again. We walked along the river admiring the famous bridges by moonlight. Then she bought me a light dinner. Once again, I could not help but feel heartened by the hospitality of the Iranian people.

As the next week would be Khomeini's death anniversary, religious police were patrolling much more assiduously in their cars with green paint and special insignia, looking for single men hanging around with single

Esfahan: More domes and architectural wonders.

women, or people who broke the law by dancing or singing. All Iranians were supposed to be mourning Khomeini the following week and more religious police were going around to make sure no one was having too much of a good time in public. I asked Maryam if we would run the risk of getting questioned by walking in public without her relatives around. She laughed, "I don't care."

» » » »

Esfahan is a city of beautiful bridges that link the two halves of the city bisected by the Zayandeh River. Esfahanis like to spend their time strolling along the river, or picnicking by the green belt on its banks. Every evening, or on the Friday rest day, the riverbanks are crowded with families and couples. At night, the bridges are lit up to create a most romantic atmosphere.

The cynic, however, would attribute this to the lack of places to hang out in Esfahan, or anywhere else in Iran. The government forbids most forms of public entertainment. Dancing and partying are prohibited. Only men are allowed to sing and only religious songs are allowed. Some members of the religious establishment believed that when women sang, men with weak minds could be tempted to commit hideous crimes or act in a manner deemed indecent by polite society. There were a few cinemas but some clergymen would love to see them closed, as they might prompt naughty un-Islamic acts. Ironically, Iranians can buy pirated DVDs or VCDs from many shops and watch them in the privacy of their homes. There was nothing wrong with such piracy as it meant financial loss for the already wealthy moviemakers of the Great Satan, as America is known to the regime.

» » » »

I visited the Imam Khomeini Square again, and also the monuments around it. Imam Khomeini Mosque, completed in 1629 during the reign of Shah Abbas the Great — the same year two exiled Dutch murderers from Batavia became the first Europeans to settle in Australia — is one of the most monumental mosques in the world. Unfortunately, a massive tent and scaffolding had been put up over its entire courtyard for ceremonies relating to the death anniversary of Ayatollah Khomeini, obscuring the magnificent inner gateway facades.

Sheikh Lotfollah Mosque is on the eastern side of Imam Khomeini Square: I thought I would be tired of mosques by now, but the interior of this mosque really surprised me. No wonder a plaque en-site described it as the most beautiful mosque in the world. The amazing interplay of light on the geometrically arranged tiles makes this an architectural wonder of great aesthetic beauty. Yes, the plaque was not too far off the truth.

Ali Qapu Palace, built in the 17th century, is a six-storey palace commanding a strategic view across the square. It was once renowned for its beautiful frescoes and was one of the finest examples of Persian painting and arts during the Golden Age of Abbas Shah. Unfortunately, fundamentalists destroyed most of its murals and frescoes during the Islamic Revolution of 1979. The fundamentalists regarded these murals not as fine art but as pornography, a symbol of the aristocratic ruling class and an abomination in light of Allah's decree against idol worship and portrayal of human images.

The walls and ceilings of the palace are bare today, except for some colourful floral tiles on the staircase and a few faded frescoes of dancing girls that hint at the exuberance of what used to exist. I was almost heart-broken when I saw what remained. Ironically, on the outer walls of the palace there

One of the few remnants of classical Persian court paintings. Many exquisite examples were destroyed during the Islamic Revolution by fundamentalists who opposed any display of "graven images".

are portraits of Supreme Leader Khamenei and Ayatollah Khomeini. I wonder whether the fundamentalists would regard these, too, to be graven images. An Iranian I met grumbled sarcastically, "Who do they think they are? The new Shahs?"

»»»»»

I went south of the river to Jolfa, Esfahan's Armenian or Christian Quarter. Armenians have always been loyal subjects of the Persian State, from the days of the Achaemenids' Persian Empire to the Islamic Republic of today. I have seen carvings of Armenian envoys bringing horses and amphoras with griffin-handles as gifts for the Persian kings at the famous 6th century BC. Apadana Staircase at Persepolis.

Armenian craftsmen and merchants have always been valued by various Persian dynasties. In the 17th century, Shah Abbas the Great transported a large community of Armenians from the city of Old Jolfa (on the border of Iran with Azerbaijan's Nakhichevan Autonomous Republic) to New Jolfa, on the suburbs of his new capital at Esfahan. They were hugely rewarded for their services to the royal court and their religious and trading freedoms were safeguarded by generations of shahs through edicts and decrees.

Today, Jolfa's Armenian inhabitants are distinguished citizens of the Islamic Republic and they have guaranteed representation in the Iranian parliament. Having such supportive Christian citizens also allowed the Islamic Republic to boast of its tolerance towards minority religions and ethnic groups, a privilege which was, however, denied to the Bahais, a religion that appeared in Iran in the 19th century and spread across the world.

The Independent Armenian Republic is also a close unofficial ally of sorts of Iran. I recall seeing Iranian products on sale in the markets of Yerevan, capital of Armenia, and of how Armenians told me that Iran, despite being an Islamic fundamentalist state, was a covert ally of Armenia in its struggle against Muslim Azerbaijan for control over the disputed territory of Nagorno Karabakh. Iran, with an ethnic Azeri population of over 20 million, is always wary of the possibility of independent Azerbaijan claiming Iran's West and East Azerbaijan provinces, which people in Baku, capital of independent Azerbaijan, call "Southern Azerbaijan". My enemy's enemy is my friend — this is the eternal truth in geopolitics. Hence the close links between Iran and Armenia.

Jolfa is today a very fashionable suburb with nice apartment blocks, travel agencies, ethnic restaurants and cafès, boutiques and a few old churches. The Vank Cathedral is an example of the marriage of Persian, Armenian and European architectural and artistic traditions. With its huge mud dome, the cathedral looks like a mosque from afar. Close-up, one sees the cross on top of the dome, plus bell towers typical of a church elsewhere in the world. The inner walls of the main cathedral building are lined with well-preserved frescoes and murals of biblical scenes, coupled with Persian mosaics and tiles of Islamic geometric patterns typical of mosques in Iran.

The cathedral museum, apart from displays of Christian art and everyday church objects, also proudly displayed the various decrees and edicts issued by Persian shahs granting rights and privileges to the Armenians, or grants of protection of persons and properties. There was also a gaudy exhibit on the Armenian genocide and of how 1.5 million Armenians were massacred in 1915 by the Turks, who had been for a long time, a geopolitical rival of the Iranians.

A common image depicting the martyrdom of Ali Asghar, Imam Husayn's infant son.

»»»»»

Across shops and bazaars in Iran, one came across portraits of Imam Husayn, the grandson of Prophet Muhammad. He is usually portrayed as a handsome, dashing figure, sometimes almost Jesus-like, on a horse, or with horsemen behind him. Killed at the battle of Karbala (in today's Iraq) on 6 October 680AD by soldiers of Yazid I, the Umayyad Caliph based in Damascus, Husayn is the foremost martyr of Shia Islam, the predominant Islamic sect of Iran. The anniversary of his martyrdom is called Ashura, and it is a day of mourning and religious observance among Shia Muslims. On this day, black flags are raised everywhere and processions are held at which participants beat their heads and chests repeatedly, whip themselves and wail to mourn this event that occurred more than 1,300 years ago.

Shia Islam sees the family and descendants of Prophet Muhammad as his rightful political and religious heirs, whose rightful inheritance of political leadership was robbed by the Umayyads (whose political position is held by today's Sunni Islam). When in 680AD, Husayn and his family and companions — including 72 adult men — marched from Medina to Kufa where many people supported his cause, Yazid I sent an army of 4,000 against them.

Husayn and his entourage were besieged in the desert at Karbala, where they ran out of water, and then were slaughtered one by one. Eventually, all 72 men and 51 children were killed, leaving only a few female members of the Prophet's family. The Battle of Karbala is a rallying cry for all Shia Muslims, and Shiite accounts of the battle include tales of individual bravery, providential acknowledgement of such courage and indescribable cruelty on the side of the enemy Sunnis (involving killing of infants, mutilation and beheading, among other acts).

The martyrs of Karbala, together with other followers and descendants of the Prophet's family who were killed in subsequent years by the Umayyads, are mourned every year and their shrines have become major pilgrimage centres. The Iranian and Shia calendar is so full of such mourning days that black flags are flown everywhere for large parts of each year. Some say Noruz, the Iranian New Year, is the only happy day on the Iranian calendar.

Husayn is sometimes shown carrying a baby in his arms, with an arrow through the baby and into his arm. The baby portrayed here is Ali Asghar, Husayn's infant son. Husayn's entourage had grown so thirsty during the siege that Husayn carried his son towards the enemy, asking them for water for the children. The enemy commander called on his archers to shoot the two but none dared — one soldier shouted that heaven would damn them if they shot an infant. So the commander lifted a bow and shot an arrow across, which went through the baby and into Husayn's arm. Ali Asghar is often described in Shia literature as the manifestation of innocence and purity, and his death is seen as evidence of the cruelty of the Sunnis, who would not even spare a baby.

There was also the story of Husayn's brother, Abbas, who went to the river in search of water for Husayn and was attacked. His companions were all slaughtered but he managed to get a bag of water though on his way back to the camp, his right hand was cut off in an ambush. The water skin (or bag) was then hung onto his left shoulder (don't ask me how) as he continued his way back. Then he was attacked again and his left arm severed as well. But he persisted, biting the water skin between his teeth, until an arrow hit and burst the water bag. Another barrage of arrows shot him off his horse. As he died, he called out his brother's name.

After Husayn was killed in the final battle during which his limbs were severed, his corpse was decapitated and his head sent to the Caliph as a trophy. His surviving female family members tried to save his torso but the Umayyad soldiers had horses stamp it into the dust instead, as Shia accounts bitterly recount.

There are other stories involving Husayn's eldest son and horse, and other individual companions, all highlighting their bravery and readiness to die for Husayn and the Prophet's family. Although graphic performances of any kind are seen as un-Islamic, passion plays similar to those performed in Christian Europe during the Middle Ages are regularly held in Iran, portraying the battle of Karbala and the terrible martyrdom of Husayn and his family and followers.

As noted in Wikipedia, "The saying, "Every day is Ashura, every land is Karbala," is a reminder to live one's life as Hussein did on Ashura, with total sacrifice to Allah and for others. This saying also implies that "We must always remember, because there is suffering everywhere""

Any Shiite is familiar with these tales and even the less religious among them will get somewhat emotional and charged when recounting this historical event. A young lady I spoke to in Shiraz, who seemed most unreligious and anti-establishment to me, almost choked with emotions and grief as she told me the story of Imam Husayn. This is hardly surprising given the mourning that goes on for much of the year, generation after generation perpetuating such feelings. The Battle of Karbala will remain a thorn between Sunni and Shia Islam, and between modern nation states such as Egypt and Saudi Arabia on one side (Sunni) and Shiite Iran on the other.

I visited Golestan-e Shohada in the southern suburbs of Esfahan. This is a cemetery for those who died in the Iran-Iraq War of 1980–1988. In all, 500,000 people from each side died in this terrible conflict which began when Saddam Hussein of Iraq invaded Iran in the wake of the Iranian Islamic Revolution, with the aim of capturing Iran's oil-rich Khuzestan Province. One whole generation in Iran, i.e., "The Lost Generation", died in this war.

Golestan-e Shohada, the cemetery for the war dead of the Iran-Iraq War.

Golestan-e Shohada, or Garden of Roses, is Esfahan's war cemetery. Most of the dead appeared to be young men in their prime, and some tombs even had photos of teenagers and children. It was a moving scene: elderly ladies placing flowers by the tombs; some whispered the latest news of the family to their long-dead husbands; others sat quietly by the resting places of their loved ones, lost in thought.

There were many huge boards with old photos of young men at war. I wonder how many of these are still alive today. Those smiling young faces holding rifles, by their cannons, in diving suits, in the swamps... sent to the battlefield as cannon fodder. Also present were images of the two chief ayatollahs and various patriotic messages rallying support for the current regime. One wonders if the war had been fought for longer than necessary, and how long the regime could maintain patriotic fervour by constantly reminding the nation of the war.

Iran of Ayatollahs and Mourners

Iran is rich enough to support revolution as an industry.
— Shimon Peres

I got onto a morning bus to Tehran. Ali, an English speaking Esfahani, sat beside me on the bus. We spoke quite a bit, perhaps too much when I was quite tired from poor sleep the night before. Although he was only 22 years old, he looked more as if he were in his early 30s. Middle Easterners seem to age quite quickly compared to East Asians. For instance, the Israelis have just released a 38-year old Hezbollah turncoat — he looked as though he was in his early 50s. Although it could well be that he had aged while in Israeli prison, I saw enough of such old-looking young Middle Easterners during the past few months in the region.

Ali was on his way to Tehran to join his parents on a holiday at the Caspian beaches. There would be five days of holidays that week — two additional days had been declared by the government over the 4th June death anniversary of Ayatollah Khomeini, 5th June anniversary of Khomeini's arrest by the Shah that marked the start of his resistance movement and the standard weekly Friday rest day. The death anniversary of Khomeini was supposed to be a solemn day of mourning and reflection, but many people, especially the middle and upper classes of Tehran, Esfahan and other large cities, regarded this as an opportunity to get away and have fun on the cool beaches of the Caspian.

"Nobody mourns anymore," Ali said. "We just want to get away from all that fake public mourning, especially on TV. We Iranians mourn too much and in public — but all you see about this is not real." Indeed, in the past few days, banners and huge black billboards with images of Khomeini had suddenly risen up everywhere, on top of those that are found all year long. Their state TV station ran documentaries of Khomeini non-stop as though he had only died the day before (instead of in 1989), interspersed with images of public memorial ceremonies in which men and women in mourning clothes marched with black flags, wailed loudly, shouted slogans or beat their chests frenziedly in typical Shiite expression of deep sadness and sorrow.

Like many young Iranians I have met, Ali did not mince his words about his dislike of the current government. "It's a dictatorship. All Iranians hate it. It is crazy, trying to make the whole world Iran's enemy. What has the government done with the economy? Nothing but talk non-stop about Khomeini, the long past Iran-Iraq war, Israel and America."

I remembered what Maryam told me. Most people, in her view, were against the current regime. "The current President, Ahmadinejad, is just a puppet of the military clique and the Supreme Leader Khamenei. The previous president, the liberal Khatami, had aroused great hopes but disappointed everyone — his hands were tied as real power lay with the unelected Supreme Leader, not the elected president. What was the use of voting? Furthermore, all candidates have to be screened and approved by the regime before they can take part in elections."

Across Iran, I saw huge portraits of not only Khomeini but also that of Khamenei, who was often shown standing next to Khomeini, perhaps in an attempt to rise on the former's shoulders. Obviously, Khamenei does not have the same standing as the long-dead revolutionary leader. A huge mural across the entire western outer wall of the Kowsler Hotel in southern Esfahan was self-evident. The English caption below the portraits of the two men said, "Obedience to Khamenei is obedience to Imam Khomeini." The message seemed to have underscored the political weakness of the former.

Maryam also told me, "Our parents had protested against the regime but that led nowhere. Now, even they have told us not to bother about politics. You can't change anything. The brave ones get sent to prison. Now we just keep quiet and get on with our lives."

An Esfahani taxi driver told me that he once worked in a sensitive professional position in Qatar but Ahmadinejad's anti-West and aggressive nuclear stance had led to him losing his job. Maryam blamed the government for what she thought to be a decline in tourism the past few years. A fellow traveler said that a Teherani told him that many Teheranis would call the main square in South Teheran "Meidan-Shah", by its old name after the overthrown Shah, instead of its current official name, "Meidan Imam Khomeini".

In spite of these comments, I wouldn't be surprised if there were a huge divide in views between the anti-regime urbanites that I met and those in the rural areas who are more religious and pro-regime, i.e., those that bothered to vote and actually voted enthusiastically for Ahmadinejad and the existing order. A tourist told me how a local pointed to a public image of Khomeini, saying, "This man is responsible for everything that is right in this country. We still love him dearly." The huge challenge for Iran is how to bridge the gap between liberals who want to see liberal democracy and respect for personal freedoms, and the rural conservatives who prefer the status quo under a theocratic regime.

The bus got into Teheran at 3pm — as punctual as ever — Ali told me that bus companies would be fined if they arrived too early (that would be evidence of speeding dangerously) or too late (customer rights), and this is monitored by police at the various checkpoints across the countryside where we stopped briefly several times on each bus journey I took.

The interior of Sheikh Lotfollah Mosque, one of the most beautiful mosques in the world.

I was in Teheran merely 10 days but the city had been transformed into Mourning Central. Black flags and banners flew everywhere, with even more Khomeini posters than ever. The taxi driver that drove me to the hotel even passed me a mini Khomeini mourning poster. However, as a local told me, the Tehranis would all go for a beach holiday this week, instead of mourning for Khomeini as the government would prefer to see.

I checked into the Atlas Hotel in North Teheran. I was curious about this supposedly upmarket area that I heard was a world of difference from South Teheran which was full of vehicle repair workshops and metal spare parts shops. In contrast to South Teheran, the streets of North Teheran were lined with shady trees and had much greenery and vegetation. Even then, the streets were dirty compared to almost spotless Esfahan, the jewel of the Middle East.

I walked around the area that also contained the Armenian St Sarkies Cathedral, and the notorious former US Embassy where the Hostage Crisis took place during the Islamic Revolution. At the height of the Islamic Revolution, radical students stormed the US Embassy and took 52 US diplomats hostage for 444 days, in an episode that continues to poison US-Iranian relations. Following the crisis, the US imposed economic sanctions on Iran, which included a freeze on Iranian assets in the US worth billions of dollars. Over the years, sanctions were extended to a ban on all business activities between the US and Iran, and the US even threatened to impose sanctions on third-country companies dealing with Iran. The hostages were only released on 20 January 1981, minutes after Ronald Reagan was sworn in as the new US president.

Today, the embassy premises, according to a 2006 *Guardian* report, are used by The Committee for the Commemoration of Martyrs of the Global Islamic Campaign, which uses "the US embassy to recruit "martyrdom seekers" — volunteers to carry out operations against Western and Jewish targets. Mohammad Samadi, a spokesman for the group, signed up several hundred volunteers in a few days." A bookshop nearby sold war and jihad propaganda, which included some rather gory posters of soldiers and martyrs blown up during wars and conflicts (and who knows, perhaps suicide bombing missions as well).

Apart from the remnants of the chiseled-off Great Seal of the United States at the embassy gates, also interesting were the murals and quotations from Ayatollah Khomeini on the embassy's outer walls, some of which were hilarious. Among them were the following:

— "The United States is too weak to do anything", which was exactly the case during the last days of the Carter administration. It sent in a helicopter rescue mission but the helicopters got caught in a sand storm and crashed before even reaching Tehran. Eight US soldiers died and Khomeini celebrated the event as evidence of providential support for his war against America.

— "Tell the US be angry with us and die of this anger."

— "The only way to defy the wild wolf of Zionism and the transgression of Great Satan (USA) is sacrificial resistance." Khomeini later used the "human wave" tactic against Iraq during the Iran-Iraqi War, killing numerous people as a result.

— "We will make America face a severe defeat."

One of the iconic murals outside the former US Embassy in Teheran.

Various images on these walls were iconic, disturbing or even funny — among them, the Statue of Liberty as a skeleton, a hostage with his arms raised in a "surrender" pose and a gun in American national colours.

That week, during the Democrat primaries Hiliary Clinton threatened to obliterate Iran if Iran attacked Israel (that is, if she went on to be elected US president) and the Iranian Foreign Minister reiterated that Israel should be wiped off the face of the Earth. The standoff over nuclear facilities continues unabated. Even the 50,000 Iranian Rial banknote has the symbol of the nuclear atom superimposed over the map of Iran.

As noted in a commentary in *Iran News*, an English newspaper, "not only Iran but other peoples in the Third World have been suffering mostly because of policies by the arrogant powers. But we should note that times are changing rapidly and that the era of those arrogant powers will come to an end." Sounds like the Shiite wait for the 12th imam, or the Mahdi, who would come to Earth with Prophet Jesus and end all injustice, bringing peace to all.

I wonder when Iran and America will reconcile with each other. How can a country develop its economy when it remains stuck in a continuous revolution and a conflict with the world's number one superpower for 30 years? I am sure a compromise can be struck, even between Iran and the US. Both Iran and the US need brave leaders who can overcome past baggage and normalize relations in a way that benefits both great peoples.

» » » » »

Iran News commented on the reasons for the current real estate boom in Iran, which has pushed prime properties in Teheran and the Caspian Sea coastal resorts to record prices, with many properties valued at well above US$1 million. Bizarrely, among the key reasons were that the UN sanctions and blacklisting of Iran's key state banks had restricted activities in many of their other economic fields. On the other hand, there had been an inflow of cash from the Iranian Diaspora which was withdrawing money from developed markets suffering from the subprime crisis. Money previously kept overseas had also been returning for fear of a freeze to be imposed on Iranian assets if more UN resolutions were passed. These factors have combined to lead to the diversion of lots of cash into the real estate sector, leading to what the paper described as a bubble. Yes, there are lots of fancy new apartments and projects across North Teheran. The question to ask, then, would be when the bubble would burst and whether the country and its banks were ready for that. Since time immemorial, what goes up must come down. That has never changed.

>> >> >> >> >>

Teheran was a dead city that day. It was a mistake to return to Teheran so soon. Everything was shut — almost all shops, many restaurants and cybercafés, even the National Museum, had closed their doors. The TV continued to play Khomeini videos, non-stop-Khomeini speeches, his life,

Greetings from the Supreme Leader and his nuclear programme.

old footage of the mass mourning at his funeral which more than 10 million people attended, and endless speeches by Supreme Leader Khamenei and a whole string of ayatollahs, cheered on by crowds of fist-clenching men in black mourning clothes. Huge banners on the streets, some showing Khamenei weeping at the death of Khomeini, others depicting Khomeini with images of revolutionary martyrs. Most Teheranis, I think, were basking on the beaches of the Caspian Sea, three hours away by car.

I switched between all five Iranian state TV channels and four of them had Khomeini images on them. The fifth looked like it had a game show on but Khomeini's photo appeared suddenly after three minutes, though in what context I knew not. I cannot imagine going through all this for one whole week, year after year. It's like attending a funeral again and again, year after year. No wonder, as a local told me, nobody watches Iranian TV. Every household that could afford it, has a satellite dish although it is illegal to own one. There are hundreds of channels to choose from, including the highly popular 15 Farsi language channels produced by the Iranian Diaspora in California.

» » » »

Fifteen days had come and gone. I left beautiful and hospitable Iran on the 19th anniversary of Ayatollah Khomeini's death. This is definitely a country I would return to and I wish this great, enigmatic nation the best.

Lebanon: Eternal Battleground In Paradise (June 2008)

Why God, should such a small country have everything – mountains, beaches and a lovely weather? God answered: but I gave the country its eternal punishment – the Lebanese people.

— Lina Mikdadi, "Letter from Beirut", the *Guardian*, 21 May 1979 [63]

For many years, before the term "failed state" began to be applied to countries such as Somalia and the Congo, Lebanon was synonymous with anarchy, warlords, massacres and chaos in general. During the period between 1975 and 1990, the country plunged into a terrible civil war that destroyed what used to be known as the Paris of the Middle East and a regional financial centre, safe heaven and tourism hub. Many of Lebanon's eighteen official religious communities and myriad political persuasions formed their own militia to fight over scarce resources and territory. Foreign troops marched into the land on various pretexts, further deepening the already tightly stretched religious and ethnic fault-lines of this country.

Even today, Lebanon appears to be on the edge. In May 2008, the country's rival factions — pro-Western Sunni Muslims and Maronite Christians on one side versus a coalition of pro-Iranian and pro-Syrian Shia Muslim groups on the other — fought on the streets of Beirut, almost tipping the country into a renewed civil war. An agreement has since been signed among the factions to agree on a new president — Lebanon has had no president for seven months

---

[63] Peter Yapp, *The Travellers' Dictionary of Quotation*, p 622.

— and to attempt to resolve the issues dividing the country. It remains to be seen if the agreement would eventually work out; if it does not, this beautiful nation might just be pushed to the brink again.

»»»»»

Since the mid-1990s, I had been wanting to visit Lebanon but political events and various mishaps conspired to prevent that. Once the May 2008 fighting was over and the interim peace agreement was signed, I booked my air ticket from Teheran to Beirut. I reckoned that, there was probably a window of opportunity before further disagreement threatened to pull the country apart once more.

The flight to Beirut was full of Nepali women on their way to become domestic maids in Beirut. I was to discover that despite all the political and economic miseries Lebanon had been suffering, there was enough wealth flowing around to employ domestic workers and all sorts of foreign manual labour. During my stay in Lebanon, I also came across many Indian and Syrian construction workers and road cleaners. Is it the massive inward remittances — estimated to be US$5 billion a year or US$1,200 per person —and easy access to such transfers that created a structural employment issue here? In a country with huge unemployment and underemployment issues, perhaps the ready inflow of cash from its diaspora allowed the Lebanese to live comfortably without getting their hands dirty.

I sat beside Mona, a young Lebanese undergraduate living with her family in Damman, Saudi Arabia. Her family hailed from Baalbek and appeared to be quite well-off — she spoke a bit about holidays in Europe and buying the right cologne for her boyfriend. Although she was Sunni-Muslim, she was dressed in a bright summer dress with bare shoulders and cut in a way that most Middle Eastern *mullahs* would have disapproved. Welcome to Lebanon, the petite France of the Middle East.

Mona spoke English with an American accent, and through her I had my first exposure to the sophisticated, cosmopolitan and Westernised

Lebanese bourgeoisie, with their extended diaspora. But I was to discover later that there was a wide divide in the country. Beirut and the Christian heartland to the northeast of Beirut were clean, fashionable, well-organised and very European in outlook, while towns of the poor Shiite south looked like typically messy Arab Third World oversized villages complete with wet, dirty and crowded souks (which look rather exotic and picturesque to Western tourists). This is another symptom of the political fault-line this country has always lived with and suffered from since time immemorial.

»»»»»

It was said that Beirut was where St George slew the dragon. That the legend had occurred here was repeated many times by the Beirutis, though it could hardly be traced to any definitive evidence. In any case, did the dragon mentioned ever exist at all? And who exactly was St George? He too, is as untraceable in history as the dragon. It is uncertain if St George ever existed, or that the dragon was slain here, or if it were indeed St George that slew it; though it is certain that Beirut, the city, was killed, or rather, destroyed, many times, and every time, it became alive again[64].

A Lebanese-Brazilian from the Talal Hotel picked me up at the airport and drove me through the sprawl of Beirut across the city's impressive highways and flyovers that one hardly saw even in other non-oil Middle Eastern cities that had not gone through the destruction Beirut had experienced. The assassinated former Prime Minister, Rafik Hariri, had definitely done a fantastic job in rebuilding the country.

Located on Ave Charles Helou opposite the Port and close to Martyrs Square, the Talal Hotel was on the Green Line, the frontline between rival Muslim and Christian militia forces of West and East Beirut respectively during the Lebanese Civil War from 1975 to 1990. Indeed, traces of the devastation were obvious from the shell holes and glassless windows of the building next to this hotel. I was not sure whether these were the result of

---

[64] W.M. Thomson in *The Land and the Book*, 1859, had raised questions about the city and its legend.

the 1975–1990 Civil War, the many Israeli invasions and bombings, or the recent fighting between the government and the opposition.

Across the road was the home of a Catholic politician. The walls of this huge mansion had posters of him with the Lebanese cedar flag in the background. There were anti-bomb or anti-truck barriers all around the heavily-guarded building — I would pass a few more such buildings across Beirut, all of them under heavy military guard or even armoured carriers around them. Beirut resembled what Singapore and Hong Kong would have looked like in a war — soldiers and tanks amid a landscape of malls and skyscrapers of steel and glass.

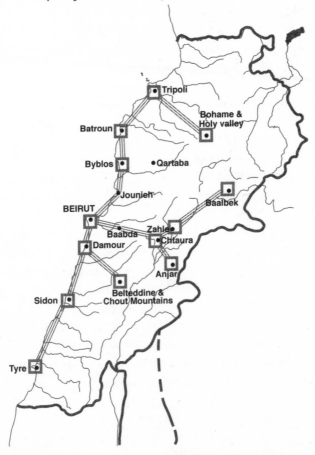

I walked around Downtown Beirut. There was a huge sea reclamation project ongoing and lots of huge skyscrapers and malls and hotels (including The Hilton) being built despite the political instability. I bet their owners were having cold sweat during the recent disturbances. I wondered why anyone would dare to invest in anything here, given the seemingly never-ending chain of war and broken peace agreements. I suspected the only people who would invest here were either the wealthy overseas Lebanese who were emotionally bound to this land and thus could sustain greater investment risk and bear lower returns than a purely profit-motivated investor; or the Gulf States and Iran, all of whom had vested interests in Lebanon's various parties and factions, and would need to commit money to rebuild Lebanon after every conflict so that these factions would continue to act as proxies for them in this eternal battleground between the pro-West Arab states and Iran, and between the Islamic World and Israel. That is why Lebanon, despite the many wars that were fought and the continuing tensions, has a first class infrastructure and impressive ongoing rebuilding and development programmes.

Many corners of the city were garrisoned with soldiers and armoured carriers. The usefulness of these soldiers is a big question mark, as evidenced by the speed with which Hezbollah, the pro-Iranian Shiite militia, took over West Beirut during the recent disturbances and the hands-off neutrality adopted by the Army.

There were a number of grand mansions built in an exuberant mix of pseudo-Moorish and Western styles. They were just as heavily guarded by soldiers. These were probably the residences of important politicians and the powerful political families that have long dominated Lebanese politics. During the May 2008 fighting, many of the pro-government politicians, such as Said Hariri, son of Rafik Hariri, and Walid Jumblatt, had to be rescued by the Army as Hezbollah rapidly took over much of Beirut. If the takeover had occurred during the Civil War days, the winning party would have tried to capture and eliminate rival leaders.

»»»»»

I walked around the rebuilt downtown area, including Martyrs' Square and the mausoleum of Rafik Hariri to the west of the square. Many Lebanese regard Hariri, a billionaire who was credited with the reconstruction of Lebanon after the terrible Civil War of 1975–1990, almost as a god today. Hariri was born to a humble Sunni Muslim family in Saida and became very wealthy after he completed within record time, the construction of a hotel for Saudi Arabia's King Khaled, thus winning the latter's trust and many other projects for the construction company which he founded.

In 1992, Hariri was appointed prime minister following the end of the civil war, when Sunni Muslims, guaranteed the prime ministerial seat by the 1943 National Pact, lacked a credible and neutral candidate. In 2005, amidst serious disagreement with Syria over Lebanese domestic issues, Hariri was killed in a bomb explosion together with 21 others. Lebanon had never existed as a country until 1920, when it was carved out of the old Ottoman province of Syria. Even to this day, Syria refuses to recognize Lebanon's independence. During the Civil War, Syrian forces entered Lebanon in support of various factions, and it has since become an arbitrator in Lebanese aaffairs.

Hariri's assassination spurred the Lebanese people into the mass protests now known as the Cedar Revolution, which led to the withdrawal of Syrian forces from Lebanon. Investigation into the assassination by the UN is still

Temporary tomb of Rafik Hariri in central Beirut.

ongoing and many people believe it would point to the involvement of Syria. In fact, a number of sources revealed that Syrian President Bashar al-Assad had threatened Hariri and Walid Jumblatt, Lebanon's leader of the Druze, that "If you and Chirac want me out of Lebanon, I will break Lebanon." Hariri was already wildly popular after a few terms in office, due to his successful revival and rebuilding of Lebanon. His assassination transformed him almost into a god, revered by all except the pro-Syrian and pro-Iranian Shiites across Lebanon. Posters and billboards bearing his likeness can be found all over the nation.

The downtown area of Beirut has been rebuilt very nicely by Solidere, the company set up for this purpose by Hariri. By agreement with the government, Solidere (Société libanaise pour le développement et la reconstruction de Beyrouth, French for "The Lebanese Company for the Development and Reconstruction of Beirut."), set up in 1994, enjoys special

Faces of Beirut: Huge, well-restored mosque with advertisement billboards, not too far away from skyscrapers damaged during the country's many civil conflicts.

powers of eminent domain as well as a limited regulatory authority codified in law, making the company a unique form of public-private partnership.

Solidere has the unusual distinction of being openly set up by the head of government of a country to develop so prime a property. I recall reading about this with skepticism at that time, and wondered if the maverick businessman-turned-politician was a fraud. In many countries, this would be denounced as corruption. However, the Lebanon of 1994 was a bankrupt country totally devastated by 15 years of civil war. No one but Hariri was willing to put money in. With his own money involved, Hariri gave credence to this project critical for the revival of the Lebanese nation. Hence, Solidere's very success won Hariri the hearts of the vast majority of the Lebanese people.

According to Wikipedia, "Solidere's shares are listed on the Beirut and Kuwait Stock Exchange, and its Global Depository Receipts trade on the London, Frankfurt and Luxembourg Stock Exchanges. Its share price on the Beirut exchange has risen sharply in recent years, from about US$5 in early 2004 to a high of US$26 in February 2006. In June 2006, Solidere approved a US$100 million dividend payout to its shareholders." On 13 June 2008, the share price was US$20.95, which is quite good considering the continuing instability in Lebanon.

I visited the National Museum. Its most interesting exhibits included the sarcophagus of King Hiram of Tyre and a number of intricately carved Roman sarcophagi and beautiful mosaics. There was also an interesting video about how the museum was restored after the end of the Civil War. The National Museum lies at a major crossroads on the Green Line during the Israeli invasion in the midst of the Civil War, and there were six armies, some of them rivals, garrisoned at that junction, ready to shoot one another at any time.

I went to Tripoli, Lebanon's second largest city, in a smart little Tripoli Express bus. We sped along the trendy central Lebanese coast and its many beach resorts, brand-name malls and glass-tower apartments. This fashionable extended sprawl of Christian Mt. Lebanon faded into smaller villas and a wild, bare rocky shore some distance north of Byblos. The bus reached downtown Tripoli in 75 minutes. This was a busy, bustling city of 500,000 inhabitants. If Beirut and its northern environs were Hong Kong or Miami, then Tripoli was a mini version of Cairo — busy streets crowded with vehicles and vendors. Loud, lively Arabic music competed with vehicle horns, whereas Western pop is more likely to be heard in Beirut. Even then, Tripoli is quite different from Shiite Saida and Tyre, which are downright depressing towns with lots of politics and little economics.

Posters of the late Hariri and his son, as well as other Sunni politicians, were hung everywhere. This was clearly their political heartland. Hezbollah has no place here, unlike parts of southern Beirut. In fact, during the May 2008 disturbances, Hezbollah supporters and pro-Syrian parties were attacked by supporters of the Future Movement. I saw a few burnt out buildings guarded by soldiers in the Old City. As usual in Lebanon, it was difficult to figure out whether the damage was caused by the latest conflict, or the many others in this country over the last three decades.

I visited the dilapidated Citadel of Tripoli, from where one could see the crowded apartment blocks of the city, closely crammed up against one another, with piles of rubbish in many places and a number of war-ruined buildings. I walked around the souk, and took some photos with local supporters of Hariri who posed in front of posters of him and his son, plus an ominous sign that read "The Truth". Will the truth of Hariri's assassination ever be known? Or would the truth behind his death be disputed forever, like a Lebanese version of the conspiracies relating to the assassination of John F. Kennedy?

》》》》》

From Tripoli, I got onto another bus, this time for Bsharre in Qadisha Valley, or Holy Valley. The bus was full and all except three passengers (including me) were Lebanese soldiers on their way to the training camp at The Cedars, where the tallest cedars, known as Arb el Rab, or Cedars of the Lord, are found. These bulky and burly soldiers were like overgrown school kids, joking non-stop throughout the journey and even throwing a ball around occasionally. A few tried to speak to me but unfortunately I could not speak Arabic and their attempts did not go very far.

Qadisha is one of the most sacred places in the world to the Maronite Christians and the patriarch of the Maronite Church used to reside in a monastery here, before the Patriarchate moved to a location nearer Beirut. The Maronites were the largest Christian community in Lebanon, and was until the Civil War, the most powerful community there. The Maronite Church is an Eastern Catholic Church, i.e., a church that preserves the traditions and rituals of the ancient churches of the Middle East and Eastern Europe, but recognizes the supremacy of the Bishop of Rome, i.e., the Pope. St Maron, an aesthetic monk who lived in Syria, founded the Maronite Church in the 5th century. The church continues to use the ancient Syriac language in its rituals and prayers, although its followers had been speaking mostly Arabic since the 15th century.

The Maronites had always been the predominant community in Qadisha and Mount Lebanon, to which the great European powers added additional Sunni and Shiite Muslim territories (to the north and south of Beirut respectively) to form the State of Greater Lebanon in 1920. Maronite

Locals in Tripoli, a pro-Hariri Sunni Muslim city .

Christians accounted for over 50% of the population of the enlarged Lebanese state, according to the population census of 1932, the last ever officially conducted, and accordingly, the 1943 National Pact was drawn up.

The National Pact of 1943, drawn up between the key ethnic-religious communities of Lebanon to spell out the division of powers after independence, according to Wikipedia, sets out the following key rules:

- the Maronites were not to seek foreign intervention and to accept Lebanon as an "Arab" affiliated country, instead of a "Western" one;
- the Muslims were to abandon their aspirations to unite with Syria;
- the President of the Republic was always to be Maronite, the President of the Council of Ministers (prime minister) to always be Sunni; the President of the Parliament to always be Shia; the deputy speaker of the Parliament to always be a Greek Orthodox; and
- Parliamentary representation was to be in a ratio of 6:5 in favour of Christians to Muslims (this was later changed to 5:5 as a result of the Taif Agreement of 1990 that ended the Civil War).

The pact also gave the Christians command of the armed forces and the then Christian majority in the population gave the community a parliamentary majority. However, with a higher Muslim birth rate and a high Christian emigration, it has long been an open secret that the Shia Muslims are probably the largest community in Lebanon, with about 30% of the population, followed by the Sunni Muslims with possibly 25% and Maronite Christians forming only 22% of the population. It was dissatisfaction over a pro-Christian political system based on outdated population proportions, as well as the influx of predominantly Muslim Palestinian refugees that drastically upset the country's delicate population structure, that led to the Civil War of 1975.

Even today, many Maronites still regard Lebanon as a Christian country, an oddity in an ocean of Muslims in the Middle East. Maronites resent the fact that they are no longer the majority — some even deny the fact outright, and they see the Shias as foreign — the Iranian "Fifth Column" out to destroy Lebanon, the Christian land. Michel, a Maronite from Bsharre, said, "the dirtiest people in Lebanon are the Shia, and wherever they moved in huge numbers, everyone would want to move out of that area, which forms part of the Shiite plan to capture strategic parts of Lebanon for Iran." He said the Beqaa Valley used to be more Christian but many Christians moved out as more and more Shia people moved in. I would later have to admit that the Shia regions did indeed look dirty and the contrast was particularly glaring when I walked into the Christian quarter of Tyre.

Michel added, "To hell with Hezbollah. All everybody wants is to work and feed the family. Who cares about the liberation of Jerusalem and Palestine? Why mess up the whole country by fighting Israel when Israel is no longer occupying Lebanese land?" This is a sentiment I would hear many times as I travelled through Lebanon. When asked about Lebanon's tourism season, Michel said, "The whole year used to be tourism season but the industry has been screwed up since Hezbollah's war with Israel. Businesses are happy whenever they see a few tourists."

The bus went uphill and then entered a canyon. For most of the journey, we were on a good but winding road along the top eastern edge of the valley. What a scenic view! Monasteries and churches were scattered in different parts of the valley. The Maronite Christians, after the defeat of the Crusaders, retreated to these remote mountains where they could defend themselves against the Muslim lowlanders. Here, religious men also built monasteries where they lived secluded lives, meditating and contemplating God. Today, the valley and its monasteries have become a UNESCO World Heritage Site.

I got off the bus at Cedars. According to Wikipedia, the forest at Cedars "is said to contain 375 individual trees, two claimed to be over 3000 years old, ten over 1000 years in age, and the remainder at least centuries-old." This meant that the oldest trees were young when the Phoenicians had just invented the alphabet, China's Zhou dynasty was newly founded and Troy fell as a result of Ulysses' trick with the wooden horse.

The Cedars were really cold because of the altitude, which I hadn't expected as I was only wearing a T-shirt. I had a quick overpriced lunch and then took photos of the cedar trees from the outside. No point paying to go in when you could see the trees from outside. I enquired about taxis going 6km downhill to Bsharre and the local taxi mafia gave a rip-off quote. I decided to walk instead.

Three hundred meters downhill and a young Lebanese named Paulo drove past and stopped to ask if I wanted a lift. He even offered to take me to a panoramic viewpoint overlooking the Holy Valley. Qadisha, he said, was his favourite part of Lebanon. He came here every few months, he said, to relax and to breathe the fresh air. I asked him about the huge portraits of a bald man with a moustache hung everywhere in the Bsharre region. "That's Samir Geagea," he said, "the former head of a Maronite Christian militia called Lebanese Forces which was a major participant in the Lebanese Civil War." Geagea was a local son here, and, according to Paulo, was unfairly put in prison for alleged war crimes when all the other politicians got away with major human rights violation. The real reason for his incarceration, in his opinion, was his opposition to Syrian control and manipulation of the Lebanese government. Geagea was held in prison for 11 years in solitary confinement and released after the Cedar Revolution of 2005. He is now a leader of the March 14 Alliance that opposes Syria and Hezbollah.

During winter, the whole Bsharre region becomes a ski resort. The Lebanese are fond of saying Lebanon is the only country in the

Bsharre, The Cedars: Billboard depicting Samir Geagea.

Mediterranean where one can swim in the morning and ski in the same afternoon. However, as Robert Fisk had commented in his book *Pity the Nation*, he had never actually known any one who had achieved such a feat.

"Half of what I say is meaningless, but I say it so that the other half may reach you."

— Khalil Gibran

Paulo drove me to Bsharre's Gibran Museum and Mausoleum. Khalil Gibran (1883–1931) was Lebanon's greatest poet, though he spent most of his life in the US and wrote his greatest work, *The Prophet*, as well as various other poetic inspirational works, in English. An article in *The New Yorker* claimed that "The Prophet", as he is also called, is the third best-selling poet in history, after William Shakespeare and Lao Tse.

According to Wikipedia, "In the book, the prophet Almustafa who has lived in the foreign city of Orphalese for 12 years is about to board a ship which will carry him home. He is stopped by a group of people, with whom he discusses many issues of life and the human condition. The book is divided into chapters dealing with love, marriage, children, giving, eating and drinking, work, joy and sorrow, houses, clothes, buying and selling, crime and punishment, laws, freedom, reason and passion, pain, self-knowledge, teaching, friendship, talking, time, good and evil, prayer, pleasure, beauty, religion, and death."

Set on a cliffside just outside Bsharre, the Gibran Museum was a moving, dignified and serene place where personal belongings of Gibran and his paintings, mostly nudes, were displayed. I'd never heard of Gibran but was now curious to find out more.

Interestingly, Wikipedia also has it that: "Gibran was a prominent Syrian nationalist. In a political statement he drafted in 1911, he expresses his loyalty to Greater Syria and to the safeguarding of Syria's national territorial integrity. He also calls for the adoption of Arabic as a national language of Syria and the application of Arabic at all school levels."

I wonder how this sat in with those Lebanese who were Christian, but people and politics change with time and history. Even the Lebanese national identity did not exist in 1911. The boundary of today's Lebanon was only drawn up in 1920 and if Gibran were alive today, he might have been an ardent anti-Syrian Lebanese nationalist.

»»»»»

With Ding, a Chinese backpacker I met at the Talal Hotel, I got into a service taxi to the Kola station in the southern suburbs of Beirut — the word station was a misnomer. There was no bus station there, only lots of taxis, buses and mini-buses parked under a flyover. For a country that has an impressive road infrastructure, Lebanon had no proper bus terminal that allowed people to buy tickets at the right price from the right people, and no waiting or resting area and other amenities one normally associated with major urban bus terminals. Perhaps, Lebanon's Gulf donors did not find it glamorous to build bus terminals. I hated Kola, not just because of the lack of amenities, but also because of the taxi mafia who hung around there and lied blatantly that there was no bus to wherever you wanted to go. Only taxis go there, they would lie, so that one engaged them for an overpriced journey.

Tanks and military installations everywhere in Lebanon.

From Kola, I got into a mini-bus for Saida (Sidon), a large city to the south and once a great Phoenician centre, passing the Shia southern suburbs of Beirut. The beach resort coastline typical of Beirut and the north came to an end some distance south of the city. We took about an hour to reach Saida. It was 8:45am and the Sea Castle, symbol of Saida, was yet to be open. We took a few photos from this very pretty Crusader castle. Linked to the city by an ancient bridge, the Sea Castle was very picturesque indeed. We walked around the narrow lanes of the old city. Unlike Beirut which was very European, Saida was a typical Middle Eastern city with a lot of noise, dirt, and a pervasive damp decomposing smell that might appeal to those looking for the exotic.

We also visited the Khan el Franj, the impressively restored caravanserai that once played host to merchants of the Mediterranean. The Grand Mosque was similarly impressive, with its Crusader stained glass and high church vaults — this was once a cathedral built by the Crusaders, which was later converted to a mosque upon the city's reconquest by the Muslims. However, the nice young men who took us around the mosque denied the Christian past of the building, and instead subjected us to a painful lecture on the need for us to seek truth in Islam. "Do you know the meaning of life? Do you know who created us and what comes after death? Do you believe in that nonsensical Darwin talk about men descended from dinosaurs?"

It could well have been the preaching of an equally annoying evangelical Christian either from the American South or Singapore! They all say the same thing, anxious to tell me I would burn in hell even if I had done good all my life. And this gentleman at Saida mosque declined to shake hands with Ding, citing religious reasons, and seemed to display a condescending attitude towards her. Could he have realized that this very act was indicative of the attitude many of the more extreme among his community have for women and their social status in general? Did he know that half his evangelical efforts got swept into the dustbin the moment such attitudes were displayed?

»»»»»

We returned to the bus station and took another mini-bus to Sour (pronounced Sur), better known as Tyre, a city whose merchants the Bible called 'princes' [65]. We crossed the Litani River into the south, once a hot battleground between Palestinian and Shiite guerrillas of Amal and Hezbollah on one side, and Israel and its puppet South Lebanon Army on the other. There were more Lebanese army check-points, increasingly supported not just by armoured carriers but also battle tanks. However, as recent events had shown, we were not certain how effective these Lebanese soldiers would be at defending their democracy when the Hezbollah next raised hell.

Hezbollah forces were nowhere to be seen but they were certainly everywhere, on banners, billboards and posters. They showed Hezbollah secretary-general Sayyed Hassan Nasrallah with his boofy hat and Kim Jong-Il-like smile; the enigmatic Musa Sadr, the long missing spiritual leader of the Lebanese Shias; Ayatollahs Khomeini and Khamenei of Iran, Hezbollah's major backer; and Imad Fayez Mughniyah — senior Hezbollah military commander and alleged mastermind of a number of terrorist attacks (such as those on the US Embassy in Beirut in 1983 and on the Israeli Embassy in Buenos Aires in 1992) and the kidnapping of Westerners — who was assassinated by Israel in Damascus in February 2008.

The yellow flags of Hezbollah, or the "Party of God", hung from many lampposts, perhaps as many as the Lebanese cedar flag. On the Hezbollah flag was the stylized form of the party's name in Arabic, with the first letter of "Allah" reaching up to grab a rifle, plus a globe, a book, a sword and a leafed branch. According to Wikipedia: "The text above the logo reads in Arabic, "Then surely the party of God are they that shall be triumphant" (*Quran* 5:56). Underneath the logo are the words 'The Islamic Resistance in Lebanon'".

That is a fitting representation of the aims of the organization, which is to spread the Islamic revolution worldwide through armed struggle or otherwise. Unlike other armed groups in Lebanon, Hezbollah's declared objectives are not just the freedom of Lebanon but also the elimination of the State of Israel and the reclamation of Jerusalem and the Holy

---

[65] The Bible, Isaiah 23:8

Land for Muslims. That is also why Hezbollah continues to attack Israel despite the departure of Israel from all of Lebanon except for a tiny piece of disputed land that is not really Lebanese but possibly Syrian. It is for this pan-Arabic objective of Hezbollah that the Lebanese people continue to suffer attacks from Israel.

Sour was known as Tyre in ancient times. Tyre, then an island (now merged with the mainland) was one of the most important Phoenician

Shias showing a poster of Hezbollah secretary-general Sayyed Hassan Nasrallah and arm tattoo of Imam Hussayn and Zulfiqar, the legendary double-tip sword of Imam Ali, Shia Islam's most sacred saint. The sword was supposed to have been presented to Ali by the Prophet himself and is a symbol of honour and martyrdom to the Shias. Interestingly, tattoos are forbidden in Islam.

trading ports and city states 3,000 years ago. It was Tyre's traders that founded Carthage in what is today Tunisia, and from Carthage, capital of a new maritime empire that once rivaled the power of Rome, Phoenician traders founded other cities and ports such as Leptis Magna and Sabratha.

The wealth of Tyre attracted many invaders, including Nebuchadnezzar, King of Babylon, who besieged the city for 13 years from 586BC, and Alexander the Great, who only conquered the city after building a causeway across to the island fortress and a seven-month siege. The latter was so angered by the city's resistance that he not only destroyed half of it, but had the entire city's inhabitants massacred or sold into slavery.

Tyre's recent history is less glorious but no less tragic. Tyre is a smaller town than Saida, and it looked dirtier and more chaotic. This was not surprising, for this ancient city had long been Lebanon's frontline town, and had suffered from numerous attacks not only from Israel; the huge Palestinian military presence here even before the Civil War led to a "Wild South" scenario in which various Palestinian factions battled one another for control of the city, which for a time was even renamed by extreme left wing factions as the "People's Republic of Tyre".

Today, tourists visit Sour for the extensive ruins of old Tyre, which is a UNESCO World Heritage Site. We walked around the piles of stones, the ancient necropolis, the broken columns by the seaside and the huge hippodrome, all right at the city centre. We also walked through the city's Christian Quarter, marked by much cleaner and wider streets, which seemed to manifest a degree of civic pride that a Christian we met said was lacking among the country's Shiite population. Throughout my stay in Lebanon, as much as I hate to admit it, the Christian areas of Lebanon resembled Northern Europe with its accompanying order and cleanliness, while the Muslim areas, in particular, the Shia ones, seemed to be more typical of the Third World, which is often associated chaos and dirtiness.

Vehicles bearing the sign "UN" were seen in many places in Sour. The United Nations Interim Force in Lebanon (UNIFIL) was created in 1978 to confirm Israeli withdrawal from Lebanon and restore Lebanese government authority in the south. However, three decades after the "interim" force arrived, their duties remain uncompleted. Israeli forces had withdrawn but Hezbollah forces remained a powerful presence here, and from time to time, launched attacks on Israel and provoked a vigorous response from it as a result. The ones who suffer from such actions, inevitably, have always been innocent civilians. Isn't this the case everywhere in the world when armies clash?

» » » » »

From Beirut, I travelled to Byblos and Dog River to the north on a sleepy Sunday morning. All of Beirut was almost dead because it was Sunday. Unlike the rest of the Middle East, which has its rest day on Friday, Lebanon, as it is nominally a "Christian country" (even though Christians probably do not account for more than 25% of the population — no one really knows as no population census has been conducted since 1932), has Sunday as a rest day, like the rest of the world.

It took less than an hour to get to Byblos, 42km north of Beirut. The coastline, alternating between huge rocks and fine sandy beaches, was like the most beautiful of the Amazons, the legendary women warriors of Colchis, armed with the qualities of ruggedness as well as great beauty, which made them attractive as well as deadly. Behind all were the soaring heights of Mt. Lebanon, green and inviting, so unlike the normally bleak, often dramatic and tortured rockface of mountains found across this part of the world. The moving clouds, pushed along gently by the cool breeze from

Details on the sarcophagus of King Hiram of Tyre, a great Phoenician king, at the National Museum in Beirut.

the Mediterranean this time of the year, constantly painted and repainted the changing shades of green that characterized these mountains. It was no wonder that, for years, I had met Arabs, especially the Gulf Arabs, who told me that the most beautiful country in the Middle East was Lebanon.

The Lebanese, well-known to be entrepreneurial as they once hailed from the Phoenicians, the world's first maritime traders, have crowded much of the coastline between Beirut and Byblos with beach resorts, clubs and entertainment complexes of every description. Many of them, at least when viewed from a distance, looked quite posh. And they were all full as well on this sunny Sunday morning. Mona, the Lebanese girl I met on the flight, said that the moment the recent fighting ended, the Gulf Arabs and Lebanese immigrants all rushed to Lebanon for their summer vacations. Interestingly, the place looked more like a posh Mediterranean beach resort than a tacky Middle Eastern one. Despite all the political instability, it was remarkable that money still flowed into the country; building all that infrastructure despite the edgy possibility that civil war could return at any time. Perhaps, to some of these immigrants living in godforsaken West Africa, which I had visited a few months before, this did indeed look like heaven.

Lebanon is a country with not much arable land and most of the coastline was full of skyscrapers — whether commercial or residential – squeezed in that flat, narrow strip between the sea and the mountains, and many buildings were built on terraces on the rising slope.

Byblos itself is but a part of the almost continuous line of skyscrapers and resorts stretching north from Beirut. I alighted on the highway and walked to the old town. I visited the archaeological site which included a museum in the Crusader Castle. The site itself was just lots of stones, a few columns and lots of holes probably dug out by archaeologists. One had to use a lot of imagination to figure out what used to be there. Whatever it was, one must not overlook the historical importance of Byblos.

Byblos was an ancient city-state, first inhabited 7,000 years ago and believed to be the oldest continuously inhabited city in the world. When its first inhabitants built their mud houses, rice was cultivated in Southeast Asia for the first time, the plough was introduced in Europe, the water buffalo was domesticated in China, beer was brewed for the first time by a farmer in the mountains of West Iran and the wheel was invented in Mesopotamia. More importantly, Byblos was also where the Phoenicians invented the alphabet which was then adopted by the Greeks and the Romans, and then taken up by most languages worldwide. The city supplied ancient Israel and Egypt with cedar wood, which was used to build the Temple of Jerusalem and many of the Pharaoh's temples and palaces. Ancient Byblos also supplied Egypt with papyrus, which was then sold to the Greeks. The first bibles were written by the Greeks on papyrus from Byblos, hence the corruption of Byblos into "bible".

Today, Byblos is a small prosperous Christian town thriving on tourism — not just because of the archaeological site but also for the fabulous beaches nearby. Here I found the greatest concentration of souvenir shops I had seen so far in Lebanon, some of them selling what they claimed to be fish fossils supposedly chipped from quarries at a nearby mountain. I expressed surprise that so many fossils, rare in other parts of the world, were found here in a mountain. The shop owner, however, could not provide me with a satisfactory reply.

Another interesting attraction was the Persian fortress at Byblos, built by the Persians who ruled Byblos as a vessel state during 538–332 BC. According to the plaque at the site, this made Byblos an important part of the Persian defence system. In a perverse sense, this remains the case today, as Iranian-supported Hezbollah has in recent years emerged as the most powerful militia in Lebanon, and constantly attacked Israel from Lebanon. Critics say such battles are proxy wars fought by the Iranians against pro-US Israel. I even read a report that described the Hezbollah as Iran's aircraft carrier in the Mediterranean. If the US deployed many warships and aircraft carriers to the Gulf region, why couldn't Iran do the same in Lebanon?

I got onto a bus towards Beirut but later got the driver to drop me off at Nahr El Kalb, or Dog River. Here, for over 3,000 years, conquerors and armies passing through Lebanon would leave inscriptions and stele on the rockface at the canyon near the mouth of Nahr El Kalb. Among them were: Egyptian Pharaoh Ramses II, the one whose forces, which according to the

Bible, hurried after Moses into the parting Red Sea; several Assyrian kings from what is today northern Iraq; Babylonian King Nebuchadnezzar II — who was mentioned in the Bible as the destroyer of the Temple in Jerusalem and the builder of the Hanging Gardens of Babylon, one of the seven wonders of the Ancient World; a Roman emperor; a Byzantine governor; a Mamluke Sultan; French Emperor Napoleon III's expedition and other French armies; various British military expeditions, and lastly the Lebanese Republic on the evacuation of foreign military forces from Lebanon in 1946, which to the Lebanese marked the independence of the country. Sadly, this ideal remains unfulfilled as Lebanon's recent history, too, has long been marked by repeated foreign interventions and incursions after independence.

» » » »

I got into a service taxi to the Airport Bridge in south Beirut to take a bus to Baalbeck. The Airport Bridge was a modern flyover which was destroyed by Israeli bombing in the 33-day 2006 Lebanon War. In 2006, the kidnap of a number of Israeli soldiers plus repeated bombing of Israel's northern frontier by Hezbollah, Lebanon's pro-Iranian Shia militia, led to an Israeli

The magnificent ruins of Roman Baalbeck.

invasion and massive bombing of Lebanon. Israel did not achieve any of its objectives – destruction of Hezbollah and the rescue of its missing soldiers. Instead, not only did Israel have to withdraw from Lebanon with Hezbollah's military strength virtually intact, Hezbollah was now seen as a rare military victor over Israel. The biggest loser, however, were the Lebanese people — more than 1,000 killed, the nation's infrastructure, only recently rebuilt after the Civil War of the 1970s and 1980s, devastated, and tourism ravaged during the peak summer season.

The bridge was being rebuilt at the moment, with funding from the Gulf and Iran. Lebanon, even after the end of the Civil War in 1990, had to endure several rounds of invasion and devastation from Israel. Every time, the Gulf States and Iran would pump in cash to rebuild what had been destroyed. In a perverse manner, I suspected the fact that the other Middle Eastern states did not have to bear Lebanon's burden as the frontline state actually encourages them to adopt the most belligerent stand towards Israel. After all, they just need to pay up for Lebanon's losses. Any damage that did not include human lives was cheap, especially with oil price levels so high.

I got onto a mini-bus for Baalbeck, Lebanon's famous monument in the Beqaa Valley. The bus went up a winding road to the heights of Mount Lebanon with a beautiful panoramic view of Greater Beirut and its skyscrapers. Pine trees were everywhere. Initially there were many buildings, some of which looked like hotels but most were residential. Many, however, looked unoccupied and I wondered if they belonged to absent Overseas Lebanese. It was interesting that rather tall buildings were built even up in the mountains.

Eventually, the mini skyscrapers disappeared and we began to see more military posts and communication towers. There were also half-destroyed bunkers — from which of the many wars in previous decades I did not know — and fortified buildings, which like many structures across Lebanon of a military nature were painted in bright national colours. Sometimes, I believe that it is countries that have weak or disputed national identities which put up their national flags more often than those confident of who they are.

The Beka'a is I think the boundary between the Levant and Asia.
                                    — Freya Stark, *Beyond Euphrates*, 1951[66]

After passing the peak of the Mount-Lebanese Range, the road began its downward descent. A new highway with bridges across mountain crests and ridges was being built and will no doubt enable Syrian tanks to reach Beirut in record speed. Before long, the bus reached the famous Beqaa Valley, a very fertile vale once controlled by the Syrian Army and now garrisoned by Hezbollah.

This fecund valley in eastern Lebanon has 40% of the country's arable land. It used to be occupied by the Syrian Army between 1977 and 2005, and is currently a major base of the Hezbollah militia. This was the scene of many battles between Israel and the Palestinians and Syrians, and between Syrians and the Palestinians. The Greek Orthodox city of Zahle at the heart of the Beqaa Valley (often nicknamed the "Bride of Beqaa"), which the bus also passed, was during the Civil War the subject of a bitter half-year siege by Syria. That led to a brief Israeli attack on the Syrians in support of the Christians, thus triggering a major international crisis which potentially could have led to an all-out war between US-backed Israel and Soviet-backed Syria. Only the urgent peace-making efforts of Ronald Reagan produced a temporary truce between the two sides and preserved the Great Powers' desire not to fight each other in this valley, a fact little known by most people until recently.

Today, Zahle is better known for its wine and the good food of its river-side restaurants. Away on the horizon were mountains — the Mount Lebanon range to the west — parts of which remained snowcapped even on this day in June — and the Anti-Lebanon range which forms the Syrian-Lebanese border to the east.

Upon reaching Baalbeck, I walked around this famous site. It was huge but unfortunately, its grandness was partially eclipsed by the new city just next to it. It could have been a magnificent sight if the complex stood unobstructed on the plains, as it once probably did. The site was guarded by many young soldiers who seemed to be having fun in the shade, joking and laughing away. A few Syrian labourers were clearing weeds and cleaning the site. A number of local people wore the typical *kerrifya*, common throughout the Arab World but the first time I ever saw it in Westernised Lebanon.

I had roast chicken for lunch and then took another bus to the road junction town of Chtaura where the road to Baalbeck branches off from the Beirut-Damascus highway. Chtaura was also where the Syrian Army once had its Lebanese headquarters. Today, it is a sleepy junction town with predatory taxi drivers all fighting for the chance to tell the dumb foreigner that there was no bus to wherever he wanted to go and that he should take their over-priced taxis.

By this time, I was tired and anxious to go quickly to the old Umayyad city of Aanjar, located close to the Syrian border. Instead of waiting for the bus, I tried my best to bargain and eventually obtained an acceptable price from the taxi drivers. The taxi driver, an unshaven Shiite man in his fifties, was a keen supporter of the Hezbollah. As we passed a huge billboard of Hezbollah's Nasrallah, he turned to me with his right hand, thumb upwards in a sign of approval, "Hezbollah, Good!" I asked, "Hariri?" The taxi driver laughed scornfully, "No good," drew a line across his throat, then tweaked his thumb downwards. The mischievous soul in me probed further, "Syria? Bashar Assad?" He raised his dark eyebrow, "Very good! Allahu Akbar!"

»»»»»

Built in the 7th century by the Umayyad dynasty, the first of the Islamic empires in the Middle East, Aanjar is an important regional centre renowned for its many symmetric arches and the unique red-white stones that were used to build many of its structures. I loved the emptiness of the place, which, despite its UNESCO World Heritage status, was hardly visited by the many tourists who also visited Baalbeck an hour away.

The modern Aanjar of today is an ethnic Armenian town, whose inhabitants are descendants of Armenian refugees from Musa Dagh ("Mountain of Moses") in southern Turkey's Hatay Province, who were relocated to Aanjar with the help of the French when Hatay, originally a French Mandate territory, was annexed by Turkey, historical enemies of the Armenians, in 1939. Aanjar has six villages, each named after the six Armenian villages of Musa Dagh, immortalized in the Hollywood movie *Forty Days of Musa Dagh*, which dramatized the forty-day-resistance of Musa Dagh's Armenians in 1915 against the Turkish Army's order to massacre its inhabitants and deport any survivors. The relocation of Musa Dagh's Armenians saved them from slaughter by the Turks but did not spare one-tenth of them from dying of malaria in Aanjar's swamps. It took many years before the swamps were drained and turned into the fertile land of milk and honey it is today. There are now 150,000 ethnic Armenians in Lebanon representing more than 5% of the population, and Lebanese-Armenians were guaranteed six seats in Parliament.

During the Civil War from 1975 to 1990, Lebanon's Armenians formed the Armenian Secret Army for the Liberation of Armenia (ASALA), which took the opportunity of those lawless days to train and launch terrorist attacks on Turkish diplomats worldwide, with the objective of, as stated in a US government document, compelling "the Turkish Government to acknowledge publicly its alleged responsibility for the deaths of 1.5 million Armenians in 1915, pay reparations, and cede territory for an Armenian homeland". Altogether, ASALA launched 84 attacks in which

The great Umayyad ruins of Aanjar near the border with Syria.

46 people died. The group only lost much of its organization and impetus when the Israelis invaded Lebanon in 1982. The incursion forced the Palestinian Liberation Organisation, one of ASALA's major backers, to withdraw from Lebanon.

Due to the close proximity of Aanjar to the Syrian border, it was formerly the headquarters of the once-feared Syrian intelligence in Lebanon. It was said that Rustum Ghazzali, head of the Syrian intelligence in Lebanon, was at that time the most feared person in all Lebanon. Aanjar also played host to many Syrian *mukhabarat*, or secret agents, who accounted for as much as half the local population, until April 2005, when all Syrian forces were compelled to withdraw as a result of the Cedar Revolution following the assassination of Hariri. Beyond the bare brown mountains to the east, against which Aanjar is nestled, is Syria, where the *mukhabarat* are probably waiting to return at the slightest provocation.

I met a middle-aged Lebanese-Brazilian at Aanjar who drove me back to Chtaura, where I got onto a bus for Beirut. There are 8 million Brazilians of Lebanese-descent, much greater than the population of Lebanon, which has only 4 million. I met a few of these Lebanese-Brazilians at Talal Hotel, and saw Brazilian flags hung from many Lebanese homes. The 15-million strong Lebanese Diaspora is found worldwide — from the supermarkets, grocery stores and restaurants across West Africa which I toured a few months ago, to the fashionable suburbs of Paris and Bordeaux, where they are seen as an important part of the French national fabric. A young Frenchman once told me that he thought the French public would support any involvement of the French Army to uphold the sovereignty of Lebanon.

»»»»»

I visited the Chouf Mountains with Brandon, a bright young Californian about to start his political science PhD at UCLA, by taking a bus which drove southwards onto the coastal plains of the Lebanese Mediterranean. Just before the bus turned inland into the Chouf Mountains, we passed Damour, site of a terrible Palestinian massacre of a few hundred Maronite

Christian civilians in 1976 during the Civil War, which involved rape and murder of women, mutilation of the dead and desecration of ancient tombs, described in shocking detail by Robert Fisk in his book *Pity the Nation*.

The Chouf Mountains are the historical heartland of the Druzes in Lebanon, a religious community who sometimes described themselves as a sub-sect of Sunni Islam, though some Muslims would not consider them Islamic at all. There are between 250,000 to 400,000 Druzes in Lebanon and possibly up to 1 million in Syria. Persecuted by other major branches of Islam across the centuries, the Druzes have always guarded their heritage and religious beliefs jealously and often with great secrecy. Although they maintain, at least officially, that they are also Muslims, their beliefs contain many non-Islamic elements. For instance, the Druzes believe in reincarnation, celebrate the Noruz, the new year for Iranians and Kurds, and practise monogamy. They also believe in the divinity of the sixth Fatimid caliph, Al Hakim Hamzah, who declared himself the reincarnation of Allah. While the Caliph was, according to other Muslim sources, murdered in 1021, Druzes believe that he had merely gone into hiding and would return in 1000 years' time. The Druzes are very secretive about their religion and only formally initiated members are given full access to the wisdom and knowledge of their faith.

I recalled my conversation with Samir, a Druze businessman in Beirut, about his faith and belief in reincarnation: The Druzes believe

Beiteddine Palace in the predominantly Druze Chouf Mountains.

that the total number of Druzes has been the same throughout history and that there is a secret Druze community in China. Every Druze that dies would be replaced by a Druze born at the same time. Their belief in reincarnation is similar to that of Hinduism or Buddhism — if one had done good deeds, one would be reborn in a better life, and vice versa. However, the Druzes believe that humans would only be reborn as humans, not animals or insects, which is possible in eastern religions. The whole rebirth process would end on judgment day when al-Hakim would return together with the secret Druze community in China, to conquer and bring justice to the world.

Some Druze families had their own stories of rebirth — of how individuals realized, often through dreams, that they were reincarnations of someone else who died, and that the two families involved would meet and become close through this strange link. Samir told me about his father's story of being born again: The previous life of Samir's late dad was as his own elder brother, who died at the age of six in an accident caused by his sister. At the moment the elder brother died, Samir's grandmother gave birth to Samir's father, and he was given exactly the same name and simply took over the birth papers of the dead elder brother, as the family was still grieving over the death of their eldest son.

Some years later, when he was still a little boy, Samir's father suddenly "remembered" the accident that caused the death of his previous life and announced to the family that he was actually the reincarnation of his dead elder brother. He even recalled that the death was caused by his sister and throughout the rest of his life, would refuse to speak to that sister. Strange, isn't it? Samir said there were a number of other stories of reincarnation among the Druze but that it was generally rare for people to "remember" their previous reincarnation. However, given the Druze belief in constant population size and the inherent small size of the entire community, stories like that do emerge from time to time.

»»»»»

Apart from the Druze, there were also huge Maronite Christian communities in the Chouf Mountains. Both communities had not always lived in peace, and it was the bitter civil war between them in the 19th century that led to European intervention and the resulting formation of the *sanjak* or autonomous state of Mount Lebanon within the Ottoman Empire; that eventually formed the nucleus of the Lebanese state of today after the fall of the Ottomans. During the 1975–1990 Civil War, the Maronite Lebanese Forces and the predominantly Druze Progressive Socialist Party (PSP) led by the Jumblatt family (who were traditional tribal chieftains) fought bitterly in these mountains. More recently, during the clashes in May 2008, Hezbollah attacked and captured villages controlled by Walid Jumblatt, current head of the PSP, in the Chouf Mountains and forced it to surrender these villages to the Lebanese Army.

Palestinian symbols at Shatilla refugee camp / a friendly Palestinian teenager posing in front of war ruins.

We took about an hour to reach Beiteddine, after walking through the splendid grounds of the luxurious Mir Amin Palace Hotel. From the high ground of the hotel, the Beiteddine Palace was just below, we had a perfect sniper's position overlooking what was the Lebanese President's official summer palace. This might just be fine for the Prince of Liechtenstein, but certainly not a desirable hangout for any Lebanese president. Wikipedia.org has a special entry for "List of assassinated Lebanese people" which named 19 political figures from 1979, including a president, a president-elect and two former prime ministers.

Whatever the case, the magnificent Beiteddine Palace was the official summer residence of the Lebanese president, and was, as a result, very well-maintained. Built between 1788 and 1818 by Bashir Shihab II, the Maronite emir of Mount Lebanon, Beqaa Valley and Jebel Amil under the Ottomans, this is a magnificent example of mixed Moorish, Byzantine, Omayyad and European architectural styles, designed by, interestingly, Italian architects. The palace was severely damaged by the Israeli army during their invasion of 1982, and was later taken over by Druze forces who turned it over to the government in 1999 to be converted into a museum.

We walked through the complex, awed by the intricate carvings and Andalusian-Moorish aesthetics, combining in a most tasteful and graceful manner, the flow of water in the courtyard fountains and those on the inner walls. There was also an interesting mosaic museum here, with well-preserved Byzantine and Roman mosaics from a church in Jiyyeh, a coastal town just south of Damour. According to Wikipedia, "The Prophet Jonah was said to have landed on its shores when he was spat out of the giant fish described in the Old Testament, and a temple was built which stands until today. It was known at the time of the Phoenicians as a thriving natural seaport. This natural seaport continued functioning and remains up to the present times. Many invaders passed... such as Tohomtmos the Egyptian who landed his soldiers... Alexander the Macedonian relaxed on its shore preparing for the attack on Tyre. St Peter and St Paul also walked through Jieh several times."

During the Civil War, Maronite Jiyyeh was repeatedly attacked by Israelis, Palestinians and Druze. Jumblatt's forces captured it a few times and horrific massacres had occurred here. Jumblatt's Druze forces, in particular, had been accused of "taking no prisoners" (in Robert Fisk's *Pity the Nation*) and dynamiting churches in Jiyyeh. Interestingly, a commemorative plaque at the Mosaic Museum at Beiteddine Palace acknowledged the generous donation of Walid Jumblatt, respectable cabinet minister of public works, for all these exquisite mosaics. I wondered where he obtained them.

From Beiteddine, we took a service taxi to Deir el Qamar, once the capital of the Emirate of Mount Lebanon and the long-time residence of Emir Fakhreddine II the Great (1572–1635), an enlightened leader and reformist who brought much of what is Lebanon today, under his rule, angering the Ottomans who eventually executed him and his family. Couched against the mountain slopes overlooking a deep picturesque valley, Deir el Qamar was a pretty if sleepy place, and another UNESCO World Heritage Site. We strolled around for a while and had some difficulty finding transport out of town. The town is today Maronite Christian, hence our efforts to find any Druze house of worship didn't bear much fruit. In any case, a taxi driver told us that Druze houses of worship weren't open to outsiders, which was probably true, considering the secretive nature of their religion.

»»»»»

I joined Adrian, a young and friendly aspiring French journalist on a visit to the dirty, messy slum that is the notorious Palestinian refugee camp, Shatilla. This was where, in 1982, Christian militias massacred thousands of unarmed Palestinian refugees, right under the nose of the Israeli army, shortly after the assassination of the baby-faced President-elect and Christian Phalange warlord Bashir Gemayel.

Walking through the squalor of the camp, I was amazed how people could live in such terrible conditions for 60 years. Shame on the Arab countries for not offering these Palestinians citizenship and allowing them to work legally. Even the West, which the Arabs are fond of accusing of being racist, was a lot more accommodating to refugees. We took many photos of Fatah, Arafat, Hamas and other political groups we were not familiar with. The people we met at the souk area of the camp were friendly and some even posed for us, pointing out on a Palestinian map where they were originally from — Jaffa, Ramallah, Hebron, Jenin, Bethlehem — the list went on — plus many villages whose houses and olive groves had long been flattened and whose names no longer existed on the road maps of Israel. The sad thing was, most of these people were probably born in the refugee camp, and even their grandparents who were born in Palestine, had left Palestine as children.

More Palestinian symbols and posters at Shatilla refugee camp: A struggle that has gone on for too long.

The camp, as expected in places of this kind, was full of various factions and groups, with clear if unmarked lines and boundaries. A little boy warned us, "Mafia, mafia", as we left the busy Palestinian souk area for what appeared to be more residential areas of the camp. We found ourselves in an area with lots of green flags and photos of an Iranian mullah. A group of walkie-talkie men surrounded us and asked what we were doing. Just tourists, we replied. They made a few calls and told us we were no longer in Shatilla but in the Lebanese Amal territory.

Amal is a Shia militia that first fought the Maronites, then the Hezbollah, on the side of the Syrians during the Civil War. They are now allied with Hezbollah in a pro-Syrian, anti-Western alliance. As with Hezbollah, the icon of Amal is the Iranian-born cleric Musa Sadr who disappeared mysteriously in Libya in 1978. Many believe that Musa Sadr was killed by Libyan leader Gadaffi over disputed funds, though Libya claimed that Musa Sadr had left Libya safely for Italy. For many Shiites in southern Libya, Musa Sadr was akin to the mysterious 12th imam of the Shia faith, who would reappear on judgment day to bring justice to the world.

We had no choice but to leave the area. I did not fancy being taken hostage or kidnapped by a renegade faction — in such places, certain groups sometimes committed crimes and blamed it on others. Politics is too complicated, especially in places like Lebanon. We walked through the bazaar again, and once more, got stopped by yet another group of plainclothes men, probably as we had again crossed another invisible boundary. At another location, just outside what appeared to be a party office of some kind, a young man hurled himself at me as I snapped a photo of a political wall mural. "No photo!" he shouted. I supposed it was because photos of Palestinian party offices could well be used for target practice planning by the Israeli Air Force.

As we left the area, we came across a friendly vehicle repair shop owner and his friends. They asked, "Palestine good?" We replied, "Yes, Palestine good, very good." They were very happy and we took a few photos of them. They joked and played with each other, and called two among them "Yahud", meaning 'Jew'. It looked like the word 'Jew' had become a bad word. It is tragic that the longstanding political hatred of the Palestinians because of the loss of their homeland, has deteriorated into racism and deprecatory attitudes.

»»»»»

The Daily Star, a Lebanese newspaper, reported on the continuing efforts among all parties in Lebanon to form a cabinet in accordance with the Doha Accord that ended the recent fighting. The report referred to the various politicians by their current titles and positions, such as Speaker Berri, MP Walid Jumblatt and MP Michel Aoun, all of which sounded very respectable. Anyone who has read modern Lebanese history, would know that these men were once active participants in the Civil War, and whose forces had killed many people during the bitter 15-year-conflict. Many journalists had, during those days, referred to them as warlords, which I supposed, was a designation they would have preferred to have shaken off. Whatever it was, as recent events have shown, these men, as well as the chief player in Lebanon today, the Hezbollah, retain considerable firepower and could, at any time, plunge the country into civil war yet again.

Even then, as a Lebanese told me, if one really wanted peace, then one should give these guys the benefit of the doubt and close one's eyes to what happened during those years of conflict. One should always look ahead and hope for the best.

I liked this country and wished it well, but its contradictions appear so huge that I wondered if there would ever be peace. Even in the Phoenician Golden Age of the past, this was never a united land. The Phoenician city-states were divided and mere pawns in the big game between the Egyptians, Persians, Assyrians and Babylonians. Other conquerors had looted this land and raped its women — Alexander the Great, the Romans, French and many others. Today's Lebanon is divided — its 18 communities guard their own turfs jealously, switch their alliances at the blink of an eye, and often seek external help to kick their rivals. Nothing seems to have changed the last 4,000 years.

Epilogue

In the old days, everything took a long time: the siege of Troy lasted 9 years; the Peloponnesian War lasted twenty-seven; the siege of Tyre by Babylon went on for 13 years and The Hundred Years War between Britain and France lasted 126 years.

But everything takes a much shorter time these days. The ground campaign of the First Gulf War of 1991 lasted only 100 hours. The 2003 invasion of Iraq took less than two months. Though its roots were much longer, the subprime crisis took less than a few weeks to crush most of the top Wall Street banks.

The journeys in this book took place between 2002 and 2008, but within years, the political and social-political landscapes of some of these countries have changed dramatically.

Let's begin with **North Korea**. Since 2006, North Korean relations with the world have followed this pattern: months of crisis followed by a sudden resolution with the injection of more US and South Korean cash, before the next nuclear crisis breaks out again. As some observers have noted, the US would probably have invaded by now if there were oil in North Korea.

In June 2008, North Korea destroyed a water-cooling tower at its nuclear facility in Yongbyon, which symbolized its decision to terminate its nuclear programme. In August 2008, however, it suddenly announced that it would soon restore the facility. This, strangely, was soon followed by rumours that Kim Jong-Il might have fallen seriously ill or even died. Although there have often been rumours about Kim's health, the recent one seems to be more sustained and probable. Reports indicated that he had suffered a severe stroke and would take a long time to recover. Despite the US and South Korea's history of bickering with him, Kim's sudden non-appearance on the political scene has become a major concern about stability in North Korea, since no obvious political successor is in sight. In October 2008, the US removed North Korea from its list of states that sponsored terrorism, in a move that may slightly calm the sometimes-turbulent relations between the regime and the rest of the world.

In May 2009, however, North Korea suddenly announced a major nuclear test, which according to the Russian Defense Department, had a blast yield equivalent to the size of the nuclear explosions that destroyed Hiroshima and Nagasaki in 1945.

Macedonia still stays united, though its racially-based politics continue to stir many prophets of doom. The name dispute with Greece remains unresolved but in 2005, Macedonia officially became a candidate for EU membership and the nation has applied for NATO membership as well.

In March 2006, former **Serbian** dictator, Milosevic died of a heart attack in a cell at the War Crimes Tribunal in The Hague, leaving angry Serbs to accuse the West of murdering him, while many Croatian, Bosnian and Albanian victims of his vicious wars felt cheated of the justice they deserved. In June 2006, Montenegro declared independence after a referendum, which marked the breakup of the much-reduced federal state. Yugoslavia has finally been consigned to the dustbin of history. In 2008, Kosovo declared independence as well, in a move that Serbia vowed never to accept. Serbia has remained in a bizarre state of denial, trapped in its unredeemable past. Will Serbia march towards a prosperous future within the European Union, or will it continue to heckle for a past that can never be reconciled with the future?

Meanwhile, the EXIT festival of Novi Sad has become one of the most important music festivals in Europe. In 2008, it won the UK Festival Award for Best European Festival. According to Wikipedia, "Icelandic singer Björk was scheduled to play at the 2008 edition EXIT Festival, but her show was canceled due, according to the management of the singer, to Björk's recent support of Kosovo independence. The organizers of the EXIT Festival, however, denied these claims, even though they conceded the email evidence was authentic. Later, they publicly claimed to have extended a new "open invitation" for Björk to perform at Exit.

Inter-ethnic gay relationships during wartime Yugoslavia were the key focus of the 2005 movie, *Go West*, directed by Ahmed Imamovic, and jointly developed by a studio in Bosnia and another one in Croatia. The movie was about two gay lovers, a Bosniak (i.e., Bosnian-Muslim) and a Serb, who lived in Sarajevo during the war and their hardships trying to escape from the city. The movie has won awards in the US, Canada and Spain. The BBC called it the story of Romeo and Romeo.

Srpska has survived as a political entity despite pressure to merge its institutions including its army and police force with that of FBiH. The political leaders have continued to bicker with those of FBiH and the European Union. With the declaration of independence by Montenegro and Kosovo from Serbia, Srpska leaders have threatened to hold a referendum, too, and secede from Bosnia. The European Union High Representative warned that he might remove from office the Srpska prime minister if he continued such rhetoric. It remains to be seen if Srpska can retain its current state of political existence in the years to come.

Economically, however, Srpska is praised by foreign observers. It takes only a few days to incorporate a company in Srpska but several months in FBiH. The Sarajevo Stock Exchange has stagnated while the Banja Luka Stock Exchange has attracted interest from some international funds as well as praises for its transparency and progressiveness. From a longer-term perspective, ultimately, it is politics that counts. Unless all of BiH, whether Srpska or FbiH, get their act together, this region will be nothing more than a punt for the non-mainstream exotic investor.

The **Federation of Bosnia and Herzegovina** (FBiH) continues to hobble along, with politicians from all sides of the ethnic divide trading insults with each other and occasionally, with the European Union High Representative as well. No armed conflict has broken out, quite possibly, because everyone is so sick of war.

Economically, the FBiH has become a dinosaur of sorts, trapped in its myriad bureaucracies. In June 2008, it was reported that only 221 Euro (yes, less than the cost of an hour-long international flight in most parts of the world) remained in the budget of this entity, as a result of over-spending. A local paper reported that, despite the pathetic state of finances, the FBiH government even purchased a motorboat for its exclusive vacation resort on the Croatian Adriatic coast. The empty state treasury has already led to the delayed payment of social benefits, which triggered protests by war veterans.

In 2005, a Bosnian-American declared the discovery of pyramids in Visoko (northwest of Sarajevo) which he claimed were more ancient than the Egyptian ones, and the local government and local businesses, which anticipated a marked increase in tourism immediately, supported his claim. Visiting archaeologists, however, found no evidence that the hills locals called 'pyramids' were anything more than local geological formations, thus consigning the whole affair to a growing list of local fiascos.

More promising has been the war reconstruction process. The Old Bridge of Mostar was completely rebuilt in 2004, and tourists are continuing to return to Bosnia. In 2006, *Lonely Planet* ranked Sarajevo as the 43rd best city in the world in its *Cities Book*, which makes it the best city in the Balkans, after Athens. The emotional scars of the war, however, would take a longer time to heal, and it remains to be seen if the political fracture in this country would recover as quickly as its physical infrastructure.

Croatia has continued to transform itself. With the extradition of Croat war crime suspects to the international courts, Croatia is now a candidate for the European Union and is expected to join NATO soon. As tourists return to the Adriatic coasts and income levels continue to rise, memories of the war are fast fading away.

In May 2006, **Montenegro** held a referendum to decide on the long-debated independence issue. Some 55.5% voted for independence, narrowly passing the 55% threshold needed to validate the referendum under rules set by the European Union. On 3 June 2006, independence was declared and Montenegro's independence has been recognized not only by all UN member states but also Serbia.

In 2006, Aman Resorts of Singapore was granted a lease over Sveti Stefan and would develop the island town into a world-class luxury resort. Let's watch this space in the years to come.

On 17 February 2008, **Kosovo** declared independence and was recognized by most Western and European Union countries, including the

US, UK, France and Germany. Serbia has vowed never to allow Kosovo to be independent, even though Serbia recognized Montenegro's independence which was approved by a much lower proportion of the population (55.5%) compared to Kosovo's 90% Albanian majority who are vehemently pro-independence.

Russia and China have condemned the move as illegal as they are concerned about the implications of separatist movements in their territories, which means that Kosovo's prospects for full international recognition is next to nil. Many Kosovars believe that independence could mean resolution of the territory's legal status and hence would promote economic development and foreign investment. The fulfillment of this objective is clearly uncertain at the moment.

In 2004–2006, Dečani Monastery, as well as Gračanica Monastery, were placed on UNESCO's World Heritage List as Medieval Monuments in Kosovo, and also on the List of World Heritage Sites in Danger, due to the constant threat of Albanian destruction. In 2007, a grenade attack was made on the Dečani Monastery. Although there was no damage, it further highlighted the threat these ancient monuments face.

In spite of the predictions of many doomsayers, **Albania** has neither imploded politically nor become a regional hellhole of organised crime. The country has remained one of Europe's poorest but its economy has been developing rapidly with annual growth rates averaging 5–6%. In 2006, the European Union and Albania signed the Stablisation and Association Agreement which sets out a reform and development process which would eventually lead to membership in the European Union. In June 2008, Albania was reclassified by the World Bank as a middle income country, which signified the significant progress made in its economic reform process.

Yemen briefly entered world headlines in January 2008, merely two months after my visit, when two Belgian tourists were killed in Wadi Douan together with their guide and driver, by terrorists affiliated to Al-Qaeda. Two further attacks on the US Embassy took place in 2008. Once again, the Yemeni tourism industry has been dealt a terrible blow.

The country continues to muddle along. It is a pity that conservatism, illiteracy, the country's addiction to *qat* and prolonged rule by inept leaders seem to be condemning the nation to perpetual poverty.

Further west of the Middle East, **Libya** continues to expand its contacts with the West, although this was dealt a setback in July 2008 when Swiss local authorities arrested Hannibal Gaddafi, son of the Colonel, and his wife for the alleged injuries inflicted on two of their Swiss-based North African staff. Since then, Libya has demanded an official apology, whilst two Swiss nationals were detained in Libya, and Swiss companies there were ordered to be closed. Libya also ceased issuing tourist visas to Swiss citizens.

In July 2008, the International Criminal Court issued an indictment and arrest warrant for **Sudanese** President Omar al-Bashir, for alleged war crimes in Darfur. Sudan then warned that cooperation with the international community would end with this move. Meanwhile, an arms race is building up between Khartoum and the Government of South Sudan, in the run-up to the independence referendum. A ship from Ukraine allegedly carrying 33 tanks ordered by South Sudan was hijacked by pirates off the coast of Somalia, which further highlights the rising tension between north and south.

Iran's leaders have continued to spurn Western efforts to get its doors open to international nuclear inspectors. When high inflation associated with high oil prices and the subprime-induced global financial crisis hit the rest of the world in 2008, Iran's leaders laughed and reiterated their conviction that the downfall of Western capitalism was near. But with oil prices suddenly plunging to US$60, the economic crisis has come home to Iran as well. Inflation surged and Iran's property bubble burst. The shopkeepers of the Teheran bazaar went on strike to protest government harassment and harsh new accounting rules.

On the other side of the Arabian Peninsula, **Lebanon** hobbled along, sporadic factional fighting and car bombs rocked the northern city of Tripoli from time to time, though never seriously enough to bring the country to an all-out civil war. Would sectarian differences tip the scales towards disaster again, or would good sense prevail and nudge the nation towards stability and development? Perhaps some things never change in the Levant.

And so the wheel of life moves on.

About the Author

Tan Wee Cheng is Singaporean and a self-confessed travel junkie who has been to over a hundred countries over the last decade. He is listed in the 2008 *Book of Singapore Records* as the Singaporean who has been to the most number of countries. He has a weak spot for controversial places and a tendency to get into minor troubles, such as getting arrested by corrupt police in Bulgaria, Kyrgyzstan, Russia and the rebel state of Transdniestria (Moldova). He has survived road accidents in Albania and floods in Ecuador, getting mugged in Jerusalem, St Petersburg and Bucharest, and almost getting into a fight with a Cypriot gangster.

Wee Cheng has worked in the financial sector in Singapore, the UK and China, as an auditor, investment banker, financial regulator and as the chief financial officer of a listed company. He is currently an adjunct associate professor of accounting at a university in Singapore. These days he spends his leisure time planning more travels, working on his travel website (http://weecheng.com), helping to organise travel talks for the *SgTravelCafe. com* travel forum and having endless slices of good old *kaya* toast.

His first book, *The Greenland Seal Hunter*, also a collection of travel stories, was published by Marshall Cavendish in 2005.

Wee Cheng invites readers to email him at *letters@weecheng.com*